THE AUTHENTICITY
OF THE
SACRED SCRIPTURES

THE AUTHENTICITY OF THE SACRED SCRIPTURES

By

CORNELIUS HAGERTY, C.S.C.

Lumen Christi Press
P. O. Box 13176
Houston, Texas 77019

Nihil Obstat

WARREN F. DICHARRY, C.M.

Imprimatur

+JOHN L. MORKOVSKY, S.T.D.
Apostolic Administrator
Diocese of Galveston-Houston
March 19, 1969

Grateful acknowledgment is made to the following publishers for permission to use quotations: George Allen & Unwin, Ltd., London; Princeton University Press, Princeton, New Jersey; McGraw-Hill Book Company, New York; B. Herder Book Company, St. Louis; Charles Scribner's Sons, New York; The Macmillan Company, New York; Sheed & Ward, Inc., New York; The Society of Authors, London; The Liturgical Press, Collegeville, Minnesota; Burns & Oates, Ltd., London; Oxford University Press, New York; The Weston College Press, Weston, Massachusetts; Beauchesne et ses Fils, Paris; American Tract Society, Oradell, New Jersey; The Jewish Publication Society of America, Philadelphia; Joseph F. Wagner, Inc., New York; Lutterworth Press, London; Benziger Brothers, New York; Ernest Benn, Ltd., London; Fleming H. Revell Company, Westwood, New Jersey; The Newman Press, Westminster, Maryland; The Catholic University of America Press, Washington, D. C.

"One of the worst aberrations of our time is the widespread notion that the Bible is too antiquated to be a religious guide for the 'modern' human spirit. This point of view may be said to dominate the entire secular academic scene today . . . . Many want us to substitute for Biblical faith introspective psychological 'insights'—which have neither empirical nor experimental validation—and existential philosophies based on these 'insights.' . . . ."

—William F. Albright, in *History, Archaeology and Christian Humanism* (McGraw-Hill Book Company, 1964)

AUTHOR'S PREFACE

Study of the Bible, regarded as an inspired book and the Word of God, should be preceded by some knowledge of philosophy and history which provide motives of credibility. Divine revelation supposes that a supernatural God exists, and that he has spoken to men. Christians believe that he spoke through the Hebrew prophets; that he spoke through Jesus Christ.

Many are disposed to skepticism by reason of theories taught in universities, colleges, and high schools. Pragmatists, empiricists, positivists, and agnostics are everywhere. They deny universal ideas and principles, limiting human knowledge to the sense-perceived world. They hold that man cannot prove the existence of a supernatural God; they assert that miracles and prophecies cannot occur: therefore they are not historical facts.

Communists abhor spirits, souls, saints, angels, devils, and spiritual manifestations of every kind. Pantheists deny plurality of individual substances. The God of materialists is evolving Nature, i.e., the Cosmos; the God of pantheists, the God of Spinoza, is one all-inclusive substance. Sound philosophy demonstrates that all these theories are false; it shows the unreasonableness of their premises, and proves, from self-evident principles and obvious facts, the existence of a personal God, Creator and Exemplar of Nature.

If neither God nor substantial souls can be proved to exist, even natural religion is without foundation. Supernatural revelation presupposes the existence of a supernatural God who has spoken to men. Our purpose in this book is to show that the Bible is composed of reliable historical documents. We intend to assure ourselves of their authenticity, integrity, and veracity before we rely on them or ask anyone else to rely on them as sources of divine revelation. The main motives for Christian faith are the existence of a personal God known by reason, and the historical fact that he has spoken through prophets whose words are recorded in the Bible.

In the nineteenth century, Rationalism invaded German universities, and spread to England and France. Scholars who claimed a new erudition attempted to desupernaturalize the Bible. Under the influence of Hegelian philosophy, they tried to prove the books of the Bible were the product of natural evolution: that accounts of miracles and prophecies were myths and fables, the work of Hebrew religious poets. Leo XIII, in *Providentissimus Deus,* directed attention to the seriousness of this attack on supernatural religion.

The Higher Critics, as they called themselves, were men of erudition and acumen whose influence on European thought can hardly be overestimated. They were Naturalists and evolutionists, enemies of supernatural religion. They used as weapons their knowledge of Semitic languages, oriental history, archaeology, comparative religion, astronomy, geology and biology. Leo XII asked the Bishops of the Catholic world to provide defenders equally well versed in these sciences. "There is nothing more needful," he said, "than that truth should find defenders more powerful and more numerous than the enemies it has to face." Modern specialized research was being used to make the Bible appear a product of natural evolution; defense of the Bible demanded scholars of ability who had leisure for specialized research. Theologians and exegetes needed the help of natural scientists because the attack on the Bible came not only from exegetes, philologists, theologians, historians and philosophers, but also from astronomers, geologists and biologists.

The Biblical Commission was set up to keep watch on scholars and, when necessary, to lay down directives to guide their course. Pius X continued Leo's policy by establishing the Institute for Higher Biblical Studies in Rome, inviting Bishops to send students to it. He hoped to provide competent, orthodox teachers for diocesan seminaries and Catholic universities—teachers who would offset the influence of Rationalists and Modernists.

An immediate result of this action was the writing, by Catholic scholars, of introductions to the Bible which treated inspiration, authenticity, integrity, veracity, transmission of text, history, and environment in which the books were written, in the light of modern research. Works like Father Michael Seisenberger's *Practical Handbook for the Study of the Bible,* first published in 1911, made available the erudition of specialists. These introductions, together with splendid lives of Christ—many of them written in France—were tremendous weapons for the defense of supernatural religion against Rationalist attack.

Unfortunately, some Catholic scholars who specialized in Scripture were neither philosophers nor theologians. They became Modernists and Rationalists without being aware of it. The remedy is strict supervision of writings on Scripture by sound theologians appointed by Bishops, and no books used in Catholic schools without careful inspection. It is a pity that so many who really love Christ should be influenced by dangerous books when there are truly magnificent replies to attacks on Scripture by reverent Catholic and Protestant scholars.

The author spent many years teaching philosophy, apologetics, and dogma to undergraduate students at the University of Notre Dame. This book is a revision of part of his course in Christian Apologetics. There is some rearrangement of material, some changes in wording in the interest of clarification, and addition of footnote references which call attention to recently published works. The content, however, is essentially the same. There was really no need to "update" it beyond the abovementioned changes, for the most recent archaeological findings and the most reliable recent scholarship has served to confirm the traditional view of the authenticity and historicity of the Sacred Scriptures.

The author claims that for the purpose he aims at he has an advantage in not being a specialist. Having taught philosophy and theology he is alert to the danger to which Scripture specialists are exposed of treating the Bible as a product of natural evolution. He is strictly a defender of supernatural religion. He insists that the Bible is a book that came down from heaven—the Word of God, divinely revealed truth, one of the main sources of supernatural theology and religion.

Cornelius Hagerty, C.S.C.

Notre Dame, Indiana
January 28, 1969

RECOMMENDED FOR FURTHER READING
INTRODUCTIONS TO THE BIBLE

Lattey, Cuthbert, S. J. *Back to the Bible*. London: Burns, Oates, and Washbourne, Ltd., 1944.

Laux, John J. *Introduction to the Bible*. New York: Benziger Brothers, 1932.

Seisenberger, Michael. *Practical Handbook for the Study of the Bible*. New York: Joseph F. Wagner, Inc., 1933.

Steinmueller, John E. *A Companion to Scripture Studies*. 3 volumes. Houston: Lumen Christi Press, 1969.

OTHER BOOKS ON THE BIBLE

Bea, Augustin. *The Study of the Synoptic Gospels*. New York: Harper & Row, 1965.

Bea, Augustin. *The Word of God and Mankind*. Chicago: Franciscan Herald Press, 1968.

Keller, Werner. *The Bible as History*. New York: William Morrow & Company, 1956.

Ricciotti, Giuseppe. *The Acts of the Apostles*. Milwaukee: Bruce Publishing Company, 1958.

Rome and the Study of Scripture. St. Meinrad, Indiana: Abbey Press, 1964.

LIVES OF CHRIST

Farrell, Walter, O.P. *Only Son*. New York: Sheed and Ward, 1953.

Fernandez, Andres, S.J. *The Life of Christ*. Westminster, Maryland: The Newman Press, 1959.

Fillion, Louis C. *Life of Christ*. 3 volumes. St. Louis: B. Herder Book Company, 1929.

Fouard, Constant H. *The Life of Christ*. New York: Guild Press, 1960.

Grandmaison, Leonce de, S.J. *Jesus Christ, His Person,*

Message, Credentials. 3 volumes. New York: Sheed and Ward, 1934.

Lagrange, M. J., O.P. *The Gospel of Christ.* 2 volumes. London: Burns, Oates and Washbourne, 1938.

Lebreton, Jules, S.J. *The Life and Teaching of Jesus Christ Our Lord.* New York: The Macmillan Company, 1957.

Maas, A. J., S.J. *The Life of Jesus Christ.* St. Louis: B. Herder Book Company, 1948.

O'Brien, Isidore, O.F.M. *The Life of Christ.* Paterson, N. J.: St. Anthony Guild Press, 1946.

Prat, Ferdinand, S.J. *Jesus Christ, His Life, His Teaching, and His Work.* Milwaukee: Bruce Publishing Company, 1950.

Ricciotti, Giuseppe. *The Life of Christ* (unabridged edition). Milwaukee: Bruce Publishing Company, 1952.

ARCHAEOLOGY AND HISTORY

Albright, William Foxwell. *History, Archaeology and Christian Humanism.* New York: McGraw-Hill Book Company, 1964.

Daniel Rops, Henri. *Jesus and His Times.* New York: E. P. Dutton and Company, Inc., 1954.

Kopp, Clemens. *The Holy Places of the Gospels.* New York: Herder and Herder, 1963.

O'Connell, Patrick. *The Origin and Early History of Man.* Houston: Lumen Christi Press, 1968.

O'Connell, Patrick. *Science of Today and the Problems of Genesis.* St. Paul: Radio Replies Press, 1964.

Ricciotti, Giuseppe. *History of Israel.* 2 volumes. Milwaukee: Bruce Publishing Company, 1956.

Unger, Merrill F. *Archaeology and the Old Testament.* Grand Rapids: Zondervan Publishing Company, 1956.

TABLE OF CONTENTS

"The one true God can be known by the light of unaided reason, but he is actually known, much more perfectly than reason could know him, by his free revelation of himself in the Jewish and Christian religions. It is necessary up to a certain point to observe the distinction between philosophical and theological Theism—between the God of reason and of revelation. For it is clear that, if the acceptance of Christianity is to be justified as a reasonable act of faith, the human mind must be capable of knowing naturally that a God exists who is free to reveal himself supernaturally, in such wise that men may be certain that he has done so through the ministry of Jesus Christ."

Patrick J. Toner, D. D.

CHAPTER I

Revelation

To reveal is to disclose to others what was unknown to them. The Latin word *revelatio* is equivalent to the Greek Apocalypse, which means unveiling of what before was concealed or covered. God is invisible to men's eyes, so that any knowledge of him may be called revelation in a general sense. He manifests his existence and attributes through his creation. Men can come to the knowledge of a personal God by attending to the visible things of this world. The cause is revealed in the effects; the works reflect the nature of their Creator. Such knowledge of God is natural revelation. Supernatural revelation means knowledge gained by direct speech of God to man. God can convey a message to men by oral or written teaching. Communication of this kind is beyond man's natural way of knowing. It presupposes inspiration by which God assures a prophet that he is directly speaking to him; and for those who hear the prophet, miracles which certify that he is truly a teacher sent by God.

In all the historic religions revelation is regarded as the primary source of religious truth, and intuition and reason are secondary. And this is true in the sense that positive, historic religion is

3

always primary, and philosophic or theological religion is the result of a secondary reflective activity. The concept of revelation is as old as religion itself, since the most primitive types of religion always rely on the authority of an immemorial tradition and (or) on some supernatural means of communication with the higher powers.[1]

Millions of Jews for centuries have believed that their Scriptures contain divine revelation. Christianity is based on belief in revelation from God, as recorded in both the Old and New Testaments.

The only people who deny the possibility of divine revelation are pantheists and materialists who recognize no personal God. If there is a personal God who knows all languages and has all ideas, what is to prevent him from communicating ideas to men? Any intellect is in potency to receive from a teacher more than it can learn by observation and experiment. Faith is a natural, as well as a supernatural, way of acquiring knowledge. Children learn from parents and teachers. Indeed, most of what scientists know is received by faith in other scientists. If men learn from other men, why can they not learn from God? Every mature person knows that human minds learn from teachers more easily than they discover truths by research. The better the teacher, the more his disciples learn. God is an incomparable teacher. He cannot reveal to man's limited intelligence everything he knows; the veil can never be lifted from all mysteries. However, there is a wide chasm between knowing nothing about God and knowing everything about God. One can always learn more without exhausting the subject. Every intellect has the capacity for being elevated by special divine assistance to receptivity beyond its natural power.

Some mysteries so transcend man's natural ability to know that he could never, unaided by God, discover them. God can reveal them without revealing them fully, just as a human teacher can explain electricity without explaining it fully. No professor of physics clears up all the mysteries of light; neither does a professor of theology clear up all the mystery in the Trinity. As much can be known about light without knowing *all* about it, so much can be known about the Trinity without ever learning all about it. The Trinity could not be known by the natural resources of human reason, and even after it has been revealed it cannot be fully comprehended. The veil is partially removed, but the truth remains obscure by reason of its excess of light. On the other hand, the ten commandments could be known by unaided reason. Had they not been revealed, however, the majority of men would not have exerted themselves sufficiently to arrive at a clear knowledge of them. Human teachers are prone to disagree over moral laws, whether it be because of their own weakness and concupiscence, or of their intellectual limitations. To have the ten commandments revealed by God and thus placed above cavil and compromise is a great boon to the majority of men.

Revelation may be public or private. Private revelations are made to particular persons for their guidance and sanctification. Prayer presupposes the possibility of communion between man and God. The more a person cultivates the habit of prayer, the more sensitive he becomes to the presence and activity of God. Public revelation is addressed by God to all mankind. Although made through individuals, it is not for their own benefit but for the enlightenment of others. We are not concerned here with private revelation or with the psychology of prayer, but with public revelation.

The revelation made by God through Moses and the Hebrew prophets, culminating in the revelation made through Jesus Christ, is specifically what we mean by public revelation. The first sentence of the Epistle to the Hebrews sums it up: "God who, at sundry times and in divers manners, spoke in times past to the fathers by the prophets, last of all, in these days has spoken to us by his Son." Recorded revelation began with Moses and came to an end with St. John. Christ commissioned his Apostles to teach all nations. The Apostles learned their doctrine directly from Christ, assisted by the inspiration of the Holy Ghost. Both Christ and the Holy Ghost are regarded by Christians as Divine Persons. What they revealed is therefore revered as divine revelation. The Bible, both Old and New Testaments, is a written record of public revelation.

Inspiration

Inspiration is treated here only to clarify the meaning of revelation. It is a doctrine that belongs to dogmatic theology. However, rationalistic critics of the Bible have so often identified revelation, inspiration, and infallibility that we are obliged carefully to define these terms. They are not synonymous.

We do not hold that everything in the Bible was revealed. Much of what Moses wrote he learned by experience. He needed no special communication from God to tell him what road the Israelites followed through the desert. He may have been inspired to move here and there, but his *knowledge* of what occurred on the way was natural knowledge. St. Luke describes, toward the end of Acts, a shipwreck. Since he participated in it, he had no need of a revelation to know what occurred; yet he may have been inspired to write his account of it. When we say he was inspired, we mean he was so effectively assisted by God that he added nothing, omitted nothing, and misrepresented nothing that God wanted him to transmit to posterity. Inspiration of this kind is supernatural; it is more than the natural inspiration of poets, painters, orators, and other men of genius.

Inspiration does not necessarily give new knowledge, whereas revelation does. Inspiration acts on the will of the writer to move him to write; it acts also on his intellect to enable him to discern what God wants written; it does not demand that he write only what has been supernaturally revealed. He may know naturally what he relates. An inspired writer remains in possession of his faculties; he is aware of what he is doing; is free to use his own style, his own vocabulary; but he is moved by God to say what God wants said—nothing less, nothing more.[2] Leo XIII says:

> Inspiration is a supernatural impulse by which the Holy Ghost urged and moved the sacred writers to write, and assisted them while they wrote, in such a way that they understood exactly, willed to report faithfully, and expressed with infallible truth all that God ordered and only what he ordered them to write.[3]

If ideas or facts God wanted written were unknown to the writer or could not be learned from natural sources, God revealed them. Revelation is direct communication of ideas; by it man learns from God.

An inspired writer was not necessarily conscious of God's inspiration. St. Luke asserts that he inquired diligently of eyewitnesses and earwitnesses and in every way tried to come into possession of the history of Christ. It does not appear that he received any of his information directly from God. There is no evidence that he ever met Jesus Christ. He had access to Paul, to other Apostles, to the mother of Christ, to Cleophas, and to others who had seen and heard Jesus.

Luke reported what he had learned from them. He wrote what eye and earwitnesses preached. He may not have been aware that he was inspired by God to write either of his books. St. Luke had all the natural advantages of a scientific historian; it is not necessary for us to maintain that he was aware of a divine impulse or inspiration to write either of his books.

> In the Bible there are books whose contents comprise truths and facts unquestionably taken from the writer's own stores of knowledge; there are other truths and facts which might have been revealed, but which may not have been revealed, and which lie side by side with truths that were revealed—and all of them—revealed, unrevealed and doubtful—are closely interwoven so as to form the texture of one story that is complete and organically whole. This story, we maintain, is inspired, not merely in the gross, scope and substance, but in all its parts and entirety. We hold, therefore, that the character of the contents, as revealed or unrevealed, has no direct bearing on the question of their inspiration.[4]

Christianity is a revealed religion; but it is also a historical religion. The historical facts concerning Christ and his Apostles can be ascertained before we raise the issue of whether our historical records are inspired and free from all error. Once we are sure we possess a reliable historical account of the words and deeds of Christ, we are in a position to judge his claim to be a teacher come from God. The Christian religion is founded on the historical fact of the resurrection of Jesus of Nazareth. It assumes the history of Israel recorded in the Old Testament. To know that Adam and Eve were the first man and woman; that they were elevated by grace to participate in supernatural life; that they sinned, involving their whole family in loss of supernatural dignity; that a redeemer born of a woman was promised—all this presupposes reliable historical records.

No one can defend Christianity intelligently without defending the Bible as a historical book.

To approach the study of the sources of supernatural religion with arrogance is inexcusable. Christianity is a great historical fact deserving serious examination. Whatever one's judgment about it, its concrete reality cannot be brushed aside. The Jewish people preserved their writings; Christians kept records of what Christ said and did. We are about to examine these as historical documents; to test their authenticity, integrity, and veracity.

Any person of prudent judgment will approach the study of the Bible with respect. At the very least, it is the oldest and most influential book in the possession of mankind.

Infallibility

If God willed to call men to a supernatural end; if, as a means to that end, he made a revelation; if he willed not only to preserve this revelation in written records but to have it preached and taught orally, it is reasonable to suppose that he would take measures to prevent errors from creeping into it as it was handed down from one generation to another. An intelligent God would not let official teachers change his message. If he willed to reveal truths upon which the supernatural happiness of rational creatures depends, he could not be indifferent to their exact transmission. As he inspired writers to say what he wanted said, so he took precautions that erroneous interpretations be excluded.

Infallibility is not the same thing as inspiration. Its purpose is to safeguard the purity and integrity of revelation already given. Whereas inspiration is positive, infallibility is negative. Inspiration moves a writer to say what God wants said; infallibility preserves revelation from infiltration by human opinions. It is not the gift of making new revelations; it is not inspiration; it is supernatural assistance to messengers sent by God, to prevent them from mixing errors with the supernatural message. Without this assistance, men would have been bewildered and could not be blamed for failing to recognize their obligation to believe the word of God.

Necessity of Revelation

Besides considering the possibility of supernatural revelation, which is a philosophical question, and the truth of revelation, which is a historical problem, it will be useful to discuss briefly the advantages, the utility, and even the necessity of divine revelation.

It is a boon to humanity to have the conclusions of sound philosophy concerning man's origin, nature and destiny confirmed by divine revelation. Men have always sought help from God and have desired to be taught by him. However sensual the orgies in which they have celebrated the feasts of their gods and however cruel the sacrifices by which they sought to appease them, history shows that men have sought enlightenment concerning their relationship to God from supernatural or preternatural sources. The sad history of philosophy shows that reason did not succeed in providing mankind with a satisfactory natural religion. To what extent the various races of men have received their religion by tradition and to what extent they have worked it out by reason is difficult to determine. The evidence of history goes to show that they have not depended on philosophers more than on prophets, priests and magicians to keep up their religious life.

Plato said men need a divine teacher to answer their questions concerning the spiritual world. They learn easily from a teacher, while most of them have little inclination to solve religious mysteries by abstract thinking. Even in regard to such essentials as the nature of God and the principles of morality, men have felt the need of tradition and leadership. History witnesses to deception by malign spirits. Most men are too busy, too lazy, too ignorant, too egotistical, too sensual to discover for themselves the truths of natural religion and morality. They are too weak to endure the stern discipline necessary to work out for themselves an adequate philosophy of life. St. Thomas Aquinas tells us:

> The truths about God that can be attained by natural reason are to a great extent also content of revelation and faith. This is wise. If men were exclusively dependent on their natural abilities for attaining truth only a few could possess sufficient knowledge of God. The majority of men for various reasons would be unable to devote themselves adequately to energetic thought, and arrive at these truths through their own mental labor.... The period of youth, so full of excitement and emotion, would be least given to a searching scrutiny of such profound truths. Finally, a purely natural knowledge of God is always liable to error. Many proofs of this are furnished in the history of philosophy. Hence it is well for a kind and wise Providence to include also natural truths in the sphere of revelation and faith. Thus all men with more ease possess a knowledge of God devoid of doubt and error.[5]

There is, however, an even more serious reason why men need divine revelation. Are men called to a supernatural end? This is the decisive historical question which underlies the notion of salvation as understood by Christians. If men are called to the beatific vision, as Christians believe, how else could they find it out except by revelation? Without supernatural knowledge, there could be no supernatural life. God is a spirit; he knows and loves; such is his life. Natural knowledge does not suffice for supernatural life. Christianity invites men to participate in divine life. But men cannot know supernaturally except by faith. Faith comes by hearing. It is preserved by tradition; it is a social inheritance.

> Supernatural religion may be defined as the sum of the new relations which elevate man to the dignity of a child of God, and assign him as final end the beatific vision, the sight of God face to face in heaven, as well as the duties which result from these supernatural relations.[6]

The main purpose of revelation is to inform men of the wonderful union of friendship with God to which the family of Adam was invited, of its loss by sin, and of its restoration by Christ. As we see them in history, men have always risen above or fallen below natural religion and morality. Everywhere there are men who are better or worse than the naturally good. A profound aversion toward God or a strong attraction toward him is discernible in human lives. The mystery of evil becomes intelligible in the light of supernatural revelation. The tradition that original sin disordered human love illuminates the sordid history of mankind.

The First Vatican Council said of the need for revelation:

> It is owing to this divine revelation, assuredly, that even in the present condition of the human race, those religious truths which are by their nature accessible to human reason can easily be known by all men with solid certitude and with no trace of error. Nevertheless, it must not be argued that revelation is, for that reason, absolutely necessary. It is necessary only because God, out of his infinite goodness, destined man to a supernatural end, that is, to a participation in the good things of God, which altogether exceed the human mental grasp; for "eye has not seen nor ear heard, nor has it entered into the heart of man, what things God has prepared for those who love him" (I Cor. 2:9).[7]

Rationalistic Criticism

For several centuries, divine revelation has been under attack by men who look upon any book that records miracles as unhistorical. Miracles do not occur, they say, because they cannot occur. Rationalists assume that there is no supernatural order; but no attempt is made to establish this fundamental postulate, despite the fact that Rationalist critics claim to be scientific historians

We, on the contrary, hold that if miracles did occur, they are facts and must be reckoned with. If Christ did rise from the dead, no amount of *a priori* reasoning based on pantheistic philosophy can prove that he did not. True scientists and historians find out the facts before philosophizing about them.

The central fact upon which Christian revelation depends is the historical Jesus Christ. Whatever interpretation is put upon his doctrine, example, and influence, it is a fact that he lived and that he influenced the history of mankind as no other man has influenced it. As Father Lattey declares:

> No amount of juggling with supposed sources has succeeded in making the conclusion plausible that Jesus was a nobody, who did nothing in particular: that after spending two or three years in uttering some beautiful morality and some mistaken prophecy, he was executed on account of some points in his teaching that seemed to favour revolt from Rome. Such a conclusion does not explain the tremendous upheaval accomplished in that short time, the bitter opposition of his enemies and the fervent devotion of his followers: nor yet the still greater upheaval in the world's history, the rapid development of a movement which soon became the most important factor in the world's history and has remained so ever since, in spite of all the learning and cunning and brutal violence turned against it.[8]

The history of Christ is contained chiefly in the Gospels,

the Acts of the Apostles, and the Epistles of St. Paul. We must show these to be authentic. The apologist's first task is to guarantee the books of the New Testament to be reliable historical documents. From these, he shows that Jesus of Nazareth claimed to be the Son of God, and that he established his claim by his life, doctrine, and miracles.

The reasonableness of the Christian faith depends upon the authority of the historical Christ. It must be settled on the field of history, not by the authority of the Church. The authority of the Church is a consequence of the divinity of Christ; and whether the Bible is inspired in all its parts must be decided by authority. But whether Jesus Christ said and did the things attributed to him is for history to decide. We are not concerned at present with either inspiration or infallibility, but with the historical reliability of the written records.

A Square Deal for Facts

Christianity is a positive religion, founded on historical facts. While it is true that the beginning, root and foundation of Christianity is faith or acceptance of truths on divine authority, reason provides adequate motives for faith. Reason can enable man to demonstrate the existence of a supernatural, personal God, and to furnish evidence that he has made a revelation to man. Before men can be expected to believe the word of God, they should know by reason that a supernatural God exists who has spoken through the Hebrew prophets and through Jesus Christ.

Summary

We defined revelation as God's unveiling of himself to

man through his works (natural revelation) and through direct communication of ideas by prophets (supernatural revelation). God made a supernatural revelation to Moses when he spoke to him from the burning bush, commanding him to deliver a message to the Hebrews and to Pharao. He certified this revelation by miracles first for Moses and afterward for Pharao and the Hebrews. The miracles were evidence that Moses was a teacher sent by God. Supernatural revelation is not confined to mysteries; it embraces all that God wishes to make known to man. It consists in communicating ideas to rational creatures by speech of God himself through his certified messengers. The truths manifested by revelation were delivered to men by historical persons: Moses, David, Isaias, Jesus of Nazareth.

Our object is to investigate the historical record of what is related in the Bible; to certify the Sacred Scriptures as a trustworthy source of truth. We oppose the view of Naturalists, Rationalists, and Modernists who try to explain the Bible as a natural evolution of religious consciousness, and regard its message as subject to constant evolution and restatement. For us divine revelation is supernatural. The Bible is a book come down from heaven, giving men a participation in God's eternal and unchangeable wisdom.

NOTES FOR CHAPTER I

1. Christopher Dawson, *Religion and Culture* (New York: Sheed and Ward, 1948), p. 43.
2. Andre Robert and Alphonse Tricot, *Guide to the Bible* (Westminster, Maryland: The Newman Press, 1951), Vol. I, pp. 8-20.
3. *Providentissimus Deus.*
4. Paul Schanz, *A Christian Apology* (New York: F. Pustet & Company, 1907), Vol. II, p. viii.
5. St. Thomas, *Contra Gentiles,* I, 4.
6. W. Devivier, *Christian Apologetics,* ed. Bishop S. G. Messmer (New York: Benziger Brothers, 1903), p. 28.
7. Vatican Council, *Revelation,* Chapter 2.
8. Cuthbert Lattey, S.J., *Back to the Bible* (London: Burns, Oates, and Washbourne, Ltd., 1944), pp. 80-81.

"The experimental sciences . . . have been invoked against the supernatural element in Holy Writ; especially against miraculous interference with what are called nature's laws. Miracles are impossible, we are told, because they are an interference with the constancy and uniformity of natural laws. Now, in the first place, it must be remembered that we stand in no need of modern science to be informed that nature behaves in certain uniform ways, e.g., that fire burns and that water quenches fire. Common observation has told us as much since the days of Adam. Science has but extended and methodized common observation. Nature's uniformity is no more certain today than it was thousands of years ago. But apart from that matter, neither science nor common observation can go a step further than to declare that it is *of the nature* of water, or of fire, or of any other natural agent to behave in a certain way, and that they have *as a matter of fact* so behaved. But to declare that under no circumstances can they behave otherwise is quite beyond their province."

—Rev. M. P. Hill, S.J.,
The Catholic's Ready Answer
(Benziger Brothers, 1915)

CHAPTER II

Miracles

Before examining the evidence for the historical truth of the Gospels, a discussion of miracles is needed because many people are under the mistaken impression that science has disproved the possibility of miracles, and that consequently any book which relates miracles as facts cannot be historically reliable. A true scientist, however, is supposed to view facts objectively: he does not deny what has been observed by competent witnesses, simply because it is wonderful. The more wonderful facts are, the more deserving they are of attention.

Like every positive science, history is supposed to record facts without preconceived notions as to their possibility or impossibility. The object of historical inquiry is to find out what happened. If miracles *did* occur, they *can* occur. If miracles are recorded by Matthew, Mark, Luke and John, and if these witnesses can be proved competent and honest, there is no historical ground for denying them. The question of the possibility of miracles does not fall within the province of science or history. In broad daylight, in the

presence of thousands of witnesses, the Evangelists say that
Jesus Christ worked miracles. Five thousand men besides
women and children witnessed one of those miracles; it
was the talk of the country.

Thomas Huxley said a scientist should sit down before
facts like a little child. But scientists often have preconceived opinions. Rationalists, Materialists, and Modernists
deny miracles because they have fallen under the spell of
pantheistic philosophy. For them Nature is God; consequently there can be no supernatural order, and miracles
cannot occur because there is no supernatural cause to
produce them. If we take our stand on the existence of a
personal God who created nature and who operates both
in it and above it, the possibility of miracles presents no
problem. God did not exhaust his resources in creating
nature.

In the following statement, we have a straightforward
presentation of the Rationalist attitude:

> The first obligation imposed on us by the Rationalist prin-
> ciple, which is the foundation of all criticism, is to eliminate
> the supernatural from the life of Christ. This at a single stroke
> removes from the Gospels what are called the miracles. Para-
> lytics and lepers cured instantly, the deaf, the dumb, and men
> born blind who suddenly recover their hearing or speech or sight,
> by a mere touch or word of Jesus—in all this there is clearly
> no reality. Not only did Jesus nothing of this sort, but I make
> bold to add it was not possible for such to be believed of Him
> while He was still alive ... Inasmuch as criticism declines to
> believe in accounts of miracles it has no need to advance proofs
> in support of the denials: what is related is false simply because
> what is related could not be.[1]

A man who has such an attitude may have a good opinion of himself, but from the point of view of scientific
history, he is foolishly naive. Unfortunately, his is the fundamental assumption of much modern criticism of the Bible.

Supernatural phenomena did not occur because they cannot occur. The world was not created; it evolved. Positive evidence counts for nothing. At all costs, the philosophy of evolutionism must be maintained. Why cannot miracles happen? Because they are inconsistent with materialistic or pantheistic evolution.

The objection to miracles on grounds that they are impossible is merely an inference drawn from a false system of philosophy. It has nothing to do with either science or history.

The Christian apologist today must be prepared to encounter a great deal of ignorance. Teachers and writers with no philosophical background accept as fundamental axioms definitions and principles of men who believe in the God of Spinoza rather than in the God of the Bible. For the pantheist, Nature is everything; consequently there is no transcendent God, no supernatural order, no miracles. Of course, if there is no God except Nature, there can be no miracles. If everything evolved from one impersonal substance; if this impersonal substance expresses itself completely in Nature so that beyond Nature nothing is conceivable, then there can be no divine revelation; there can be no prophecies, no inspired books, no supernatural religion. Grant the existence of a personal God who is able and willing to act supernaturally, and all objections to the possibility of miracles disappear.

Obediential Potency

All living beings possess active and passive powers. By their actions they can influence beings around them, and they can receive influence from other beings. Nevertheless, they are not self-sufficient in the exercise of their natural powers. They need divine assistance. God is always present to every creature by his power. He does not determine free creatures to act contrary to their free will, but concurs with them according to their nature. Such concurrence is part of the natural order; all creatures need it. Nature is not a self-sufficient mechanism; it depends on divine conservation and concurrence. This is basic to theistic philosophy.

To raise any creature to a sphere of being and activity beyond its natural possibilities requires supernatural power. God can strengthen natural powers by supernatural conservation and concurrence. The supernatural causality of God in creatures operates according to the nature of the creature. God can give man supernatural grace and knowledge because man has intellect and will. He could not so elevate an irrational animal.

To work a miracle, God, naturally immanent and active in all creatures, needs only to increase his conserving and concurring activity. Natural concurrence becomes supernatural concurrence whenever God wills to do more than the exigencies of any given creature call for, or of which its powers are capable. All the divine help a creature needs to enable it to attain its perfection is natural to it. Whatever divine assistance is given that raises a creature to be and to act beyond its natural needs and powers is supernatural. It is natural for man to know God through his works; it is supernatural to see him face to face. St. Thomas says:

> In the human soul, as in every other creature, passive power is twofold: first in relation to natural agents; second in relation to the First Cause which is able to move any creature to a higher

activity than it could reach under the influence of any natural agent. And this is called the obediential potency of creatures.[2]

The laws of nature were established when God gave each creature its nature, its natural appetites, and the good toward which it moves either of necessity or freely. Nature is the totality of creatures united into an ordered system. The natural active and passive powers of creatures are limited. God is intelligent; he considers the end of the whole as well as the end of each individual. Prayer, for instance, is a law of nature for rational creatures. In prayer, men acknowledge their dependence on God and their need for help. God can answer prayers without interfering with the laws of Nature. Surgeons do not act contrary to nature when they cut out a malignant growth; neither does God act contrary to nature when he answers prayers. St. Augustine explains this further:

> Not unreasonably we say that God does something contrary to nature when he acts contrary to what we know of nature. For this is what we call nature—the customary course of nature as known to us, against which, when God does everything, it is called a marvel or miracle. But as to that supreme law of nature, which is hidden from our knowledge either because we are impious or because we are still deficient in power to understand, God can no more act contrary to it than he can act contrary to himself.[3]

Besides the natural order which includes the whole visible created universe and man with his intellect and will, there is a preternatural order consisting of good and bad angels. They are more intelligent than men; they have powers of action superior to the powers of men. They can exert an influence in our world since they are part of the ordered system of creatures. They exert good and bad influence, subject to the providence of God. In considering the cause of miracles, account must be taken of the active and passive powers of angels and devils if we wish to distinguish a true miracle which manifests the supernatural power of God from a phenomenon which manifests the preternatural power of a devil. Since devils are not elevated to the supernatural order they can do only what they are qualified by nature to do; by nature they are superior to men, and can astonish men by the phenomena they can produce.

Monists, who deny a supernatural God, also deny angels and devils. That Christ should drive a legion of devils into a herd of swine seems to them absurd. They reject everything that cannot be explained by laws of mathematics, physics, and chemistry. Free will is out of place in their system. Natural scientists who are materialists, pantheists, or mechanists mix philosophy with natural science. They think it necessary to get rid of angels, devils, spiritual souls and vital principles in animals and plants.

But if a personal God exists, a supernatural order exists. God is supernatural; angels and devils are preternatural; free human beings are spiritual; hence the real world we live in is full of supraphysical, supraorganic, supramechanical phenomena.

The capacity possessed by every created nature under the direct influence of God to do what it could not otherwise do is called, as we have said, obediential potency. God can raise the dead. He has the power to do that sort of thing, just as man has the power to define terms which irrational animals cannot do. By immediate activity, God can influence the powers of created natures to produce effects they could not produce under the influence of any created agent.

The concept of obediential potency is basic to a proper understanding of miracles. Every created nature is susceptible of changes under the immediate influence of God, of which it is not susceptible under any other causality. All creatures have powers and exigencies suitable to their respective natures. To intellectual beings, God can reveal truths they could not know by natural means of knowledge. God cannot make a square circle because a square circle is inconceivable; but he can do whatever is intrinsically possible or conceivable. He is everywhere by his presence, power and essence. He can reveal supernatural truths to men because men have a natural capacity for learning from a teacher who can convey ideas and judgments to them in words they understand.

There is nothing in the science of the twentieth century that contradicts this notion of obediential potency. The mechanical concept of the universe, introduced by Descartes and advocated by many modern physicists, has definite limitations. Mathematicians are conscious that they deal with abstractions, aloof from existential reality. Physicists do not study substances, but phenomena, observed, abstracted and reduced to formal relations. Their theories do not touch substances, natures, essences, persons. Most scientists are not systematic thinkers embracing in a single world-view the whole of nature, including spiritual souls. Many of them deny the existence of the metaphysical, spiritual, supernatural worlds because they have accepted a false theory of knowledge such as empiricism, positivism, phenomenalism or pragmatism. Materialists and pantheists, no matter what their pretensions as scientists, are not equipped to judge the historical truth of supernatural events. They have made up their minds in advance that supernatural events are inconceivable.

Definition of a Miracle

Four definitions of miracle are given by John A. Hardon, S.J., in an article "Concept of Miracle" in *Theological Studies,* June, 1954:

> Miracles are spontaneous signs of God's special intervention in the world and manifestations of his presence. The miracle may also serve to testify his approval of certain teaching or personal holiness.
>
> The Vatican Council says "miracles are divine effects ... which clearly show forth the omnipotence of God."
>
> A miracle is an event produced by God beyond the order of created nature.
>
> Miracles are extrinsic signs which God performs to witness to the truth of some doctrine or to testify in favor of some person whose sanctity he wants recognized.

Not every supernatural event is a miracle. Invisible activity of the Holy Spirit, transubstantiation, regeneration through baptism, are supernatural events known only by faith. By a miracle, we mean an extraordinary event capable of being perceived by the senses of an observer whether he have faith or not. A miracle is a phenomenon or a happening that amazes, that strikes awe in those who witness it. No reasonable explanation of it can be given except that it is a manifestation of the supernatural power of God. There can be intellectual miracles, such as prophecies, observable by the natural cognitive powers of man. A miracle makes the presence of God evident to man's intellect as well as to his senses.

Throughout their history, the Jews expected miracles to certify divine messengers. We read in Exodus:

> Moses answered and said: They will not believe me, nor hear my voice. But they will say: The Lord hath not appeared to thee. Then he said to him: What is that thou holdest in thy hand? He answered: A rod. And the Lord said: Cast it down upon the ground. He cast it down, and it was turned into a serpent, so that Moses fled from it. And the Lord said: Put out thy hand and take it by the tail. He put forth his hand and took hold of it; and it was turned into a rod. That they may believe, saith he, that the Lord God of their fathers, the God of Abraham, the God of Isaac, and the God of Jacob hath appeared to thee. And the Lord said again: Put thy hand into thy bosom. And when he had put it into his bosom, he brought it forth leprous as snow. And he said: Put back thy hand into thy bosom. He put it back and brought it out again, and it was like the other flesh. If they will not believe thee, saith he, nor hear the voice of the former sign, they will believe the word of the latter sign. (Exodus 4:1-8)

Men of common sense can tell when they are witnessing a supernatural happening. Either the fact itself or the way it is done manifests the power of God. The raising of Lazarus was a greater miracle than curing Peter's mother-in-law. (A doctor might have cured her, though not so quickly.) The sudden cure of leprosy or blindness by a word is evidently supernatural because natural cures do not occur that way. If a woman has had arthritis for eighteen years and is bowed down so that she cannot straighten herself at all, her instantaneous cure by the mere touch of a prophet is beyond the power of natural means. The sudden cure of a man with a withered arm can be explained only by creative power. A miracle, therefore, whether it be supernatural in substance or only in mode, is an effect evidently due to supernatural causality.

Devils can make a herd of swine wild, or enable a possessed man to break chains. However, there are limits to the power of devils; their nature is finite. Devils would undoubtedly produce more confusion than they do if they were permitted by God. God does not allow them to terrorize men according to their own desires and whims. They not only have natural limitations, but in the use of such power as they naturally have, they are restrained by Divine Providence.

"Anyone could foretell in what these machinations would result, the instilling of a deadly poison, the opening of locked doors, laming horses, making them weak or rendering them furious, depriving men of the power of speech, or exciting in either sex ungovernable lusts."[4] So wrote Arnobius about 300 A.D., the antics of devils have not changed. Mechanists, however, are as unwilling to ascribe observable phenomena to devils as to a personal God.

Enemies of the supernatural like to call a miracle a "transgression of a law of nature." Such a definition suggests capricious interference with established laws. It suggests that God did not do things right the first time and has to tinker with his universe. Hume says: "A miracle may be accurately defined as a transgression of a law of Nature by a particular volition of the Deity or by the interposition of some invisible agent." This definition is a caricature. God does not transgress laws; he sustains all natural laws; he is the exemplar of all laws. A miracle is an effect of omnipotence surpassing any effect created agents can accomplish: it is an effect beyond the power of created causes. To surpass the course of Nature is not to contradict Nature—no more than to teach a new science is to contradict an existing science. No natural agent, no creature, can do all that God can do. God does not transgress a law of nature when he inspires a prophet. He is always concurring with natural agents in the use of their powers; why should he not increase his concurrence?

As a result of the hue and cry against miracles that has been raised by materialists and atheists who pose as learned scientists, many timid Christians became ashamed of biblical miracles. They beat a retreat. They came to consider miracles more embarrassing than helpful to Christian faith.

> Miracles have come to be regarded by an increasing number as less and less important for Christianity. So far from being essential to Christian faith, the whole tendency of the Modernist is to regard miracles as unnecessary.[5]

This position, however, is unworthy of anyone who acknowledges the existence of a supernatural God. Monists do not believe in miracles because they do not believe in divine concurrence, conservation, and providence. They are logical in denying miracles. Anyone who professes to believe in a supernatural God has no reason to be ashamed of miracles. They are sensible evidence of the care of God for rational creatures; they are necessary to establish the veracity of divine messengers. If God wishes to make a revelation to men through a prophet, why should he not accredit his prophet by supernatural signs?

Ecclesiastical Miracles

Timid Christians dread the frown of monists posing as scientists; and they are willing to give up the miracles of the Old Testament and all ecclesiastical miracles, provided scientists will allow them to keep the miracles of Christ. These compromisers do not realize that any intrusion of God, angels or devils into Nature is intolerable to pantheists and materialists. Newman bravely took the only consistent position for a theist:

> ... Lest I appear in any way to be shrinking from a determinate judgment on the claim of some of those miracles and relics which Protestants are so startled at, I will avow distinctly that ... I firmly believe that the relics of the saints are doing innumerable miracles and graces daily and that it needs only for a Catholic to show devotion to any saint in order to receive special benefits from his intercession. I firmly believe that saints in their lifetime have before now raised the dead to life, crossed the sea without vessels, multiplied grain and bread, cured incurable diseases and superseded the operation of the laws of the universe in a multitude of ways.[6]

Writing in *La Croix,* Catholic daily published at Lourdes, Dr. Leuret replied to a newspaper attack on the "unhygienic conditions of the Lourdes baths" by declaring that "hygiene has nothing whatsoever to do with the baths and waters of Lourdes." Although the waters are only changed twice a day and hundreds of sick, many with suppurating wounds or contagious diseases, bathe in them, never in ninety years, said Dr. Leuret, has a case of transferred infection been recorded. Such a case, he added, would not have gone unrecorded, "for those who deny the supernatural effects of Lourdes have watched eagerly for some such evidence to use as a weapon against the shrine."

On the contrary, wrote Dr. Leuret, experiments conducted have shown that microbes lose their virulence when they come in contact with the Lourdes waters. Such experiments had been made, he said, by Professor Mazzeo of the Naples Institute of Hygiene. The water acts as if it contained penicillin, he asserted, but tests have shown that there is no penicillin present. Never in the history of the Lourdes shrine, the doctor insisted, has any harm come to anyone, sick or well, from immersion in the icy waters. All this is "the continual miracle of Lourdes, which cannot be explained by science and which is outside the normal laws of hygiene."

The truly religious man is sensitive to the presence of God. Whereas the atheist thinks of the world as self-existent, moved by mechanical laws under whose influence evolution occurs in a blind, mechanical way, the religious man thinks of the world as governed by a personal, omnipotent God who is everywhere present, in whom all creatures "live and move and are." Miracles appear to mechanists to be medieval superstitions, but to the spiritually enlightened they are expressions of the personal love of their all-powerful Father and Friend. It is logical, therefore, to deny miracles altogether or to look for a good many miracles.

Prophecies

Because man possesses intellect he has obediential potency to be elevated to participation in God's own life of knowing and loving. Aristotle said intellect is in potency to all things. Plato called attention to the ease with which men learn from a teacher compared with the difficulty they experience in discovering knowledge for themselves. Human teachers are limited in their ability to communicate knowledge. Men could learn more if teachers knew more. Since God is omniscient, he is the greatest teacher. From him, men can learn what would otherwise be unknowable.

Isaias' prediction that the Messias would suffer for the sins of mankind, Micheas' prophecy that the Messias would be born in Bethlehem, Christ's declaration that he would rise from the dead on the third day after his death, presuppose supernatural vision of the future. Such knowledge is possible only to God. Great minds like Pascal and Leibnitz and Bossuet were filled with awe by prophecies and their fulfillment. Prophesies are enduring miracles; anyone with intelligence can witness them. The Hebrew prophecies and their fulfillment in Christ are unassailable, historical facts. No hypothesis except divine revelation is adequate to explain them.

Quadratus, about 125 A.D., wrote:

> But the works of our Saviour were always present, for they were genuine: those who were healed and those who rose from the dead—who were seen not only when they were healed and when they were raised but were constantly present; and not only while the Saviour was living, but even after he had gone they were alive for a long time, so that some of them survived even to our own day.[7]

The physical miracles of Christ remained for years in the persons raised from the dead or cured; prophecies continue for thousands of years and are open to the observation of anyone intelligent enough to appreciate them even at the present time.

Moral Miracles

The conversion of Saul of Tarsus and the conversion of Europe to Christianity were moral miracles. Saul's conversion is intelligible if one accepts his own account of it; on any other theory it remains unintelligible. The change wrought in pagans from cruelty to their wives, slaves, and defective children to tender Christian charity cannot be explained without assuming supernatural assistance. St. Augustine says: "Deny that the spread of Christianity was accompanied by miracles and the greatest miracle of all remains to be explained—the spread of Christianity without miracles."

Miracles are so woven into the text of the Gospels that they cannot be expurgated without substantially altering the records. Either Christ's miracles occurred or his whole history is a fraud. Every attempt to give a naturalistic explanation of miracles proved to be fantastic even to Rationalists. Harnack, a distinguished scholar and a Rationalist, says: "To reject documents as utterly unserviceable or to assign them to a later period because they contain accounts of miracles arises from a prejudice. . . . We have no right to hide behind the gospel-miracles in order to escape from the gospels."[8]

The miracles of the Bible are related as historical facts. If the Evangelists were eyewitnesses or disciples of eyewitnesses, twentieth century critics have no valid reason for rejecting their reports. The critics were not present; they are in no position to judge. Their attempts to rewrite the history of Israel succeed only in producing fiction.

Certainty of Miracles

Renan argued that no one can ever be sure a miracle really happened. He did not say miracles are impossible, but that we lack sufficient evidence to establish their truth. He demanded that a miracle be worked before a learned body such as the French Academy, in order to make it credible for scholars. Hume said it is more likely those who have reported miracles were mistaken than that miracles really occurred. "The history of miracles is of a kind totally different from that of common events. It is always to be suspected."

We read that, at the command of God, Moses cast down his rod and it turned into a serpent; when, at the command of God, he took the serpent by the tail it changed back into a rod. Could not Moses be certain of such an experience? If Moses put his hand into his bosom and took it out full of leprosy, then put it back and it was restored to health, how could Moses forget what happened? The career of Moses is essential to the history of Israel. The miracles he worked in Egypt affected the lives of hundreds of thousands of Egyptians and Israelites. If the miracles did not occur, how explain the influence of Moses? The law of parsimony is invoked by critics of miracles; phenomena should not be called miracles if they can be attributed to a natural cause. But the only hypothesis that makes sense of the history of Israel is the truth of the miracles of Moses.

On one occasion Jesus is reported to have fed five thousand men besides women and children with five loaves and two fishes. Five thousand witnesses perceived this miracle by sight, touch, and taste. They did not need great learning to know that they were hungry, that they were fed, that there was no place to buy food in the wilderness where the event occurred. Such a quantity of bread and fish could not have been concealed. Eyewitnesses were so impressed that they wanted to make Jesus their king. This miracle is narrated by the four Evangelists. After the miracle twelve baskets of fragments were gathered up. How could so many people have been deceived? Could not anyone who disputed the fact have ascertained from some of the five thousand witnesses what really happened? This miracle was preached throughout Palestine from 29 to 44 A.D. The Gospels of Matthew, Mark, and Luke were in circulation during the lifetime of many eyewitnesses. If any trust is to be placed in human testimony, this miracle is a historical fact. If it did not occur, why were there no contemporary denials? Why did the enemies of Christ maintain silence? If there is any valid history, the testimony of eyewitnesses must be accepted.

Good Will

The cognitive powers of man do not determine themselves; they are determined by evidence. Witnesses of a miracle know what they saw. Thomas did not doubt that he saw and touched the risen Christ. The enemies of Christ were nonplussed at the raising of Lazarus; even to them it was an evident miracle. Because they are extraordinary phenomena, miracles attract attention. In the time of Christ, no one denied that he worked miracles. He healed the sick, raised the dead, and everyone knew it. Why was it that in an environment fiercely hostile to Christ no one attempted to deny his miracles? Annas, Caiphas, and the Pharisees, Scribes, and Sadducees were anxious to silence Peter and John after they cured the lame man at the gate of the temple.

> What shall we do with these men? For indeed a miracle hath been done by them, known to all the inhabitants of Jerusalem. It is manifest; and we cannot deny it. . . . For the man was above forty years old in whom the miraculous cure had been wrought. (Acts 4:16-22)

Enemies of Christ would have been eager to deny his miracles, but there were too many witnesses. A man born blind, an illiterate, put to confusion priests and officers of the temple when they argued that Christ was a sinner because on the Sabbath he restored a blind man's sight.

> Why herein is a wonderful thing that you know not from whence he is and he hath opened my eyes. Now we know that God doth not hear sinners: but if a man be a server of God and doth his will him he heareth. From the beginning of the world it hath not been heard that any man hath opened the eyes of one born blind. Unless this man were of God he could not do anything. (John 9:30-33)

NOTES FOR CHAPTER II

1. Havet, *Revue des Deux Mondes*, April 1, 1881, p. 587, quoted by Louis C. Fillion, *Life of Christ* (St. Louis: B. Herder Book Company, 1929), Vol. II, p. 647.
2. St. Thomas Aquinas, *Summa Theologica*, 3a, q. 11, art. 1.
3. St. Augustine, *Contra Faust*, XXVI, 3.
4. *Adversus Gentes*, 2, 43.
5. A. C. Cotter, S.J., *Theologia Fundamentalis* (Weston, Massachusetts: Weston College Press, 1940), p. 71.
6. John Henry Newman, *Lectures on the Present Position of Catholics in England* (New York: Longmans, Green and Company, 1891), pp. 312-13.
7. Eusebius, *Historia Ecclesiastica*, IV, 3.
8. Louis C. Fillion, *Life of Christ* (St. Louis: B. Herder Book Company, 1929), Vol. II, p. 649.

"When you are really instructed in the Divine Scriptures, and have realized that its laws and testimonies are the bonds of truth, then you can contend with adversaries; then you will fetter them and lead them bound into captivity; then of the foes you have made captive you will make freedmen of God."

—St. Jerome

CHAPTER III

Great Religious Facts

In our defense of the Bible against Rationalists, Modernists, and others who deny either the possibility or the fact of supernatural revelation, we desire to make clear at the outset that we use the scientific method, not the method of authority. We intend to verify the historical reliability of the books of the Bible, and then to demonstrate that no theory can explain the facts they relate without postulating a supernatural cause.

Those who are committed to the view that God is not only immanent in Nature but identical with Nature are not free to observe supernatural happenings objectively. They must deny, *a priori*, supernatural facts, and insist that the Bible is a product of natural evolution. They are philosophers first and historians afterwards.

Now if there be no transcendent God, there can be no supernatural order; if there is no supernatural order, there is no divine revelation. Supernatural activity is impossible without a supernatural cause. The God of the Bible is a supernatural God who invites men to supernatural happiness. Rationalists are convinced before they examine the lives of Moses or Jesus of Nazareth that neither of them ever worked a miracle. The Bible teaches that God created the world; pantheistic and materialistic evolutionists know, *a priori,* that he did not. Any Biblical critic who postulates that the world originated by evolution out of some eternal substance is disqualified from using the scientific method in dealing with facts related in the Bible. He assumes that miracles are impossible; he infers that they did not occur. Therefore, he says, the Bible must be expurgated.

Christian Apologetics Does Not Debate Theism

Christian Apologetics does not debate theism; this is a matter for Natural Apologetics. No one but a theist is prepared to study Christian Apologetics. Divine revelation implies the existence of a personal God, immanent in the world, but not limited by it, conserving the world and concurring with its inhabitants in the exercise of their natural powers, always able to increase his conserving and concurring activity. Faith is motivated by knowledge of God's existence. This motive must be supplied by reason. No one can have rational grounds for believing a divine revelation unless he admits that there is a personal God to make such a revelation.

From Genesis to Apocalypse, the Bible assumes that God, the Creator, can speak to men and can accredit his messengers by giving them power to work miracles. Demonstration of the existence of God is the work of Natural Apologetics; demonstration of the historical truth of Christ and his miracles is the work we are now engaged upon. Our business is to establish the historical truth of the Gospels concerning the life, death and resurrection of Jesus Christ. Anyone whose philosophy does not permit him to believe in miracles or in supernatural revelation is cut off from making an honest inquiry concerning these historical facts. Such people's minds are closed; they know for certain that the miracles of Christ did not occur because, according to their philosophy, miracles cannot occur.

The Bible records miracles. If Moses did not converse with God, the Pentateuch is a myth. If Jesus Christ did not work miracles, Christianity is a fraud. Every Christian apologist must be alert to the dishonesty of critics who pretend to approach the Bible as impartial, scientific historians while in reality they are apostles of materialistic or pantheistic evolution.

There is no use trying to prove the veracity of the Bible to a pantheist or materialist; the Bible relates happenings that could not occur unless God created this world and watches over it with intelligent love. A reasonable discussion of the historical value of the Bible presupposes open minds. No doubt there is no such thing as an unbiased attitude toward Christ; people are always for him or against him. Frankly we are for Christ and for supernatural religion; we do not conceal it.

Truth needs no more than a fair hearing by an honest mind. On the other hand, profound subconscious hatred of everything supernatural is an impediment to the use of scientific method. Our fundamental disagreement with Higher Critics, Rationalists, Naturalists and Modernists is not over scientific method or historical criticism. We object, rather, to their lack of objectivity: their failure to use unbiased scientific method.

Jesus Christ a Colossal Fact

The actual existence of Jesus of Nazareth, surnamed the Christ, founder of the Christian religion, crucified under Pontius Pilate about 29 A.D., is not debated by scholars. Christianity is a historical fact, patent to everyone. The scientific historian cannot explain Christianity without its founder, Jesus of Nazareth. His divinity may be denied, his virgin birth ridiculed, his theological system attributed to St. Paul and St. John, but his real existence as a historical person is unquestioned and unquestionable.

Christianity has nineteen centuries of history behind it; it has been the chief agent of Western culture. The Israelites are a fact; they have almost four thousand years of history behind them. Their sacred literature was known in Egypt and Babylon before the coming of Christ. Whatever be said about their inspiration, the sacred books of the Hebrews, are a fact. Scientific method consists in observing facts and trying to explain them by reasonable hypotheses. The foreground of Jesus of Nazareth is the history of Christianity; the background is the history of Israel.

The full light of history shines on Jesus Christ. He is not a legendary figure rising out of the mist of folklore. What he said and did during his brief public life influenced men more than the words and deeds of any other man. Ever since his tragic death on the cross between two thieves outside the walls of Jerusalem, men have thought about him, talked about him, written about him, fought about him and died about him. He bestrides history like a colossus. Years are counted in both directions from his birth. After nineteen centuries he, more than any philosopher, poet, statesman or soldier, is in the minds of men. Whether you are for him or against him, you cannot deny his historical prominence. His example has been an inspiration and his doctrine a light to countless millions. Grandmaison writes:

> Unlike Buddha Sakyamuni, Jesus did not come into the world during a period half-known, in which history and legend dispute over names and facts; nor was he born, like Mahomet, in a remote district of Arabia. The Jewish world of the first century, particularly the Palestinian world, is well known to us; its national vicissitudes, its complete political system, the flow of ideas and influences within its borders, all are in the full light of history. Its immediate surroundings, too, are an integral part of ancient civilization in one of the most brilliant and best known periods . . . Born under the rule of Augustus and dying under that of Tiberius, Jesus was the contemporary of Philo the Jew, of Titus Livius and Seneca. Virgil, if he had lived to normal age, might have seen him, while Nero, Flavius Josephus, Plutarch and Tacitus belonged to the generation which immediately followed him.[1]

Ever since 1835 when David Strauss wrote his *Life of Christ,* Rationalists have tried to explain Christ and Christianity as products of natural evolution; but their theories proved unsatisfactory not only to Christian scholars but to later Rationalist historians. Everyone who has tried to write a serious life of Christ has been forced to declare him beyond human comprehension. Biographers who set out to analyze him and his influence, to show his strong points and his weak points, to show the limitations of his doctrine, to synthesize his system, to exhibit his inferiority to modern thinkers, were put to confusion. They ended by confessing that no one ever surpassed Jesus Christ. Strauss, Renan, Harnack, Bousset, and many other Liberal theologians paid tribute to the surpassing excellence of Jesus of Nazareth. They admitted that, in spite of centuries of evolution, no one has equalled him in doctrine, in example, or in influence. They try to explain Jesus Christ without admitting his divinity; but their attempts have been futile. Jesus Christ was too big for them; they could not master him. One indication of this inadequacy has been their failure to satisfy other Rationalists.

Early Rationalists attempted to show that the Gospels were not written until late in the second century; and that until the canon of the New Testament was defined in the fourth century they were increased by additions and corrections until only a faint and uncertain trace of the historical Christ remained. But historical research completely reversed this opinion. Every competent historian came to realize that the epistles of St. Paul could not be questioned. Magnificent research, both in the field of textual criticism (Lower Criticism) and in the field of investigating the authenticity and veracity of individual books of the New Testament (Higher Criticism) paved the way for the Rationalist Harnack to declare that the Gospels belong, in all essentials, to "the primitive Judaic period of Christianity, to that short) period which we may call palaeontological." Their unique character, he said, is undeniable. In the Gospels, we are "face to face with primitive tradition."[2]

This does not mean that deniers of the existence of a supernatural God and of supernatural revelation have been converted to Christianity. They are still dominant in the universities of Europe and America. But historical research and textual criticism have forced historians to recognize most of the Epistles of St. Paul and the first three Gospels to be authentic historical documents. Those who pretended that the Christ of faith was a product of second century evolution were exposed as willful men who searched not for truth but for evidence to bolster up their denial of a supernatural order. The task of the Christian apologist is easier now than it was at the end of the nineteenth century. Historians have confirmed Christian tradition. Our task will be to record the findings of scholars who spent their lives investigating the historical truth of the books of the New Testament.

That there can be no completely unbiased attitude toward the historical foundation of the Christian religion is to be expected. Everyone has an attitude toward the existence of a personal God and personal immortality. The issue is tremendous and no one can be indifferent. The hypothesis of original sin and redemption by the incarnate Son of God is opposed not only to the hypothesis of either materialistic or pantheistic evolution but to all forms of Naturalism or Rationalism. Nevertheless the strictly historical question as to the reliability of the Gospels as sources of information concerning the life of Jesus of Nazareth can be examined on its merits. We shall try to be impartial, but we cannot respect opponents who claim to follow the modern scientific method of induction but who in truth would not admit a miracle if they observed it with their own eyes.

What the people of the twentieth century know about Jesus of Nazareth has been handed down to them by witnesses no longer living. Reliable witnesses ought to be believed. Social progress is impossible without historical tradition. Man is born into society and receives a social inheritance from parents and teachers. If he cannot trust his parents and teachers, he cannot become a cultured man. History takes this law of solidarity for granted. Revealed religion, like all other human institutions, depends on historical tradition.

Background of Jesus Christ

Jesus Christ is a fact no matter what hypothesis is offered

to explain him. Christianity, with its ancient, world-wide organization, is a fact, whether it be considered supernatural or the product of natural evolution. The sacred books which comprise the Old Testament are an obvious fact to be explained by deniers of supernatural revelation. No one can question the ancientness of these books since they were translated into Greek at least two centuries before Christ. At the time of Josephus (first century) they were revered as sacred and venerable. They are a literary and historical phenomenon of prime importance.

Seisenberger writes, with regard to this background of Christianity:

> The Christian religion, and with it the whole civilization of Christian nations, is based on Israel. The modern world, which calls itself Christian, is inseparably connected with the people of Israel, and the new covenant between God and man, instituted by Christ, is only the extension and development of the old Israelite covenant. Out of Israel proceeded the Saviour and salvation for the whole world. Amidst the Israelites grew up the body of literature that both Jews and Christians venerate as *Holy Scriptures*. What Greece and Rome received from the East they passed on with their own additions to the West, and thence the benefits of salvation have been spread abroad over the whole world. . . . No one can attain a full comprehension of the documentary evidence for our faith without taking into consideration the circumstances of the early history of the Jewish race and the course of events affecting this people.[3]

We do not intend to enter into an examination of the historical value of each book of the Old Testament. This is not necessary. If we can show that Jesus of Nazareth is a teacher sent by God, his authority will establish the credit of Moses, the psalms and the prophets as inspired writings.[4] We shall concentrate on proving the historical reliability of the Gospels, the Epistles of St. Paul, and the Acts of the

Apostles, because these are the main sources of information about Jesus Christ.

Nevertheless, our readers must know enough about the Old Testament to be aware that the Hebrews preserved the tradition of the creation of the world out of nothing, the special creation of man, of his elevation and fall. Otherwise, the mission of Christ will not be understood. Had there been no fall from a supernatural order, and no law of solidarity, there would have been no need for a Savior to rehabilitate the human family. All early Christian apologists endeavored to prove that Jesus of Nazareth fulfilled the Hebrew prophecies. This argument does not impress people who are ignorant of the Old Testament. Indeed, to do justice to it one should know well the history of Israel. For example, God told Moses he would raise up a prophet like unto him. If one knows nothing about Moses, he cannot understand how the deliverance of the Hebrews out of Egypt typified the deliverance of the human race from the bondage of sin.

We are not going to presume that everyone who has finished high school, even Catholic high school, knows enough about the history of Israel to appreciate the argument from the prophecies for the divinity of Christ. We are sure this is not so. The Bible is given little attention in American schools, whether public or private. Our experience in and out of the classroom has made us aware that many are pitifully ignorant of the principal characters as well as of the principal ideas of the Old Testament, or they have been taught distorted views based on the theories of the Higher Critics.

We propose, therefore, to preface our study of the authenticity, integrity and veracity of the New Testament with a bird's eye view of the history of Israel. Introductions to the Bible have been one of the chief means by which Rationalists have destroyed respect for the Bible as a supernatural book. Pope Leo XIII pointed out in his great encyclical *Providentissimus Deus* that the best way to combat Higher Critics of the Bible is to know more about the Bible than they do. "Nothing is more necessary than that truth should find defenders more powerful and numerous than the enemies it has to face." At the time he wrote this encyclical, Higher Critics in Germany were devoting all their energies to study of the Bible, while both Protestants and Catholics were neglecting it. Thus the Higher Critics were able to undermine the faith of millions of Christians. The situation has in some respects become worse in recent years, since the views of the Higher Critics have gained acceptance in Catholic circles and are being presented as the fruits of "modern scholarship."

The more one knows about the Old Testament the better. Jesus Christ is incomprehensible to even the greatest scholars; he resembles a mighty mountain whose top is always shrouded in mists. Yet of all historical persons, study of him is most rewarding. One who knows what kind of Messias the prophets taught the chosen people to expect will have his eyes opened for aspects of Christ that could be missed by one who lacks this background. In our days prophecies do not appeal because generations brought up on newspapers and secular magazines know little or nothing about them. Nevertheless, the central idea of the Old Testament is the rehabilitation of the family of Adam by the coming of a Redeemer who was to reestablish on a firm basis the kingdom of God, that is, a supernatural kingdom on earth whose purpose is to prepare men for permanent membership in the everlasting kingdom of heaven. The crucifixion of Christ is the center of human history. To appreciate the crucifixion one should try to learn what led up to it, as well as its effect on human society.

Reading the Bible

Anyone ambitious to improve his mind should read the Bible. No other book will reward so richly time spent upon it. Every now and then a Catholic bobs up who says no one ever told him to read the Bible. We refer him to the encyclical of Pope Benedict XV on St. Jerome, in which he strongly recommends founding societies in honor of St. Jerome to promote reading of Holy Scripture. St. Jerome says to Eustochium: "Read assiduously and learn as much as you can. Let sleep find you holding your Bible and when your head nods let it be resting on the sacred page." Pope Benedict concludes: "We shall never desist from urging the faithful to read the Gospels, the Acts and the Epistles so as to gather thence food for their souls."[5] Pope Leo XIII granted a special indulgence to all who read the Bible fifteen minutes a day. The Bishops of the Third Council of Baltimore exhorted American Catholics: "The most highly valued treasure of every family library and the most frequently and lovingly made use of should be the Holy Scriptures." Pope Gregory I referred to the Bible as "a letter addressed by Almighty God to mankind." In 1952, Pius XII, blessing the work of the Confraternity of Christian Doctrine, urged "the faithful of the United States to give themselves in increasing numbers to a more frequent reading of the Bible."

What a paradox! Higher Critics, opposed to belief in supernatural religion, devoting all their time to the study of the Bible in order to destroy men's faith in its divine inspiration, while Catholic schools, supposed to be defenders of the Bible, devote their energies to secular studies! Pressure is put on religious schools in the United States by accrediting agencies to conform to secular curricula, with the result that such basic subjects as Bible history and Church history are often ignored. The encyclical *Providentissimus Deus,* in 1893, called attention to the necessity for Biblical studies, and since then there has been a revival. But this revival has not produced the results that Leo XIII expected. Many Catholic priests who specialized in Holy Scripture assimilated the errors of Rationalism and Modernism, and introduced them into Catholic colleges and high schools.

Enlightened educators recommend reading a chapter of the Old and a chapter of the New Testament every day as an invaluable habit for one who wishes to inform and improve his mind. The Bible has inspired generation after generation of men of every nation; it has furnished artists with gorgeous imagery, saints with knowledge, statesmen with enlarged vision, orators with power and writers with literary charm. Poets, painters, sculptors and architects make so many allusions to the Bible and borrow so much from it that anyone ignorant of it cannot appreciate the literature and art of Europe. Certainly no one can claim to be deeply and widely cultured without familiarity with the Bible. The cathedrals are said to be the Bible in stone. Illiterates in the Middle Ages knew more about the Bible from what they saw and heard than most Americans know from what they have read.

NOTES FOR CHAPTER III

1. Leonce de Grandmaison, S.J., *Jesus Christ: His Person, Message, Credentials* (New York: Sheed and Ward, 1935), Vol. I, p. 3, translated from the original work, *La Personne de Jesus et ses Temoins* (Paris: Beauchesne et ses fils).

2. *Essence of Christianity* (New York, 1904), p. 32.

3. Michael Seisenberger, *Practical Handbook for the Study of the Bible* (New York: Joseph F. Wagner, 1933), p. 3.

4. For detailed information concerning the history of each book in the Bible, see John E. Steinmueller, *A Companion to Scripture Studies* (New York: Joseph F. Wagner, Inc., 1942-1962; Houston: Lumen Christi Press, 1969). Volume I is a General Introduction, Volume II deals with the Old Testament, and Volume III with the New.

5. *Spiritus Paraclitus.*

"It is clear from the Old Testament that God did, indeed, visit His people, and that these visitations took place in history. . . .

". . . If our study is to be truly biblical, it must come to grips with the fact that God—the living and true God, the triune God—did in fact reveal Himself to Moses at the burning bush. The revelation took place in history. It took place on a certain day of our calendar and at a very definite spot in the Sinai wilderness. There was a man named Moses, and there was a specific bush. The bush burned with fire, but, unlike other bushes which burn, this particular bush did not burn up, and the reason for this strange phenomenon was that God performed a miracle. Unless these historical facts are presupposed, we shall waste our time if we try to study the significance and meaning of what is narrated."

—Edward J. Young, *The Study of Old Testament Theology Today* (Fleming H. Revell Company, 1959)

CHAPTER IV

History of Israel

We may divide Bible history as follows: (1) From the creation of the world to the call of Abraham; that is, from the beginning of time to the year 2000 B.C. All the Bible has to say about this immense epoch is told in eleven chapters. Genesis, the first book of the Bible, relates the call of Abraham in chapter twelve. (2) The formation of the families of Abraham, Isaac and Jacob (Genesis 12-50). (3) Moses and the organization of Israel (Exodus, Leviticus, Numbers and Deuteronomy). (4) The settling of the twelve tribes in Palestine (Josue). (5) The Judges. (6) The first kings, Saul and David (I and II Samuel). (7) History of the ten tribes until their exile in 722 B.C.; history of the two tribes to their exile in 586 B.C. (III and IV Kings; I and II Chronicles). (8) Babylonian captivity; return under Zorobabel in 536 B.C.; influence of Esdras and Nehemias (Esdras and Nehemias). (9) Rise of the Machabees (I and II Machabees); Hasmoneans; Herod. (10) John the Baptist. The Hebrews divided the Bible into the Law, the Prophets and the Psalms (Sapiential Books).

51

Principal Dates[1]

Creation to Abraham (Genesis I-XI) . . . . .all dates uncertain
Abraham . . . . .about 2000 B.C.
Moses . . . . .about 1450 B.C.
David . . . . .about 1000 B.C.
Building of the Temple by Solomon. . . . . .about 969 B.C.
Division of Kingdom. . . . . .about 932 B.C.
Destruction of Northern Kingdom. . . . . .about 722 B.C.
Babylonian Exile . . . . .about 586 B.C.
Return from Exile. . . . . .about 536 B.C.
Arrival of Nehemias. . . . . .about 445 B.C.
Rise of Machabees. . . . . .about 168 B.C.
Subjection to Romans. .about 64 B.C.
Death of Herod I. . . . . .about 4 B.C.
Birth of Jesus Christ. . . . . .about 5 B.C.

Creation of the World

The first sentence of the Bible is: "In the beginning God created heaven and earth." God created; that is, he produced the whole substance of the material world out of nothing. The world did not evolve out of God's own substance; before it was created it did not exist, either actually or potentially. The God of the Bible transcends the world he created; he created freely; he was not constrained to create to satisfy any need of his own for activity, perfection, happiness or companionship. The God of the Bible is intelligent, free, distinct from the universe. He is a self-existent person. On him all creatures depend for their origin and continued existence. They all began to be. God did not begin to be.

What the Bible has to say about the creation of matter, the formation of the solar system, the origin of plants and animals, is told on one page. Anyone who has the notion that the Bible is full of Hebrew myths and legends concerning astronomy, geology, zoology and botany can disabuse himself of this error by noting that the Bible covers the whole subject of the creation of the sub-human world, including sun, moon, plants and animals, in one chapter. The Bible states that all things were created by God out of nothing. It does not condescend to details; it ascribes the origin of the visible universe with all its inhabitants to the free activity of a self-existent First Cause; it does not tell how God created; it simply records the fact. Moses had no intention of writing a scientific cosmology. He made a long story short.

The Creation and Fall of Man

The Bible gives more information about the origin of man. God formed man's body out of the slime of the earth and breathed into it a rational soul. He made man to his own image and likeness; he gave him intellect and will. The first man was able to talk, to name the animals, and to make a graceful speech when God presented to him his specially-created wife. Adam was monogamous. He was not a cave-man or barbarian. The first woman was beautiful and able to carry on an intelligent conversation. Adam and his wife enjoyed God's personal friendship. They lost it by deliberate disobedience. In mercy, God promised to put enmity between the woman and Satan who seduced her.

The first three chapters of the Bible are the oldest historical record in the possession of man. What is set down there is not myth or legend. It is a very old tradition preserved by Abraham and transmitted to Moses by the patriarchs, or revealed to him by God. It antedates Israel. What is related in these three chapters is of prime importance for everything that follows. The creation of the world at the beginning of time; the special creation of man;

the special creation of the first woman; the unity of the human race; the original happiness of the first man and woman in a state of justice, integrity and immortality; the divine command laid upon them to test their obedience; their disobedience at the instigation of Satan under the form of a serpent; their fall from their primitive state of innocence; the promise of a future redeemer.[2]

The Biblical account of the origin of the world and of man is inconsistent with most theories of evolution. Creation out of nothing implies the existence of a supernatural, personal First Cause; and the punishment of man for disobedience implies a First Cause who is a moral ruler, concerned about the conduct of men as well as about the progress of Nature. The elevation of man to the personal friendship of God implies the state of grace which was lost by Adam's disobedience and restored by the promised Messias.

From Adam to Noe

The first man disobeyed God. His oldest son, Cain, murdered his brother because his brother was more pleasing to God than he was. Cain was a rebel and an ingrate. God did not put him to death, but placed a mark on him and banished him from the rest of his father's family. The fifth chapter of Genesis gives a list of Seth's descendants, remarkable for antediluvian health and long lives. Although their ages when they begot their first-born sons are recorded, we are not sure all of Noe's ancestors are listed, or only the most prominent. Moreover, manuscripts do not agree on numbers. Nothing is definite as to the time that elapsed between Adam and Noe.

Cain was a husbandman and Abel a shepherd. Both knew how to offer sacrifice, to care for domestic animals, to make a fire and to talk intelligently. According to the Bible, men did not pass through a period of many thousands of years during which they lived as savages, not knowing their right hand from their left, unable to distinguish between right and wrong, without tools or fire. From the beginning they were sinners, but not barbarians. Making due allowances for anthropomorphism, the first men described in the Bible are credited with a vivid realization of the presence of God, ability to understand what they were told, and conscious of their duty to obey.

Noe and the Deluge

God showed mercy to Cain, but his descendants continued in the footsteps of their father. Their imaginations and passions were bent on evil. Giants were born of the sons of God and the daughters of men. The Septuagint translates "sons of God" as "angels," as if the wicked giants were half-angels. Most commentators understand the giants to have been offspring of sons of Seth and daughters of Cain. They were giants inasmuch as they lived for centuries and became very wicked and cruel in the course of their long lives. Because of their wickedness, God decided to destroy all men with the exception of Noe, who was good and just, and his family. Noe preached penance for a hundred years while he built a great ark. Finally, he entered the ark with his wife, his three sons, and their wives. The deluge came: "all the fountains of the great deep were broken up, and the floodgates of heaven were opened." It lasted for a year. We cannot tell exactly how much of the surface of the earth was inundated; we can be certain, however, that there was a very great flood.

The Chosen People

God promised Noe not to destroy mankind with another flood. Nevertheless, men sinned again, and again incurred the wrath of God. Monotheism imposes self-restraint; it obliges men to live under the eye of a Moral Ruler who notices their good and wicked deeds. In Mesopotamia, as well as in Egypt, men turned away from the true God who created heaven and earth, to make for themselves gods according to their own corrupt desires and imaginings. For all their advanced civilization, Babylonians and Egyptians became polytheists and idolators, unmindful of their tradition of monotheism. They made gods of gold, silver, stone and wood. Devil-worship, animal-worship, magic, sacrificing of human victims, even of their own children, orgies of cruelty and sensuality disfigured religious worship. Instead of destroying the race again and starting over, as he did in the time of Noe, God selected one man who understood his ways and walked in his paths, to found a chosen people, a community of saints, separated from idolators.

In Ur of Chaldea Abraham heard the call: "Go forth out of thy country and from thy kindred and out of thy father's house and come into the land which I shall show thee. And I will make of thee a great nation, and I will bless thee and magnify thy name and thou shalt be blessed. . . . and in thee shall all the kindred of the earth be blessed" (Gen. 12:1-3). Abraham obeyed, taking with him Thare, his father, Sara, his wife, and Lot, his nephew. He journeyed northwest along the Euphrates until he came to Haran, where Thare died. Then Abraham, at the age of seventy-five, turned southwest, crossed the Euphrates, and entered the land of Chanaan.

Eminently prudent and reasonable, noble of mind, refined of heart, and having profound reverence for God, Abraham was well fitted for his vocation. "Walk before me and be perfect," God told him. The people among whom he so-journed learned to respect him and to recognize God's care of him. As yet Abraham had no child. Following a Babylonian custom, Sara requested an heir by Agar, her servant. Thus Abraham became the father of Ismael. Sara, a beautiful woman, an aristocrat, was treated disrespectfully by Agar, now that Agar had borne a child by Sara's husband. God promised Abraham a child by Sara. Sara laughed when she heard the angel announce this, because she was old. But she did have a child, who was called Isaac. Lot, who had parted from Abraham, became father of the Moabites and Ammonites after the destruction of Sodom where Lot had taken up his abode. To try Abraham's faith, God commanded him to sacrifice Isaac when the boy was twelve years old. Abraham obeyed and was about to kill Isaac when an angel intervened. Later on, Abraham sent to Haran for a wife for Isaac. She was Rebecca, who became the mother of Esau and Jacob. Esau married a Chanaanitess and in other ways rendered himself unfit to head the chosen people; Jacob inherited the promise.

Jacob fled from Esau's anger to Haran, where he fell in love with Rachel, his cousin. Laban, her father, an astute man, drove a hard bargain with Jacob for his beautiful daughter. Jacob was obliged to tend Laban's sheep for seven years. On the night of the marriage, Laban, with fatherly solicitude for an older and less beautiful daughter, substituted Lia for Rachel. With astonishing meekness, Jacob served seven years more for Rachel. All these years seemed to him as so many days because of the greatness of his love. Lia gave birth to Ruben, Simeon, Levi, and Juda before Rachel had a child. From Lia was to come the most distinguished of Israel's sons. From Juda descended King David. From Levi came Moses and Aaron. Childless and desolate, Rachel said to Jacob: "Give me children, or I die." He answered: "Am I God that I can give you children?" Then she begged him to take her servant, Bala, and have a child by her. Thus Jacob became father of Dan and Nephtali. Lia, not to be outdone, requested children by her servant, Zelpha; Gad and Aser were added to Jacob's family. Afterwards Lia bore Issachar and Zabulon. At long last Rachel gave birth to Joseph. Jacob loved Rachel more than his other wives; and he loved Joseph more than his other children. Rachel died giving birth to Benjamin, Jacob's twelfth son. From these twelve sons of Jacob sprang the twelve tribes of Israel. Jacob was given the name Israel by an angel who wrestled with him all night.

Moved by jealousy, Joseph's brother sold him into slavery and he was taken to Egypt. Later on, in prison in Egypt, Joseph interpreted a dream of Pharao: it foretold an approaching famine. So impressed was Pharao with Joseph's intelligence that he appointed him ruler over Egypt in order to prepare for the famine. The land of Chanaan was not spared and Joseph's brothers came to Egypt in search of food. Before making himself known, Joseph tested their good will toward Benjamin, his brother by the same mother. Afterwards he invited his father and all his family to reside in the land of Goshen, a part of Egypt well-adapted to their habits as shepherds. There they dwelt for four hundred years and multiplied into a great people.

Lia was buried with Jacob in a double cave at Mambre, near Hebron, purchased by Abraham as a burial place for Sara. Rachel was buried near Bethlehem, a mournful, mysterious figure in the history of Israel. God consoled Abraham, Isaac and Jacob with good wives. Sara, Rebecca and Rachel shed a radiance of culture and beauty over the cradle of the chosen people. The fidelity of Sara, the prudence of Rebecca and the amiability of Rachel are still proposed as ideals for Christian wives.

Moses

The children of Israel multiplied so fast that the Egyptians became alarmed, and thought to diminish their number by hard labor. When this proved ineffective, they forbade male children to be reared. The mother of Moses, after concealing him as long as she could, put him in a basket among the rushes by the Nile, with his sister watching. Pharao's daughter found him, adopted him, and hired his mother for his nurse. Thus Moses had a mother's care and the best education Egypt could give him. Mathematics, art and literature flourished in Egypt at this time. Moses was providentially prepared for his work as legislator and historian of Israel. At the age of forty he sided with his own people against their oppressors, and was obliged to flee. For forty years he resided in the land of Madian, tending the sheep of Raguel (Jethro) whose daughter he married. This woman was not exactly a heathen. The Madianites were stem-brethren of the Israelites, having Abraham for their father. Raguel himself was a priest and an intelligent man, helpful to Moses.

When Moses was eighty, God appeared to him in a magnificent theophany. The time had come for Israel to be organized not only as a family but as a nation. Moses was chosen by God to deliver the Israelites from bondage in Egypt and to legislate for them as God's holy people. A separated people, dedicated to the worship of the true God, needed special laws and ordinances and an environment in which they would be free to observe their feasts, their customs, and their form of worship. Israel was to be God's own people and they were expected to walk before God, like Abraham.

Moses was reluctant to accept such responsibility. He objected to both Pharao and the Israelites would scoff at his pretensions. God revealed his name: Yahweh (I am who am) and wrought signs to convince Moses that Pharao and the Israelites would recognize his authority. Moses pleaded he was not a fluent speaker; God appointed his brother Aaron to be his orator.

Moses went to Egypt, and by a series of miracles persuaded the people of Israel and Pharao that he was acting under the inspiration of God. Nowhere in the annals of history is there such a record of supernatural happenings, except during the life of Christ. When Aaron threw down his rod before Pharao, it turned into a serpent. Pharao called his magicians and they did likewise; that is, they threw down rods and each turned into a serpent. But Aaron's serpent ate up the serpents of the magicians. Ten plagues were needed to convince Pharao. They are summarized in Psalm 77:

> He changed into blood their streams—
> their running water, so that they could not drink;
> He sent among them flies that devoured them
> and frogs that destroyed them.

He gave their harvest to the caterpillar,
  the fruits of their toil to the locust.
He killed their vines with hail
  and their sycamores with frost.
He gave over to the hail their beasts
  and their flocks to the lightning.

. . . .

He smote every first-born in Egypt,
  the first fruits of manhood in the tents of Ham;
But his people he led forth like sheep
  and guided them like a herd in the desert.
He led them on secure and unafraid
  while he covered their enemies with the sea.
And he brought them to his holy land
  to the mountains his right hand had won.
And he drove out nations before them;
He distributed their inheritance by lot
  and settled the tribes of Israel in their tents.[3]

Instead of destroying men for their wickedness as he did at the time of Noe, God formed for himself a chosen people, dedicated to the practice and preservation of monotheism and revealed truth. To convince Egyptians and Israelites that Moses knew what he was about, God worked many more miracles. The ten plagues were astonishing, the crossing of the sea on foot more astonishing, but most astonishing were the phenomena at Mount Sinai. Amidst thunders and lightnings, God promulgated a law for his chosen people. The people begged Moses to speak to God and to excuse them. Moses himself trembled at God's majesty.

The law regulated the morals of the people by the ten commandments. It prescribed sacrifices, ceremonies and ordinances. It legislated for the lives of the chosen people as the founder of a religious order lays down rules for the lives of his subjects. The Israelites were to be a holy people, a community of saints, setting an example to the Gentiles and showing how God should be worshipped. From among the twelve, the tribe of Levi was selected to give all its attention to guarding and fostering liturgical worship.

In the desert, the Israelites often rebelled. When they complained of lack of food, God fed them miraculously for forty years with manna. When they complained of thirst, Moses struck the rock and water flowed in abundance. The whole sojourn in the desert was filled with supernatural manifestations. On the march, the people were guided by a pillar of fire at night and during the day by a miraculous cloud. Their shoes never wore out. God provided for them as if they were his children, yet they angered him by their lack of faith, their cowardice and their sensuality.

Moses was a magnanimous man. He lived intimately with God. For forty years he received divine revelations and communicated them to the people. He led the Israelites out of Egypt and organized them religiously, politically and socially. He wrote the first five books of the Bible. He was an eyewitness of what he recorded in Exodus, Leviticus, Numbers and Deuteronomy. For the material in Genesis he depended on tradition, both oral and written; perhaps in part on direct revelation from God. Jews and Christians have always affirmed the Mosaic authorship of the Pentateuch.[4] Modern enemies of the supernatural deny it. The law of Moses is the law according to which the Hebrews lived from the time they conquered Palestine. No one can give a reasonable explanation of their origin without recognizing the part played by Moses. He was mediator between God and the chosen people, a towering personality. "There arose no more a prophet in Israel like Moses whom the Lord knew face to face" (Deut. 34:10).

Josue

Moses died before entering the land of promise, viewing it from a mountain east of the Jordan. He was one hundred and twenty years old and "his eyes were not dim and his teeth were not moved." He appointed Josue to conquer the Chanaanites and to divide their land among the twelve tribes. Three tribes requested portions east of the Jordan, i.e., Ruben, Gad, and half the tribe of Manasses. The large tribe of Juda received the hilly country west and south of the Jordan, including the site of Jerusalem. Ephraim, another large tribe, was located north of Juda, with Benjamin, a small tribe, between them. Simeon was to the south of Juda. The other four tribes were given land north of Ephraim between the Mediterranean and the river. Special arrangement was made for Levi, the priestly tribe. The northern limit was the Lebanon mountains. Miracles attended the conquest of Chanaan. The Jordan piled up its waters, as if dammed, to permit the people to cross; the walls of Jericho collapsed of themselves. God led his people with a strong hand and a mighty arm.

The Israelites were ordered by God to exterminate the inhabitants of Palestine because of their wickedness. God had as much right to do this as he had to drown the wicked at the time of the deluge. He knew the cruelty, sensuality and idolatry of the Chanaanites; he knew they would be a bad influence upon his chosen people. However, the Israelites carried out this order imperfectly. They made a league with the Gabaonites, permitted the Jebusites to hold Jerusalem, and never proceeded against the Philistines who lived on the fertile plain between the mountains of Juda and the sea. Moabites and Ammonites, Lot's descendants, held the country east of the Dead Sea with the Edomites (Esauites) to the south of them.

Judges

God was the invisible ruler of his chosen people. As long as they obeyed his laws, kept his feasts, fulfilled his ordinances, he protected them from enemies and abundantly supplied their temporal needs. There was to be no central government; the people were to be free from burdensome taxes and conscription for military service. God seems to have followed the principle that they who are governed least are governed best. When the people disobeyed his laws, especially when they fell into idolatry, God allowed enemies to overcome them. But when they repented, he raised up inspired leaders to rout the foe. Among these leaders were Gideon, Jephte, Samson and Samuel. They also judged the people and settled dissensions among the tribes; hence the name "judges."

The Monarchy

God intended Israel to remain a theocracy—a kingdom ruled by himself; but the people became secularized. Observing the nations around them governed by kings, and seeing the advantage of a strong central government in time of war, they petitioned Samuel for a king. They did not appreciate immunity from taxes, conscription, and oppression by tyrants. Samuel consulted God. God was angry because his people had so little confidence in him. Nevertheless, he told Samuel to take a horn of oil and anoint Saul, "a choice and goodly man" of the tribe of Benjamin who "from his shoulders and upward appeared above all the people." At first humble and obedient, assisted by a truly noble son, Jonathan, Saul fought bravely and conquered the enemies of Israel. But as time went on, he became stubborn, self-centered, and disobedient to the commands of God given through Samuel. When Saul understood he had lost favor with God he became morose and melancholy. David was brought to him to deliver him from his depression by playing on the harp and singing. At first Saul liked David, and Saul's son Jonathan became David's faithful friend. But when Saul understood that God had chosen David to succeed him, he became violently jealous and sought to kill him. Saul and Jonathan both died in battle.

David is characterized as "a man according to God's own heart." He deserved this title because of his profound reverence and sensitiveness to divine inspiration. He realized vividly that the authority of the king comes from God, not from the people. Long a fugitive from the jealous rage of Saul, he learned in the school of danger to value the friendship of God. Because Saul was the anointed of the Lord, David spared his life even at risk of his own. After Saul's death David united and enlarged the kingdom; drove the Jebusites out of Jerusalem; formed the Levites into choirs, wrote psalms for divine worship, honored the ark of the covenant. In general, he proved a great king. He gathered material to build a temple at Jerusalem, but was told by God to leave its construction to his son. David was fortunate to have as the general of his army Joab, who not only conquered outside enemies, but maintained discipline among the people of Israel.

Solomon, David's son, built the temple at Jerusalem

which was one of the wonders of the ancient world. He prayed for wisdom and is regarded by Hebrew and Christian tradition as one of the wisest of men. According to tradition, he wrote Proverbs, Canticle of Canticles, and Ecclesiastes. Wise though he was, Solomon's failure to follow the Mosaic law forbidding marriages with heathens caused him to fall into idolatry and to sin seriously against God.

The reader of the Bible may be scandalized at the polygamy of Abraham, Jacob, David and Solomon, and may be puzzled by the leniency shown them in contrast with God's severity toward the Chanaanites. We should note, however, that God punished David and Solomon for their sins. Women led David to murder and Solomon to idolatry. Nevertheless, David repented. The *Miserere* is his act of contrition. According to the book of Wisdom, Solomon prayed not only for wisdom but for continence. He seems to have had special grace in this respect. Nevertheless, his heathen wives had a bad influence on him and caused a deterioration of his faith. The Bible makes no mention of his conversion.

David must be regarded as a holy man. His psalms reveal the heights and depths of mystical experience. The Church uses them for public prayer. David passed through a dark night of purgation and illumination before achieving intimate union with God. God's grace was given to him abundantly, and inspired in him gratitude, humility, love and contrition. David was a great mystic.

The Northern Kingdom

Under David the kingdom of Israel extended from the desert on the south to the mountains on the north, and from the sea on the west to Euphrates and the desert on the east. Philistines, Moabites and Ammonites lived in quiet subjection; Jebusites were routed out of the stronghold of Jerusalem; Egypt, Ninive and Babylon treated David with respect. After Solomon's death, in punishment for his disloyalty to the law of God, ten tribes, under the leadership of Jeroboam, rebelled against Roboam, the son of Solomon, and established a kingdom of their own. Only Juda and Benjamin remained faithful to the house of David. The northern kingdom was called Israel, the southern kingdom Juda.

Fearing the effect of pilgrimages to Jerusalem for the feasts of the Pasch, Pentecost, Tabernacles and Atonement, Jeroboam set up idols in the northern kingdom. The proximity of Tyre and Sidon encouraged idolatry. The situation went from bad to worse. God sent prophets to warn kings and people to mend their ways if they wished to avoid destruction. Amos warned Jeroboam and Samaria; Osee predicted the Assyrian captivity. During the terrible reign of Achab, who married Jezabel, daughter of the king of Sidon, Elias campaigned for God with burning zeal. Jezabel left nothing undone to turn Israel to the worship of Baal and Astarte. Elias opposed her with a spirit that awed Achab and his subjects. At his prayer, rain ceased for three years. He dared the priests of Baal on Mount Carmel to an open contest. Carcasses were laid on adjoining altars before the assembled people. The priests of Baal called for hours on their gods to show their power, but in vain. Then Elias drenched his sacrifices with water and prayed. Fire came down from heaven and consumed the sacrifices and the wet wood. After that there was an abundant rain. Elias left this world in a fiery chariot and is expected to return to earth as precursor of the second coming of Christ. No prophet except Moses performed more miracles than did Elias. Although author of no written prophecy, the "spirit and power" of Elias became proverbial."

The northern kingdom degenerated rapidly. The powerful Assyrian empire gradually subdued it and forced it to pay tribute. "Ephraim is a partaker with idols—let him alone" (Osee 4:17). Salmanasar, infuriated by Samaria's refusal to pay tribute, conquered the country and carried the rebels into captivity in 722 B.C. Little more is said in the Bible about the ten tribes. From other sources, we learn that the poorer people were left in the land and that colonists consisting of Cuthites, Arabs and other peoples were brought thither. These colonists carried their own goods into Palestine, but had so much luck that they developed a fear of Yahweh and asked to be instructed concerning his worship. Thus developed the Samaritans, a nation prominent in Palestine at the time of Christ. They respected Moses and kept their own version of the Pentateuch.

The Southern Kingdom

God promised David: "I have sworn to David my servant: thy seed I will establish forever and will build up thy throne unto all generations." The southern kingdom consisted of the large tribe of Juda and the small tribe of Benjamin. Unlike the northern kingdom it had a stable dynasty, and was sheltered from invasion from the north and east by its mountains. In general, its kings were less idolatrous than the kings of the north. However, Roboam,

Abia, Achaz, Manasses and Amon were not good. Joram married Athalia, daughter of Jezabel. Athalia herself ruled seven years in the style of her mother. She killed all the descendants of the royal family of David except Joas, a boy who was concealed and raised by Joiada, the high priest. Joas had a long reign and permitted no idolatry until after the death of Joiada. Isaias, the great prophet, flourished during the reign of Ozias and Ezechias and exerted a profound influence for good. Ezechias, son of Achaz, ruled twenty-nine years after the manner of David, listening to the advice of Isaias, zealous for the worship of the true God. He gained a miraculous victory over Sennacherib, a powerful Assyrian king who openly blasphemed the God of Israel. Unfortunately, Manasses, son of Ezechias, imitated his grandparents rather than his pious father.

Josias came to the throne about 640 B.C. He began to rule when he was eight years old and was taught by the high priest Helcias and the prophet Jeremias to revere the law of God. He undertook to repair the temple, and it so happened that during work on one of its walls, the high priest found a copy of the law of Moses. Josias had the book read to him and was deeply affected. He realized that the very miseries his people were experiencing had been predicted by Moses. The chosen people had proved unfaithful to Yahweh. Josias brought about a reform. When he was killed at Mageddo, however, his successors, Joachaz, Eliakim, Joakim and Sedecias ruled badly. The measure of the sins of Juda was filled up and, as Jeremias had warned, God delivered Juda into captivity in Babylon. The first deportation by Nabuchodonosor took place in 605 B.C. when Daniel was carried off as a mere boy. A second deportation occurred in 597 B.C. Finally, in 586

B.C., Nabuchodonosor, enraged by the failure of the Jews to obey orders, destroyed the temple of Solomon and turned Judea into a wilderness. The lamentations of Jeremias over the ruins of Jerusalem are full of grief: "Oh, all you that pass by the way, attend and see if there be any sorrow like unto my sorrow." Note that the destruction of the temple and the mingling of the Hebrews with the Babylonians occurred about the time of the rise of philosophy in Greece, of Confucius in China, and Zoroaster in Persia. Exiled Hebrews, in the providence of God, became a light to the Gentiles.

Babylonian Captivity

The children of Abraham had been chosen to preserve monotheism and the Messianic hope for the whole of mankind. Tempted by idol-worship and the sensuality connected with it, they imitated the vices of the Gentiles; but always a remnant of faithful to Yahweh. Even in the north, in the days of Achab, God said to Elias that he still had seven thousand men in Israel "whose knees have not been bowed before Baal" (III Kings 19:18). Tobias, an exile from the northern kingdom, set an admirable example of piety and charity in Ninive.

The Hebrews were chastened. In exile they revived the ideal of a people dedicated to the worship of Yahweh. "By the rivers of Babylon they sat and wept when they remembered Sion." Many, indeed, lost their faith; but those who persevered in their tradition were spiritualized. Some of them became very influential in Babylon, especially Daniel. The prophet Ezechiel did much to maintain faith in the people.

The Diaspora

As a result of the scattering of the Jews caused by the two exiles, many descendants of Abraham left Palestine never to return. Babylon became and remained a center of Hebrew culture. The Babylonian Talmud shows how intellectual life flourished there. In Egypt Hebrews settled in great numbers—especially after the conquest of Alexander. They formed populous districts in Alexandria; there they translated their sacred books into Greek. When Seleucus I founded Antioch, Jews congregated there, as well as in Damascus. Everywhere they displayed talent as traders and merchants and found themselves at home in the seaports along the Mediterranean. Although some of these dispersed Jews became secularized, many others returned religiously as pilgrims for the feasts in Jerusalem. At St. Peter's first sermon there were present in Jerusalem Jews from Parthia, Media, Elam, Mesopotamia, Asia Minor, Egypt, Libya, Crete, Arabia, and Rome. These Israelites, dispersed among the Gentiles, had an important influence in disseminating knowledge of divine revelation and hope of salvation through the coming of an expected Messias.

Return from Exile

In 538 B.C. Cyrus, Persian conqueror of the Babylonians, declared a policy of permitting peoples who had been violently deported to return to their homes. He was friendly to the Hebrews and not only allowed them to return, but restored the sacred vessels taken from the temple by Nabuchodonosor, promising financial help toward rebuilding the temple. Zorobabel, of the royal family of David, led back about 50,000 Jews in 536 B.C. Upon reaching Jerusalem, he quietly rebuilt the altar of holocausts and offered sacrifices to God. The Samaritans volunteered to help rebuild the temple but their offer was rejected. This infuriated them and they complained to the Persian king that the rebuilding of Jerusalem would be a menace to the peace of the empire. So much opposition developed that work on the temple was halted. Two prophets, Aggeus and Zacharias, encouraged Zorobabel and his followers to finish the building. This they did, and the temple was consecrated about 517 B.C.

Esdras—458 B.C.

For about sixty years after the completion of the temple under Zorobabel, the environment proved hostile to further progress in realizing the ideal of a separated people entirely devoted to the service of Yahweh. Separation from the Gentiles and their culture was not easy. Jews who had remained in Palestine had been deeply influenced by the pagan life around them. They had intermarried with Samaritans. The returned exiles began to imitate their example. Laxity about observing the Sabbath, doing business with Samaritans on feasts, and marriages with Gentiles weakened Hebrew morale. The wealthy showed themselves hard of heart toward the poor; priests became lax; the people were attracted by the sensuality of pagan life around them.

News of the failure of the expedition of Zorobabel to measure up to expectations reached Babylon and greatly disturbed Esdras, "a scribe skilled in the law of Moses," a priest who in his heart cherished the ideal of Israel as a community of saints. He was a scholar, respected by Artaxerxes I, from whom he received a commission to return to Jerusalem with men and money. Accordingly, about 458 B.C., accompanied by 1500 men, their wives and children, and with a great sum of money, Esdras travelled from Babylon to Jerusalem. His plan was to instruct priests and people in exact knowledge of the law of Moses.

At the season when Jews celebrate Yom Kippur (the Day of Atonement) and the Feast of Tabernacles, Esdras read the law of Moses to the assembled and explained it. He read it every day during the octave of the feast, holding up the ideal of Israel as a community of saints separated from Gentiles: that is to say, from the pagans. Especially did he lament mixed marriages, showing his grief by rending his garments and pulling out his hair. The people were deeply moved and promised to reform. Esdras demanded the dissolution of mixed marriages. The people bound themselves by oath to comply with this demand, but opposition developed when the time came for them to separate from their wives. Esdras was hated by the Samaritans and Idumeans because he was causing Jews to divorce their daughters. To protect himself and his reform, Esdras decided to rebuild the walls of Jerusalem, but the Samaritans marched to Jerusalem and pulled down what he had built, and sent a complaint to Artaxerxes that Esdras exceeded his authority.

Esdras and his work should be observed with care, because Higher Critics have attempted to prove that he and Helcias, the high priest, who educated Josias, were the real authors of the law of Moses. In their opinion, he brought with him from Babylon a redaction of a primitive code of laws, very much improved by what he had learned in

Babylon. This is wishful thinking. The law of Moses dates
back much farther than the captivity of Babylon. Esdras
read the law and explained it, but he did not write the
law, nor did he change the law of Moses. Heinisch observes:

> That Law had been given by God on Mt. Sinai. Already at
> the time of the judges, Israel had disobeyed it; against it kings,
> officials, priests and common people had sinned. It was not some-
> thing new, it was not composed in Babylonia. Nor was it the so-
> called priestly code (P), for it contained legislation found only
> in Deuteronomy, e.g., rules governing mixed marriages, and the
> payment of debts in a Sabbath year.[5]

Nehemias—445-433 B.C.

News reached Babylon of the predicament of Esdras.
All who had supported his expedition were grieved, and
considered means of sending him assistance. Nehemias, cup-
bearer and favorite of Artaxerxes, pleaded with the king
to have himself named governor of Jerusalem. By this ap-
pointment, he acquired the authority Esdras lacked to rebuild the walls of Jerusalem and to fortify the holy city.
Nehemias was a great executive. He surveyed the walls,
divided them into forty-two sections, and put all the Jews
to work with such energy that in fifty-two days the walls
were completed, with towers and gates. In spite of Samaritans and Edomites, Nehemias succeeded. Esdras and Nehemias together accomplished together what neither of them
could have done alone. Esdras was a spiritual leader, zealous for the law and the Hebrew ideal of a separated people, but he was not practical enough to rebuild Jerusalem.
Nehemias was a finished politician and prudent executive
who had his building completed before the enemy realized

what he was about. He governed Jerusalem for twelve years. During this time the reform of Esdras was accomplished.

The Machabees—180-135 B.C.

Of the history of Israel from Esdras to the Machabees, the Bible is silent. This period covers about two hundred and forty years (420-180 B.C.). In the meantime, Alexander conquered the world, including the large nations contiguous to Israel. His program called not for enslaving but for Hellenizing peoples. Alexandria in Egypt became a center of attempts to synthesize or syncretize Greek philosophy and oriental religions. The sacred wisdom of the Jews came into contact with Greek philosophy. When Alexander died in 323 B.C. his kingdom fell into the hands of his generals. The Ptolemies ruled in Egypt and the Seleucids in Syria.

Located between Egypt and Syria, Palestine felt the influence of both. Syria treated the Jews with respect, anxious to keep them from allying themselves with the Ptolemies. The Seleucids, however, followed the policy of Hellenizing Palestine, in which they were encouraged by renegade Jews. Seleucus IV, called Philopator (185-175 B.C.), was told by a Jewish Levite, named Simon, of great treasures kept in the temple at Jerusalem. Seleucus sent his general, Heliodorus, to rob the temple, but an angel prevented him. After the death of Seleucus, his son, Antiochus IV (175-163 B.C.), encouraged by Jason, brother of the high priest Onias, made a determined effort to abolish the worship of Yahweh. Jews like Simon, Jason and Menelaus, ambitious for the revenues and prestige of the office of high priest and fascinated by Greek culture, had much to do with leading the king to think he could completely Hellenize the Jews. Antiochus failed to reckon with the profound loyalty of a remnant of the Jews to their traditions and their God. The ideal of living as the chosen people of God, descendants of saints, separated from idolatrous Gentiles, fired men to resist the abomination. Antiochus took the city by force of arms, massacred thousands, and built a citadel in Jerusalem. Then, under penalty of death, he forbade the practice of the Jewish religion, ordered the sacred books burned and traditional sacrifices, feasts, and circumcision abolished. Pigs were to be sacrificed to idols in the temple; pork was to be eaten. The altar of holocausts in the court of the temple was converted into a pagan altar, and prostitutes were installed. Some Jews acquiesced in this apostasy, but others stood firm. Among them were the seven Machabees and their heroic mother, who died as martyrs.

In those days arose Mathathias, a priest, who lived at Modin in the mountains. He had five sons: John, Simon, Judas, Eleazar, and Jonathan. When Mathathias saw what was taking place, he boldly declared:

> I and my sons and brethren will obey the law of our fathers. ...Now as he left off speaking there came a certain Jew in sight of all to sacrifice to the idols upon the altar in the city of Modin.... And Mathathias saw and was grieved. And his reins trembled and his wrath was kindled ... and running upon him he slew him upon the altar. Moreover, the man whom king Antiochus sent to compel them to sacrifice, he slew at the same time and pulled down the altar. (I Mach. 2:20-25).

Judas Machabeus, third son of Mathathias, proved to be a military genius and an indomitable leader, capable, even with an inferior army, of smashing great armies sent against him by Antiochus and his successors. He drove the enemy out of Jerusalem, cleansed the temple, and, on a great occasion, had the temple rededicated to the true God. After he was killed in battle, his younger brother Jonathan succeeded him. At this time Syria was overrun with contenders for the throne. So great a respect for the prowess of Judas had taken hold of Syria that the rivals were glad to confirm Jonathan in the double office of high priest and civil ruler of Judea, and to assure him that his people would no more be hindered in the practice of their religion.

The Hasmoneans—134-40 B.C.

The government of Syria changed hands often and most of its kings were treacherous. One of these, Tryphon, invited Jonathan to a conference, took him prisoner, and demanded of Simon, Jonathan's brother, Jonathan's two sons as hostages. He murdered them all. Simon succeeded Jonathan. The Jews declared "that he should be their prince and high priest forever, till there should arise a faithful prophet" (I Mach. 14:41). This meant that his office was hereditary and that the last of the Machabees founded a royal family of high priests who were also kings. They were called Hasmoneans. Unfortunately, Simon's son-in-law, governor of Jericho, treacherously killed Simon and his sons, Mathathias and Judas, at a banquet. One son remained, John Hyrcanus, who became high priest and king in 134 B.C.

The times were evil. Uneasy lay the head that wore the crown. In Palestine, the parties of Sadducees and Pharisees contended with each other. John Hyrcanus favored the Sadducees, that is, the wealthy and worldly, against the Pharisees, zealots for the law, who added laws of their own to the law of Moses. John Hyrcanus' oldest son, Aristobul, succeeded him, showing himself soft toward Hellenic culture and luke warm toward the law. After he died Alexander Janneus married his widow Alexandra, a pious woman. Alexander Janneus was not a religious man; he was always involved in wars and politics. When he died Alexandra, twice widowed, ruled. She favored the Pharisees, who spoke of her reign (76-67 B.C.) as "the golden age."

Alexandra had favored Hyrcan, her son, a weak man, to succeed her. But the Sadducees backed his brother Aristobul. Hyrcan would have surrendered, but he was incited by Antipater, a crafty Idumean, to appeal to Pompey. The contest between the brothers was decided by Pompey, the Roman general, who happened to be in Syria after conquering Mithradates. Pompey decided in favor of Hyrcan, the weaker and more manageable of the two. He was installed as high priest, but not as ruler; Palestine was placed under the Roman governor of Syria in 65 B.C. Hyrcan was only a figurehead dominated by Antipater. Antipater and Hyrcan sided with Caesar against Pompey. In gratitude, Caesar made Hyrcan high priest and ethnarch; but he still ruled only in name: the Idumean was the man behind the throne. Antipater appointed his son, Herod, to rule Galilee, and another son, Phasael, to govern Jerusalem. After Caesar's death in 44 B.C., Herod received more territory from Antony. To silence the indignation of Jews who looked on him as a usurper, Herod married Mariamne, granddaughter of John Hyrcanus, and thus associated himself with the royal line of the Machabees. In the year 40 B.C. the Parthians invaded Syria and some of the Jews recklessly welcomed them. Antigonus, leader of the rebels, was proclaimed king by the Parthians. Antigonus cut off Hyrcan's ears so that he could no longer function as high priest, and gave him to the Parthians to carry away. Phasael, brother of Herod, ruler of Jerusalem, committed suicide. Herod escaped to Rome and on October 6, 37 B.C., the Day of Atonement, with aid from Antony, retook Jerusalem. Antigonus was put to death.[6]

Herod I—37-4 B.C.

With the rise of Herod, an Idumean, the sceptre of royal power passed from the family of Juda and David. Herod I ruled thirty-three years. At his death, he named his son, Archelaus, king of Judea. The Pharisees appealed to Rome for a form of government suited to their religious ideals. Archelaus was deposed in 6 A.D. and Judea was put under the rule of Roman procurators (6-41 A.D.). Herod Antipas, appointed by his father tetrarch of Galilee, held power from 4 B.C. to 39 A.D. It was he who beheaded John the Baptist. Herod Agrippa, 37-43 A.D., became ruler of the whole of Palestine under Caligula. He was the Herod who killed James, brother of John, and imprisoned Peter.

Herod I, called the Great, was a man of remarkable energy. Determined of will and robust of body, an alert politician, a capable administrator, and an admirer of Greek buildings and Roman efficiency, he carried out an amazing program of building. He was shrewd about keeping in the good graces of Rome. When he built Caesarea, he gave the new city the name of his patron; when he built the ancient city of Samaria, he called it Sebaste, equivalent to Augustus. He had ten wives and numerous children, some of whom, incited by his jealous sister Salome, he murdered. Patriotic Jews hated him because he was an Idumean, an alien, an intruder, willingly subservient to Rome, an advocate of pagan culture, imposing excessive taxes to carry out his extravagant building program. Moreover, he showed himself a brutal barbarian who, in trying to wipe out the family of the Machabees, killed—among others—his favorite wife Mariamne and the two sons she bore him. An ancient book, *The Ascension of Moses,* describes him as "a shameless king, an insolent and godless man, one who with the sword exterminated the nation's leaders, who murdered old and young and showed no mercy."[7] He is the one who slaughtered the innocents at Bethlehem in a vain attempt to rid himself of one he considered a rival. He deprived the Sanhedrin of political influence, and curried favor with the Romans at the expense of the Jews. To his credit, he enlarged and adorned the temple of Zorobabel, so much so that the temple he built sometimes is called the third temple. The first was the temple of Solomon, the second that of Zorobabel, and the third the one enlarged and beautified by Herod.

Herod died in 4 B.C. It seems strange to hear that the king who slaughtered the innocents died four years before the beginning of the Christian era, or, in other words, that Jesus of Nazareth was born about 5 or 6 B.C. The apparent paradox is solved by bearing in mind that Dionysius Exiguus, a Sythian monk, about 527 A.D. introduced the practice of dating historical events before and after Christ. Dionysius placed the birth of Christ in the year 753 after the founding of Rome and called this the year one. His reckoning was slightly altered by later chronologists.

The Coming of Christ

The three centuries preceding the Christian era witnessed profound changes in the government of the world. The conquest of Alexander, the general use of the Greek language, the gradual rise of the power of Rome, deeply affected the lives of peoples living about the Mediterranean. The chosen people themselves found it extremely difficult, amidst these political disturbances, to live as a separated people, dedicated to the worship of the true God. The fullness of time had come.

John the Baptist heralded the approach of the long expected Messias. He was born of a woman naturally beyond the period of child-bearing; and his father was struck dumb for not believing the angel who announced his coming birth. The angelic messenger named the child to be born to Zachary and Elizabeth: his name was to be John. Zachary recovered his speech after the birth of the child, and predicted his son's vocation: to prepare the way for the Messias.

Jesus of Nazareth was born six months after the birth of John. His mother was the Virgin Mary. His mother and foster-father, Joseph, were obliged to flee to Egypt for a time, to escape the malice of Herod. After Herod's death, they returned to Nazareth where the child grew up. At the age of twelve he displayed religious genius, amazing Jewish doctors of the law at Jerusalem. His public life began at thirty, and was announced by John the Baptist, who cried: "Do penance, for the kingdom of God is at hand." John declared he was but a voice announcing the coming of one greater than himself. John pointed out Jesus of Nazareth to his disciples as "the lamb of God who takes away the sins of the world."

NOTES FOR CHAPTER IV

1. See Steinmueller, *A Companion to Scripture Studies*. Vol. II, p. 305, for a list of dates beginning with the building of Solomon's temple. Also see Robert and Tricot, *Guide to the Bible*, Vol. II, Chapter XV, for a chronology. Early dates are necessarily estimated, and opinions differ.

2. See Instruction of Biblical Commission, June 30, 1909, on Historical Character of First Three Chapters of Genesis. This and other instructions and responses of the Biblical Commission may be found in *Rome and the Study of Scripture* (St. Meinrad, Indiana: Abbey Press, 1964).

3. Confraternity translation.

4. Monsignor Steinmueller deals at length with the Mosaic authorship in *A Companion to Scripture Studies*, Vol. II. A Protestant scholar, Dr. Oswald T. Allis, also furnishes strong support for the Mosaic authorship in *The Five Books of Moses* (Nutley, N. J.: Presbyterian and Reformed Publishing Company, 1964). We have testimony for the Mosaic authorship in other books of the Old Testament, and Christ speaks of it in the New.

5. Paul Heinisch, *History of the Old Testament* (Collegeville, Minnesota: The Liturgical Press, 1962), p. 391.

6. *Ibid.*, pp. 369-75.

7. *The Ascension of Moses* 6:2, quoted by Heinisch, *History of the Old Testament*, p. 378.

"To prove that Jesus Christ is the Messiah announced by so many prophets is, next to the demonstration of the existence of God and the immortality of the soul, to give the most important of the proofs of religion."

—Gottfried Leibnitz

CHAPTER V

Messianic Prophecies

Although the books of the Old Testament and their authors are many, a central theme runs through them all: the kingdom of God. This kingdom, first set up in Adam and Eve, was ruined by original sin; but Adam and his family were not abandoned. God promised the woman a son who would overcome her enemy and deliver her fallen family from servitude to sin and Satan. Although the majority of men succumbed to idolatry and devil-worship, a remnant always remained faithful to the one true God who desires to love men and to be loved by them in a union of personal friendship. After the family of Adam multiplied, God no longer spoke to every individual as he did to Adam; he selected persons like Noe, Abraham and Moses, renewing to each of them his promise of friendship and deliverance. God made his presence felt by visible signs, some of which are called theophanies. From first to last, the Old Testament assumes the exisence of a supernatural God who can converse with men[1]—a God who loves men and is concerned that they should try to bring out his image in their nature by obedience to his laws.

Adam did not rise gradually to a knowledge of God. As soon as he was created he conversed with God; that is, he received supernatural revelation. He was created in a state of justice, integrity, and bodily immortality. He was endowed with language and was free from disorderly emotions. After his fall, Adam's children were inclined to evil and needed constant chastisement to keep them from ignoring the true God altogether. The deluge was such a chastisement; only Noe and his family survived. When men drifted away from God again, he chose Abraham to found a family apart, a separated people, dedicated to worship of the one true God. He called himself the God of Abraham, the God of Isaac, and the God of Jacob—their friend and their exceeding great reward. Abraham was guided by supernatural revelation and walked in its light. From time to time prophets spoke the word of God to the people, recalling them from idolatry to obedience to God, always reminding them of the special love God showed Israel in Egypt and in the desert. Contrary to the mind of God, Israel demanded of Samuel that he appoint a king. God himself had been their king; Israel was taught by God and led by him. Prophets, not philosophers, were Israel's schoolmasters.

In a sense, the whole of the Old Testament is prophetic. "All things happened to them in figures" (I Cor. 10:11). In the midst of infidelity, sinfulness, idolatry and devil-worship, God took measures to preserve in Israel the ideal of a kingdom of God, a holy nation. Always a remnant remained faithful. God sent his prophets to remind kings and people that Israel had a special mission among the nations of the earth: it was to be a holy nation, ruled by

God, looking forward to the coming of a great prophet and king who would redeem the fallen family of Adam and extend the kingdom of God to all nations.

The Old Testament paints the picture of a mighty battle between the kingdom of Satan, bent upon separating men from God; and the kingdom of God, seeking to call them back into his friendship. Of themselves, men were prone to sensuality, frivolity, evil, but God fought on their side and sought their love. Noe, Abraham, Moses and David achieved his friendship. The prophets were his agents; he inspired them. They described the glory of God's kingdom which was to be perfected at the end of the world, when the great day of wrath, the day of the Lord would come. Before that day, the reign of God on earth would be extended through God's anointed, a great servant of God, on whom the spirit of God would rest, who would preach the kingdom of grace and peace to the Gentiles. As a result of this teaching: "The earth will be filled with the knowledge of the Lord, as the covering waters of the sea" (Isaias 11:9). Lagrange says:

> . . . There are men in Israel, and nowhere else, to announce to their nation a King consecrated with holy oil an Anointed One or Messias, whose role they describe, and it is especially by him that was to be effected a great religious renewal which, starting from the Jewish people, would extend to all mankind.[2]

All ancient peoples had soothsayers, augurs, diviners, magicians, medicine men, who undertook by the flight of birds or the entrails of sacrified animals to give a yes or no answer to questions concerning future events. Sibyls gave enigmatic replies while in trances induced by narcotics. But nowhere else did prophets flourish as in Israel. Their writings remain as permanent evidence of supernatural illumination. Rationalists or Naturalists, whose philosophy does not allow them to believe in divine inspiration, protest against Christians' discovering in prophets, psalms, and other books of the Old Testament genuine predictions concerning the future Messias. Such prophecy amounts to a miracle, and therefore—according to their philosophy—could not happen. Christians reply with St. Justin: "The Holy Spirit by the mouth of the prophets foretold everything concerning Jesus Christ, and if that prediction was not always made in direct and obvious terms, it at least took place by means of symbols, parables and figures." Jews before and at the time of Christ considered many passages of their Scriptures to be Messianic. Without the Messianic hope, the mission of the people of Israel and the development of the idea of the kingdom of God throughout the Old Testament would be unintelligible.

It is a pitiful mistake for unsophisticated Americans whose ancestors were devout believers in the supernatural inspiration of the Bible to let themselves be led into Naturalism by Rationalists, Naturalists, and Evolutionists, posing as enlightened critics of the Bible. Reason can demonstrate the existence of a supernatural, personal God. Arguments against prophecies, based on the assumption that they are impossible, are invalid if there be a supernatural God. We write for theists: for those who admit the existence of a supernatural God, and therefore the possibility of prophecy.

According to the Bible, the first man and woman conversed with God; they lived in intimate personal relationship with him. They were free from concupiscence. They were not ignorant because they were taught by God. They were not obliged to draw everything they knew about God from the natural world. Moreover, according to the Bible,

Adam and Eve would not have died if they had not sinned. "For God created man incorruptible, and to the image of his own likeness he made him. But by the envy of the devil, death came into the world; and they follow him that are of his side" (Wisdom 2:23-25). The Bible assumes the existence of a supernatural order; and of a kingdom of Satan hostile to the kingdom of God.

Modern Jews have split into Orthodox, Reform, and Conservative. Orthodox Jews regard the Bible as a book come down from heaven: that is, as a supernaturally inspired book. They do not countenance the theory that the Mosaic law is a product of natural evolution. Their ancient tradition is that Moses received the law from God on Mount Sinai. The party of Reform, and to a lesser degree the Conservative party, favor the theory of evolution, and thus offer a naturalistic explanation of the history of Israel. They agree with Rationalists that through the course of centuries, Hebrew religion and law evolved out of the religious experience of men of genius. Many modern Jews believe that Israel iteslf is the Messias, destined to play among the nations the role of mediator and priest. They underline the verse: "And ye shall be unto me a priestly kingdom and a holy nation" (Exodus 19:6). The salvation they hope for is the reign of natural justice, not supernatural justification and sanctification through the suffering of a personal Messias. According to one of their theologians:

> The Jewish Messianic idea whether idealized in a millenial era or incarnated in a human personality implies the concept of human perfectibility. According to Jewish teaching man must perfect his own nature to prepare the way for the Messiah. For the function of the Messiah is not to redeem a race which is incapable of redeeming itself. On the contrary, he is a symbol of man's self-redemption. The Messiah is the climax of man's ascent to moral perfection.[3]

Modern Jews, according to this Jewish theologian, deny the doctrine of original sin. They regard it as an unhappy concept. Believing in the perfectibility of human nature by natural development, they regard themselves, that is, the Jewish nation, as the Messias, the suffering servant of Yahweh, a kind of suffering victim for the sins of all men.

This is not the historical concept of the Messias. Moses, the prophets and the psalmists picture the Messias as a person sent by God through whose sufferings and merits the sins of the guilty family will be forgiven and the nations of the earth united in a kingdom of God. This kingdom is not merely the triumph of natural justice; it is emphatically a kingdom in which men will live supernatural lives, corresponding to the grace of God. The Messias will suffer and perfect a kingdom of God for all nations. All who accept him by penance and faith will be joined in holy friendship with him. The kingdom of the Messias is not a kingdom conferring worldly riches and prosperity; it is essentially spiritual, composed of those who seek supernatural union of friendship with God. The kingdom of the Messias is always opposed by the kingdom of Satan. Neither kingdom is a merely natural kingdom. The kingdom of Satan is preternaturally wicked; the kingdom of God supernaturally good. The prophet Isaias wrote: "The eye hath not seen, O God, . . . what things thou hast prepared for them that wait for thee" (Isaias 64:4).

We now give a brief summary of the Messianic prophecies as Christ summarized them for his two companions on the way to Emmaus. Moses, the prophets and the psalms pointed to a definite person, most pleasing to God, a divine teacher, a priest able to mediate between God and sinful men, restorer of a kingdom of grace which was founded for the angels and for Adam and Eve. Some of the angels sinned and were cast into hell. Adam and Eve sinned and lost the state of grace for themselves and their children. A Messias was promised who would rehabilitate the family of Adam. We select the principal prophecies: we hope our selection will be enough to show that the Messias was to be a definite person, the suffering servant of Yahweh who would volunteer to be the scapegoat for the sins of mankind. When Christ reviewed the prophecies concerning the suffering Messias, the two disciples' hearts burned within them.

The Woman and the Serpent

God asked Adam why he disobeyed; Adam replied that the woman God gave him tempted him. God turned to the woman for an explanation and she said: "The serpent deceived me." Then God said to the serpent: "I will put enmities between thee and the woman, and thy seed and her seed; he shall crush thy head and thou shalt lie in wait for his heel" (Gen. 3:13,15). This prophecy has been called the *protoevangelium*, the first good news, after the fall. The mystery of evil cast its shadow over the cradle of the human race. Adam and Eve sinned; they listened to God's enemy and obeyed his suggestion that they defy God. They incurred death and concupiscence; they fell into the power of a cruel enemy who was jealous of their happiness.

This famous text has been a subject of serious study for modern exegetes as well as for Jewish rabbis and Christian Fathers. Rationalists, who look on the Bible as a purely natural book, refuse to see in it more than a prediction of a long-continued fight between Eve and her posterity, considered collectively, and evil. On the other hand, Hebrews and Christians never considered Eve, who believed the lying speech of her enemy, and her posterity considered collectively, to be able without supernatural help to crush the head of the serpent. Eve, deprived of the state of grace, bore her children in the state of nature. The whole family was reduced to the natural order—no longer children and friends of God, but creatures and servants. They could not emancipate themselves without help of a Messias, a person in whom God was well pleased, who would restore the supernatural reign of God among men. The Messias would belong to the family of the woman; but he would be, like Adam before the fall, a son and friend of God, capable of crushing the head of the serpent.

Pius IX confidently declared that: "The Fathers and writers of the Church have taught the merciful Redeemer of the human race was clearly and openly foreshadowed in this divine oracle."[4] Christians did not invent this interpretation. The Septuagint translated *seed* not by *it* or *they* but *autos* (he), which shows the mind of the Jews in the third century before Christ. The seed of the woman who would crush the head of the serpent was to be a definite person. The same translation is found in the Targum of Onkelos (Aramaic; Bablyonian). Some manuscripts indeed have *sons* of the woman, but others have *son* (in the singular). A commentary expressive of Jewish theology is furnished by *Pseudo-Jonathan:* "And I will put enmity between you and the woman, between the seed of your son and the seed of her sons; and it will be that when the sons of the woman observe the prescriptions of the law, they will be trying to strike you on the head; when they abandon the law, you will be biting their heels. Nevertheless, there will be a remedy for them but not for you; the remedy for their heels will be prepared in the days of the Messias."[5]

Ancestors of the Messias

"Blessed be the Lord God of Sem" (Gen. 9:26). Noe singled out his oldest son for a special blessing. What this blessing was became clearer when an illustrious son of Sem was told by God: "I will bless them that bless thee, and curse them that curse thee, and in thee shall all the kindred of the earth be blessed" (Gen. 12:3). Abraham personally was blessed and his family was blessed, and through him and his family all nations would be blessed.

God entered into a covenant with Abraham, promising with an oath to multiply his children into a great nation. Although Abraham had other sons, Isaac was made heir of the promise: "thou shalt call his name Isaac, and I will establish my covenant with him" (Gen. 17:19). Isaac in turn, passing over Esau, settled the promise on Jacob, whose name was changed to Israel. Jacob designated his fourth son: "The sceptre shall not be taken away from Juda, nor the ruler's staff from between his feet until he comes to whom it belongs, whom the nations shall obey" (Gen. 49: 10). The tribe of Juda was marked for leadership among the twelve tribes. Hebrew tradition was constant in holding that the Messias would come from the tribe of Juda to which David belonged.

Moses, Type of Messias

Moses, liberator of his people, mediator between them and Yahweh, law-giver of Israel, was a figure of the Messias.

He led Israel out of Egypt into the promised land; he instructed his people in the law of God; he mediated between them and the anger of God: "I will raise them up a prophet out of the midst of their brethren like to thee; and I will put my words in his mouth and he shall speak to them all that I shall command him. And he that will not hear his words, which he shall speak in my name, I will be the revenger" (Deut. 18:18-18). This prophecy of Moses left an indelible impression. Moses typified the Messias. He delivered the Israelites out of the house of bondage; he sprinkled the doors of their houses with blood on the night before their departure from Egypt, thus keeping the destroying angel from entering to kill their first-born. In the desert Moses healed murmurers bitten by fiery serpents, setting up a brazen serpent for a sign.

Balaam

The king of the Moabites hired Balaam, a prophet, to curse the Israelites as they journeyed through Moab. The prophet was willing to prostitute his supernatural gift for money, but in spite of his wickedness he could not curse Israel. Instead, he uttered this blessing: "I shall see him, but not now. I shall behold him, but not near. A star shall rise out of Jacob and a sceptre shall spring up from Israel" (Num. 24:17). The star and the sceptre symbolized royal power. Jacob foretold that Juda would be father of a line that would bear the sceptre. In the second psalm a vivid description is given of the Messias, victorious over his enemies: "Why do the Gentiles rage and the people meditate vain things?" The kings of the earth rise up and the princes conspire against the Lord and his Messias . . . . But he who is throned in heaven laughs at them." The Gentiles revolt against God and his anointed; but God establishes his anointed (the Messias) in power in spite of their opposition.

Son of David

The Messias was to be a Semite, of the family of Abraham, Isaac, Jacob and Juda. From this line descended David. That the Messias would be the Son of David was universally expected by Israelites. During and after the Babylonian exile, when oppressed by foreign tyrants, they dreamed the Son of David would soon come to restore the kingdom to Israel. When Jesus of Nazareth inquired whose son the Messias would be, the Jews replied without hesitation, "David's" (Matt. 22:42). The scriptural basis for this hope is II Kings 7:16. Pleased with David's zeal for divine worship, the beautiful hymns he composed in praise of God and his desire to build a temple, God sent Nathan to tell him: "Thy house shall be faithful and thy kingdom forever before thy face, and thy throne shall be firm forever." This is the theme of Psalm 88. God will not cast off the family of David as he did the family of Saul; he promised to establish it forever. The Messias will be a son of David and will reign forever. This hope heartened Israel in dark days. The God of Abraham, Isaac, Jacob, Moses and David would not belie his promises. David himself predicted that the Messias would triumph over his enemies: "The Lord said to my Lord: sit thou on my right hand until I make thy enemies thy footstool" (Psalm 109:1). David calls his son his Lord. He also foretells, in the same psalm, that his son and Lord will be a priest: "The Lord hath sworn and will not repent: Thou art a priest forever according to the order of Melchisedech." And he foretells in another psalm that the Messias will suffer.

> But as for me, I am a worm and not a man
> The scorn of men and the outcast of the people.
> All those who see me laugh me to scorn
> With their lips they mock me and they wag their head:
> "He hoped in the Lord; let him set him free,
> Since he finds his pleasure in him."
>
> . . . .
>
> Many oxen surround me
> Fat bulls besiege me
> They open their mouths against me,
> Like a rending and roaring lion
> I am poured out like water,
> And all my bones are separated
> My heart has become like wax
> That melteth within me.
>
> . . . .
>
> A multitude of dogs surround me
> A band of evildoers encompass me;
> They dig through my hands and feet,
> They count all my bones
> They gaze on me and examine me
> They divide among them my garments
> And they cast lots for my tunic. (Psalm 21)[6]

Isaias the Great Prophet

After the division of the tribes into northern and southern kingdoms, the chosen people, especially in the northern kingdom, were sorely tempted to idolatry and defection from the covenant of Sinai. In both kingdoms inspired prophets warned rulers and people against the wickedness of forsaking Yahweh and the punishment that would follow. They denounced sin, but held out hope. Osee and Amos preached in the northern kingdom (Israel) about the middle of the eighth century. At the same time Isaias began to preach in the southern kingdom (Juda). Sirach calls Isaias the great prophet: "With a great spirit he saw the things that are to come to pass at last, and comforted the mourners in Sion. He showed what should come to pass forever, and secret things before they came" (Ecclus. 48:27-28).

During the past century, German exegetes and their followers in England and America have tried to give a naturalistic explanation to everything in Holy Scripture. They were hard pressed when they sought to show that the kingdom of God described by Isaias is merely the reign of natural justice (with peace consequent upon it). Still harder pressed were they to tell why the child born of a virgin should be called *Emmanuel,* that is, God with us, and *El Gibbor,* that is, God Almighty. Their temerity reached its zenith when they asserted that the suffering servant of Yahweh, by whose humiliations and wounds the sins of mankind are to be expiated, is no more than a personification of the people of Israel taken collectively. Israel is "a kingdom of priests and a holy nation," who by its virtues and sufferings will redeem and sanctify all nations.

Prince of Peace

The sixty-six chapters of Isaias teem with references to the kingdom of God. The Messias will extend the kingdom of God to all mankind, excluding only the wicked. Beginning with the second chapter, the Gentiles are pictured as flocking to Jerusalem to be instructed; and after they learn the ways of the Lord, they will "beat their swords into plowshares and their spears into sickles." After describing the pride, avarice and idolatry prevalent during the reign of Achab (chapters 7-11), Isaias foretells the coming of a divine child who, living in poverty and eating only curds and honey, will exercise a world-wide influence.

The child will be born of a virgin (Isaias 7:14). The spirit of the Lord will be upon him: "the spirit of wisdom and understanding, the spirit of counsel and fortitude, the spirit of knowledge and piety, and he shall be filled with the spirit of the fear of the Lord" (Isaias 11:2). Through him "the earth will be filled with the knowledge of the Lord as the covering waters of the sea" (Isaias 11:9). He will set an example of meekness and gentleness. The effect of his teaching and example will be that the nations hitherto resembling lions, leopards, and wolves in their dealings with one another will be domesticated and will abide together in peace, ruled by a child. "The wolf shall dwell with the lamb; and the leopard shall lie down with the kid. The calf and the lion and the sheep shall abide together and a little child shall lead them" (Isaias 11:6). Nevertheless, "there is no peace to the wicked."

Emmanuel—El Gibbor

The child born of the virgin (Hebrew—*almah;* Greek: *parthenos)* is to be called Emmanuel, that is, God with us. Chapters 7-11 in Isaias have been called "The Little Book of Emmanuel" because throughout these chapters the Messias is described as a divine child. The strongest assertion of this divinity is this: "For a child is born to us, and a son is given to us, and the government is upon his shoulders; and his name shall be called Wonderful, Counsellor, God the Mighty, Father of the World to come, Prince of Peace" (Isaias 9:6). If anyone sits down before this prophecy like a little child (or a detached scientist) and meditates upon it, he will be filled with awe. Taken at its face value, this sentence declares that the child will be God. The American Hebrew translation gives the name in Hebrew and, in a footnote, interprets it to mean: "Wonderful in counsel is God the Mighty, the Everlasting Father, the Ruler of peace." But this is not the traditional translation, According to it, Isaias calls the child *El Gibbor:* that is, Mighty God.

A suggestion of the divinity of the Messias is also found in the second psalm which Hebrews as well as Christians considered Messianic. "Thou are my son, this day have I begotten thee." St. Paul, commenting on this verse, says God never spoke that way to any angel. *This day* sounds like the eternal day of which there is no end. Micheas (5:2) says of the Messias who is to be born in Bethlehem: "And his going forth is from the beginning, from the days of eternity."

The Suffering Servant of Yahweh

The most famous prophecy in the Old Testament is found in Isaias, chapters 50 to 53. It foretells the sufferings of the Messias fulfilling his office as voluntary scapegoat for sinful men. The prophet himself is amazed at what he sees and wonders who will believe his report.

> I gave my back to the smiters and my cheeks to them that plucked them; I have not turned my face away from them that rebuked me and spit upon me. . . . (50:6)
> Many were appalled—so marred was his visage, unlike that of a man, and his form unlike that of the sons of men. So shall he sprinkle many nations, kings shall shut their mouths because of him. . . . (52:14-15)
> There is no beauty in him, despised and the most abject of men, a man of sorrows and acquainted with infirmity . . . . Surely he hath borne our infirmities and carried our sorrow; and we

have thought him as it were a leper and as one struck by God and afflicted. He was wounded for our iniquities, he was bruised for our sins; the chastisement of our peace was upon him and by his bruises we are healed. All we like sheep have gone astray, everyone hath turned aside unto his own way; and God hath laid on him the iniquity of us all. He was offered because it was his own will, and he opened not his mouth; he shall be led as a sheep to the slaughter and shall be dumb as a lamb before his shearer and he shall not open his mouth. (53:4-7)

The unselfishness of this suffering servant of Yahweh, offering himself to be sacrificed as a victim for the sins of men, have filled with awe even Rationalist critics. Priest and victim! "He was offered because it was his own will." He volunteered; therefore, he offered the sacrifice; therefore, he was priest as well as victim. He was the scapegoat; he knew it and willed it. Himself sinless, he willed to endure punishment for all men's sins.

It is sheer stupidity to see in the Suffering Servant of Yahweh no more than the people of Israel, who never volunteered to suffer even for their own sins, to say nothing of the sins of the Gentiles. It is a fiction to ascribe to modern Jews the role of suffering servant of Yahweh. Isaias was speaking about a person holier than anyone who had ever yet served the cause of mankind.

Micheas

Micheas was a contemporary of Isaias. He foretold the place of Christ's birth—a very definite prophecy. "And thou, Bethlehem Ephrata, art a little one among the thousands of Juda; out of thee shall he come forth unto me that is to be the ruler in Israel; and his going forth is from the beginning, from the days of eternity" (Micheas 5:2). This prophecy was well known to the Jews who looked for the Messias to be born in Bethlehem. Like Isaias, Micheas suggests the divinity of the Messias: "His going forth is from the beginning, from the days of eternity."

Jonas

The book of Jonas is regarded by ancient Jews and until recently by Christians as genuine history. Modern critics, with some Catholics among them, look on it as an allegory. Whether taken literally or as a parable, the story of Jonas living in the belly of the great fish in the depths of the Mediterranean and coming out alive on the third day is an amazing prophecy of the resurrection of Christ. Nor does it stand alone. Psalm 15 (16) declares: "Thou will not leave my soul in hell; nor wilt thou give thy holy one to see corruption."

Jeremias

Like Moses and Jonas, Jeremias is a type of the Messias. Opposed by rulers and false prophets, he endured persecution for delivering God's message. He was a prophet of disaster, but he consoled all who remained faithful of Yahweh. There will be a new and better covenant; a remnant of the Jews will triumph; the Gentiles will not utterly destroy the Jews until their Messianic mission is accomplished. The whole of the thirty-first chapter of Jeremias is radiant with hope. "I have loved you with an everlasting love."

Daniel

Daniel won a place of prominence with Babylonian and Persian kings because of his wisdom. His book is full of apocalyptic visions. One of these represents the Ancient of Days seated on a magnificent throne surrounded by millions of angels. "One like to the son of man," a mysterious, awe-inspiring person, presents himself before the throne and receives from the Ancient of Days a kingdom that is to last forever. This prophecy contains the title "Son of Man" which is prominent in the New Testament.

Here is the translation of the vision in the American Jewish Bible:

> I saw in the night visions,
> And, behold, there came with the clouds of heaven
> One like unto a son of man,
> And he came even to the Ancient of days,
> And he was brought near before Him,
> And there was given him dominion,
> And glory and a kingdom
> That all the peoples, nations and languages
> Should serve him;
> His dominion is an everlasting dominion which
>   shall not pass away,
> And his kingdom that which shall not be destroyed. (Daniel 7:14)

This clearly expresses the two ideas of the Messias and the kingdom of God, the central theme of the Old Testament. In spite of sin and evil, God will form a holy people beginning with the Jews and extending to all mankind, to be ruled by a Son of Man whose reign will never end. No matter how late modern critics date the book of Daniel, it is certain that this prophecy was known long before the coming of Christ. In it is contained the Messianic hope of the children of Israel. We shall not discuss here the famous prediction by Daniel of the number of years from the rebuilding of Jerusalem after the exile to the coming of the Messias, nor the abomination of desolation referred to by

Christ; but they are famous prophecies which deserve respectful attention.

Aggeus

Aggeus was born during the exile and returned with Zorobabel to Jerusalem. His short prophecy is a message of encouragement: build the temple in spite of poverty and obstacles! He warned the old men who had seen Solomon's temple not to be sad because of the simplicity of the new temple. It would be more glorious than the first temple, he told them, because the Messias would honor it with his presence. "Yet one little while and I will move the heaven and the earth and the sea and the dry land. And I will move the nations and *the desired of all nations shall come* and I will fill this house with glory, said the Lord of hosts. . . . Great shall be the glory of this last house more than of the first" (Aggeus 2:7).

Zacharias

Zacharias lived at the same time as Aggeus. He, too, encouraged the rebuilding of the temple and the city, predicting in the triumphal entry of the Messias into Jerusalem. "Rejoice greatly, O daughter of Sion, shout for joy, O daughter of Jerusalem. Behold thy king will come to thee, the just and savior; he is poor and riding on an ass, and upon a colt, the foal of an ass" (Zach. 9:9). He foresaw that the Messias would bring no more than the price of a slave. "And they weighed for my hire thirty pieces of silver. And the Lord said to me: Cast it into the treasury, the goodly price I was prized at of them" (Zach. 11:12).

Zacharias, like David and Isaias, predicted the sufferings of the Messias. "And they shall look upon me whom they have pierced; and they shall mourn for him as one mourneth for an only son . . . . In that day there shall be a great lamentation in Jerusalem" (Zach. 12:10). "What are these wounds in the midst of thy hands? And he shall say: With these I was wounded in the house of them that loved me. Awake, O sword, against my shepherd . . . . Strike the shepherd and the sheep shall be scattered" (Zach. 13:6).

No serious mind can fail to wonder at such language. The thought of a Messias humiliated, contradicted, done to death is certainly to be found in the Hebrew prophets by anyone who has eyes to see or ears to hear.

Malachias

Malachias, the last of the Hebrew prophets, was a contemporary of Esdras and Nehemias (about 450 B.C.). "Behold I send an angel and he shall prepare the way before my face" (Mal. 3:1). This prophecy resembles that of Isaias: "The voice of one crying in the desert: Prepare ye the way of the Lord, make straight in the wilderness the paths of our God. Every valley shall be filled and every mountain and hill shall be laid low and the crooked shall be made straight and rough ways smooth. And the glory of the Lord shall be revealed" (Isaias 40:3). Moreover, says Malachias: "Behold I will send Elias the prophet before the coming of the great and dreadful day of the Lord." It appears that two comings of the Lord are predicted: the great and dreadful day of the Lord is the end of the world. Whatever one makes of the prediction, at least Malachias declares that Elias, who has not yet died, will return as a herald. The whole history of Elias is unexplainable for one who denies a supernatural order.

Malachias announces that a universal sacrifice, a clean oblation, will supersede the offering of animals. In the name of God, he rebukes those who offer to God blind, lame, and otherwise blemished gifts. Then gazing far into the future, he beholds an acceptable sacrifice offered everywhere: "From the rising of the sun even to the going down, my name is great among the Gentiles, and in every place there is sacrifice and there is offered to my name a clean oblation, for my name is great among the Gentiles, saith the Lord of Hosts" (Mal. 1:11). This prophecy should be considered in connection with Psalm 109: "Thou art a priest forever according to the order of Melchisedech." The Messias, a priest according to the order of Melchisedech, will bring it about that all nations will offer to God a clean oblation.

Teacher, Priest, King

The Messias was to be a teacher come from God to instruct all men in the ways of the Lord. "Arise, be enlightened, O Jerusalem . . . . The Gentiles shall walk in thy light" (Isaias 60:1). Moses said God would put his words into the mouth of a great prophet and that all men must listen to him. "God will raise up a prophet from your midst . . . . I will place my words in his mouth" (Deut. 18:18). "Upon him shall rest the spirit of wisdom and understanding" (Isaias 11:2). "The spirit of the Lord is upon me . . . he hath sent me to preach to the meek" (Isaias 61:1). "Thy children shall all be taught of God" (Isaias 54:13). "The earth shall be filled with the knowledge of the Lord as the covering waters of the sea" (Isaias 11:9). "I will pour out my spirit on all flesh; your old men shall dream dreams and your young men shall see visions" (Joel 2:28). "And they shall teach no more every man his neighbor and every man his brother saying: Know the Lord. For all shall know me from the least even to the greatest, saith the Lord" (Jer. 31:34).

That the Messias was to be a priest is evident, especially from Isaias 53. But this prophecy does not stand alone. His priesthood is promised in Psalm 109. The description of suffering and abandonment given in Psalm 21^7 has been understood by tradition to be voluntary suffering endured by others. The sacrifices of the Mosaic law were typical, figurative of a better sacrifice to come. The scapegoat, the paschal lamb, the brazen serpent symbolized the Messias meditating between God and his sinful people.

The Messias was to be a king. This was a great expectation. In their darkest days of exile, Israelites looked for the Son of David to restore the kingdom to Israel. They were too prone to imagine a kingdom won by physical power, conferring on them wealth and luxury. They realized, however, that the kingdom was to be open to the Gentiles; that it was to be a kingdom of peace and love; that the wicked would be excluded. Isaias said plainly that the Messias-king would be meek and gentle. "The bruised reed he shall not break, the smoking wick he shall not extinguish" (Isaias 42:3).

Among Egyptians and Babylonians, it was customary to flatter the reigning king by telling him that before he came to the throne his people endured poverty, misery, slavery, and all manner of misfortune; but that he, the reigning king, had been their savior. This flattery has nothing in common with Hebrew prophecies concerning the Messias-king. The prophets of Israel looked to the future. Unlike the false prophets of Israel, they did not flatter the reigning king; on the contrary, they often brought down his anger upon themselves by foretelling his death or defeat in battle. The kingdom of the Messias was not built on flattery or humbug. He was to be holy and the people over whom he ruled were to be holy. "God is a spirit, and they that adore him must adore him in spirit and in truth" (John 4:24).

NOTES FOR CHAPTER V

1. This is recognized by objective Protestant scholars as well as by Catholics. Dr. James Barr has stressed particularly that direct communication from God to man is an inescapable fact of the Bible. See his article in *Theology Digest,* Spring, 1965.

2. M. J. Lagrange, *Revue Biblique* (1906), p. 335, quoted by Fillion in *Life of Christ,* Volume I, p. 516.

3. Neuman, *Judaism,* in *Great Religions of the Modern World,* ed. Edward J. Jurji (Princeton, 1946), p. 245.

4. Bull: *Ineffabilis Deus.*

5. P. F. Ceuppens, O.P., *Quaestiones Selectae ex Historia Primeva* (Rome, 1947), p. 212.

6. See Boylan, *The Psalms,* Volume I, p. 79.

7. In some translations, these two psalms are numbered 110 and 22, respectively.

CHAPTER **VI**

Canon of the Old Testament

Canon, a Greek word, originally meant measuring rod. Grammarians applied it to the collection of classical authors set before pupils as exemplars of fine writing. Early Christians used it to designate the rule of faith. Since Holy Scripture, with tradition, comprises the rule of faith, about the time of Origen (254 A.D.) the word canon was applied to the collection of books received by the Church as inspired and divine. This usage endured. Hence when we speak of the canon of the Old Testament, we mean the limited collection of books constituting the part of the Bible the Christian Church inherited from the Synagogue.

The word Bible is derived from *byblus,* a Greek word for papyrus plant, used in making paper. From it came the word *biblion,* meaning a book, and among Christians *Biblia,* the books *par excellence,* often with the qualification "holy." When the word was taken over into Latin the idea that the Bible was "the one utterance of God rather than a multiplicity of voices speaking for him" had gained posses-

108

sion of the minds of Christians, and the Greek neuter plural became a Latin feminine singular; and as a singular name it found its way into the languages of modern Europe.[1] Hence *Bible* as a name for the complete collection of inspired writings implies the supernatural point of view: God is the author of all divinely inspired books, and therefore they constitute one book. The same development took place with the word *Scriptures*. In course of time the plural was often dropped, and Christians spoke of "Scripture" or "Holy Scripture," thus laying stress on divine rather than human authorship. Since the rise of Rationalism the process has been reversed. Not only is each book treated as distinct from every other, but efforts have been made to discern in individual books multiple documents, authors, fragments, editors and redactors, treating divine authorship as a pious fiction.

The Hebrew word *berith* is best translated into Latin by *foedus* or *pactum,* meaning *covenant* or solemn contract; as a matter of fact *berith* made its way into Latin via Greek. The Septuagint translated it by διαθηκη (diatheke), which meant a legal instrument or will whereby property is transferred. In the earliest Latin versions διαθηκη was rendered by either instrumentum or testamentum, legal terms, one signifying any official document and the other a last will or its proclamation. Since St. Jerome translated the Old Testament directly from the Hebrew, we should have expected him to use *foedus* or *pactum,* covenant or contract, instead of *testamentum;* but he allowed *testamentum* to stand. *Covenant* signifies a bilateral contract; *testament* a unilateral contract. *Testament* lays stress on the divine goodness in giving mankind an inheritance, as it were, by will. It directs attention to the divine generosity in bestowing a library of inspired books from which men can learn of their supernatural vocation and the means to obtain it.

It is an undeniable historical fact that at the time of Christ the Hebrew people had a collection of books they revered as supernaturally inspired and of divine authority. The mentality of our age demands that we use the scientific or inductive method. There is great contempt for what is called the unscientific past; but facts must be respected. The fact here under discussion is the historical truth of divine revelation. The strategy of Rationalism has been to discredit the witness of history and to pretend that modern scholars can determine the authorship of the books of the Bible by internal evidence. The more obscure and dubious Rationalists can make the origin of the books of the Old Testament, the more plausibly they can argue for a natural evolution of what Christians hold to be revealed religion. To the orthodox Jew and the Christian, Moses is a definite historical person who relates what he experienced at the burning bush in the land of Madian; who was commissioned by God to lead the Jews out of Egypt; who for forty years acted as God's agent; who lived on terms of intimate personal friendship with the God of Abraham, the God of Isaac and the God of Jacob. The Jews believed he wrote down what God told him to write. Rationalists assert that the conversation at the burning bush, the ten plagues, the miraculous crossing of the Red Sea, the giving of the law by God at Sinai are legends, not history.

Supernatural facts, however, are verifiable. Miracles can be observed and testified to by thousands of witnesses. Scientists cannot declare the Hebrews never walked across the Red Sea, because they have no way of verifying such a statement. If six hundred thousand men fit to bear arms, besides old men, women and children did walk across it, the fact was of a kind to leave a mark in history. We admit the law of parsimony; we grant that miracles must not be multiplied without necessity. On the other hand, we maintain that the books which comprise the Old Testament are facts that merit respectful examination and reasonable explanation.

In their campaign to prove that Christianity originated by natural evolution, Rationalists have been stopped time and again by stubborn historical facts. For example, they found it impossible to deny that Paul of Tarsus wrote the First Epistle to the Corinthians. In it, Paul asserts more than five hundred people saw Christ after he rose from the dead, and that many of them were still alive at the time he was writing. In regard to the Old Testament, they are confronted with equally solid facts. Josephus (37-95 A.D.), in his well known history of the Jewish people, asserts that the Jews had books they reverenced as containing divine revelation.

> We do not have an infinite number of books which disagree or contradict each other (as do the Greeks), but only twenty-two which contain the annals of all times, and enjoy deserved credit. First we have the books of Moses, of which there are five . . . . The prophets who came after Moses wrote the history of their times in thirteen books. The last four contains hymns to God and moral precepts for mankind.

> What credence we have given to all these books of our own nation is evident from our conduct, for though so long a time has passed, no one has ever been so bold as to add anything to them whatever. But all Jews are instinctively led, from the moment of their birth, to believe that these books contain divine oracles, and to abide by them and, if need be, to die for them. . . . From the time of Artaxerxes to our own time, our history has been written down very particularly, but these books have not been considered worthy of the same credit as the books of

earlier date, because there has not been an exact succession of
prophets.[2]

According to Josephus, the Jews had a limited collection
of books, the authoritative source of their doctrine and practice; these books were written before the time of Artaxerxes
(450 B.C.); and they were studied by priests, levites, rabbis
and scribes; they formed the basis of Hebrew education and
culture. By no means were they regarded merely as "a
collection of all the relics of Hebraeo-Chaldaic literature
up to a certain period." Josephus emphasizes the reverence
of his people for their twenty-two books as "divine oracles."

The Talmud is a written record of Hebrew oral tradition.
It consists of Mishna and Gemara. Gemara is divided into
two parts, written, one in Palestine and the other in Babylonia. Hence one is called the Jerusalem Talmud and the
other the Babylonian Talmud. The Mishna was made at
the end of the second century A.D. by Juda han-Nazi and
one hundred and fifty Tannaim (teachers).[3] The Gemara
is a commentary by Amoraim (commentators). The Amoraic
period extended from the third to the sixth century in Babylonia. It was somewhat shorter in Palestine. Juda the Holy
(136-217) may be called the father of the movement to
write down what up to this time had been taught orally.
His doctrine became incorporated in Mishna and Baraita.
Baraita treated of outside matters, i.e., not directly connected with the Law.

In the Babylonian Talmud *(Baba Bathra,* fol. 14[a] and 15[b]),
a baraitha, attributed to Juda the Holy 136-217 A.D.) gives the
list of the twenty-four books which the synagogue considered
sacred and presents this last as one handed down by the Fathers.[4]

This passage voices the same tradition as Josephus: the
Jews had a collection of sacred books limited to twenty-four.

Josephus says twenty-two, but there is no discrepancy, because Ruth was sometimes numbered as one with Josue and Lamentations as one with Jeremias. There appears to have been no dispute about the five books of Moses. Among the prophets, Ezechiel alone was questioned because some thought he disagreed with Moses; but the dispute was not serious. On the other hand, it appears that the third collection of holy writings (Kethubim, Hagiographa) was not completed until long after Artaxerxes, and there did arise a serious dispute about such books as were not written in Palestine, in Hebrew and before Esdras.

> It was then that Pharisaism made ready to take over the sole leadership of the nation . . . . A stricter view was taken of the canon . . . . That body of near-scriptural writings which had hovered on the borderland . . . was resolutely pushed aside and pushed without . . . . at the memorable session at Jabneh about 90 of the common era, where Gamaliel was deposed and Eleazor ben Azariah made head of the school . . . . The closing of the canon by the excluding act which segregated the apocrypha was the work of Pharisaism triumphant.[5]

To understand what was in dispute at Jabneh or Jamnia, one should know that then as now, Hebrews classified their books into Law (Torah), Prophets (Nebiim), and (other) Writings (Kethubim). The Law consists of the five books of Moses. These are the oldest and their divine authority was never questioned by the ancient Hebrews. All believed Moses wrote what he was commanded by God to write. The last few verses of Deuteronomy, concerning the death of Moses, were thought to have been added by Josue. The Samaritans broke with the Hebrews in the fifth century B.C. and took with them the Pentateuch, which they still preserve with the greatest respect. Thus for the existence of the Law, we have the witness of the Samaritans as well as that of the Jews. The second collection consists of the Prophets, earlier and later. The earlier books of the prophets were Josue, Judges, Samuel and Kings; these were the history of Israel from Moses to the Babylonian exile, and were written, it was thought, by Josue, Samuel and Jeremias. Isaias, Jeremias, Ezechiel and the Twelve (Minor Prophets) were called later prophets. They lived before, during, and after the Exile. All of these, even the latest, flourished no later than Esdras (450 B.C.)

The (other) writings comprised Psalms, Job, Ruth, Proverbs, Canticle of Canticles, Ecclesiastes, Lamentations, Daniel, Esther, Esdras, Nehemias, and First and Second Chronicles. At the heart of this collection was the Psalms. Ecclesiastes and the Song of Songs were questions as to their agreement with Hebrew theology; but they were approved. Some of the Psalms had certainly been in use in the liturgy from the time of David. The five Megilloth (Rolls): Ruth, Song of Songs, Ecclesiastes, Lamentations and Esther were read, each on a special feast. The others were not read publicly, and their number was not exactly determined. This is evident from the extensive use of Sirach (Ecclesiasticus) in schools and for private reading both in Egypt and in Palestine. Jesus ben-Sirach wrote this book in Hebrew about 180 years before Christ; it was translated into Greek in 132 B.C. by his grandson who affixed to it a prologue of great historical value. At that time the number of books comprising the Law and Prophets was fixed; but the limits of the Kethubim or Writings had not been definitely decided because the younger Sirach thought his grandfather's book equal to other inspired Scriptures.

The Second Book of Machabees, written about the same time (125 B.C.) contains a letter from Palestinian to Alexandrian Jews telling them that Judas Machabeus, having restored peace and purified the temple, made a collection of all the sacred books he could find, following Antiochus Epiphanes' attempt to destroy them. The letter recalls that Nehemias also made a collection of sacred books after the Babylonian Exile.

> And these same things were set down in the memoirs and commentaries of Nehemias; and how he made a library and gathered together out of the countries the books both of the prophets and of David and the epistles of the kings and concerning holy gifts. And in like manner, Judas also gathered together all such things as were lost by the war we had; and they are in our possession. Wherefore if you want these things, send someone to fetch them to you. (II Machabees 2:13-15)

Both Esdras and Nehemias were zealous for the Law of Moses. Filled with holy ardor for instructing the Jews, they read the books of Moses to the people after their return from Babylon; since many could no longer understand Hebrew, Esdras was obliged to supply targums, translations into Aramaic, not written but oral. Esdras assembled the people and for the eight days of the feast of the Tabernacles he read the law to them from morning till midday. The Levites interpreted in Aramaic.[6]

The zeal of Esdras for the sacred books gave rise to legends about his own marvelous literary activity. One of these legends is to be found in the apocryphal *Fourth Book of Esdras*, written toward the end of the first century of the Christian era. In this book Esdras is said to have dictated for forty days to five secretaries the text of ninety-four books, twenty-four of which "are to be read by both the worthy and the unworthy, and seventy reserved for the wise only."[7] This apocryphal Esdras mentions twenty-four books to be read in the synagogue in the hearing of all.

Thus he testifies to the same tradition as the one we called attention to in Josephus and the Babylonian Talmud.

Closing of the Canon

From the foregoing evidence it is clear that at least four centuries before Christ the Jews possessed a limited collection of books divided into Law, Prophets, and (other) Writings. The first five, the Torah (the Law), were believed to have been written by Moses after God appeared to the people at Mount Sinai and entered into a covenant with them. The second division was called the Prophets, divided into earlier and later. Josue, Judges, Samuel and Kings continued the history of the chosen people and their relations with God down to the Babylonian captivity. These books were ascribed to Josue, Samuel and Jeremias. Isaias, Jeremias, Ezechiel and the Twelve were prophets in a stricter sense of the word: they warned the people of their infidelity to the covenant of Mount Sinai, mingling encouragement and consolation with threats. They foretold future events. Daniel is not found among the Prophets in the Hebrew Bible, but in the third division, the Kethubim. The Twelve lived from the ninth to the fifth century. Malachias, the last, flourished about the time of Esdras and Nehemias (450 B.C.). The Kethubim (other writings) consist of Psalms, Proverbs, Job, Daniel, Esther, and Canticle of Canticles. Others: Wisdom, Sirach, Tobias, Baruch, and First and Second Machabees were written after the time of Artaxerxes, or outside of Palestine, or in Aramaic or Greek.

Josephus names twenty-two books whereas the Talmud and Fourth Esdras name twenty-four. As we have noted,

Ruth was written on the same roll as Judges, and Lamentations on the same roll as Jeremias; hence Judges and Ruth were sometimes counted one book, as were Jeremias and Lamentations. The American translation of the Hebrew Bible lists twenty-eight books, counting Samuel as two, Kings as two, Ezra (Esdras) as two and Chronicles as two, whereas Josephus and the Talmud counted each of these as one.

Order of Books in the Hebrew Bible

Genesis		Psalms
Exodus		Proverbs
Leviticus		Job
Numbers		Song of Songs
Deuteronomy		Ruth
Joshua		Lamentations
Judges		Ecclesiastes
I Samuel		Esther
II Samuel		Daniel
I Kings	Hosea	Ezra
II Kings	Joel	Nehemiah
Isaiah	Amos	I Chronicles
Jeremiah	Obadiah	II Chronicles
Ezekiel	Jonah	
The Twelve	Micah	
	Nahum	
	Habakkuk	
	Zephaniah	
	Haggai	
	Zechariah	
	Malachi	

The following quotation from the Babylonian Talmud reflects Hebrew tradition concerning the origin of these books:

The rabbis taught: The order of the Prophets is as follows: Joshua, Judges, Samuel, Kings, Jeremiah, Ezekiel, Isaiah and the

Twelve (Minor Prophets).... The order of the Hagiographa is as follows: Ruth, Psalms, Job, Proverbs, Ecclesiastes, Song of Songs, Lamentations, Daniel, Esther, Ezra and Chronicles.... And who wrote these? Moses wrote his book and the section about Balaam (Num. 25f), and Job.

Joshua wrote his book and the last eight verses of Deuteronomy (narrating the death of Moses). Samuel wrote his book, Judges, and Ruth. David wrote the Psalms with the collaboration of ten Elders, viz., Adam, Melchizedek, Abraham, Moses, Heman, Jeduthan, Asaph, and the three sons of Korah. Jeremiah wrote his book, Kings, and Lamentations. Hezemiah and his associates wrote Isaiah, Proverbs, Song of Songs, and Ecclesiastes. The Men of the Great Assembly wrote Ezechiel, the Twelve, Daniel, and Esther, Ezra wrote his book and the genealogy of Chronicles down to himself, and Nehemiah completed it.[8]

The Men of the Great Synagogue

The expression "Men of the Great Synagogue" (or "Assembly," as it is in the above translation) merits attention because in the sixteenth century a Jew named Elias Levita, a contemporary of Luther, advanced the theory that the canon of the Hebrew Bible was completed and closed by "the men of the Great Synagogue," presided over by Ezra (Esdras). This theory encouraged Protestants to reject the deuterocanonical books and to adopt the Hebrew Canon rather than the traditional Christian Canon of the Septuagint.

We have already seen that the apocryphal *Fourth Book of Esdras,* composed about 100 A.D., attributes amazing literary activity to Esdras, who led an expedition from Babylon to Palestine about 458 B.C. and showed great zeal for instructing the people in the law of Moses. In consequence of this zeal, many legends sprang up concerning his own literary activity and that of a mythical Great Synagogue over which he was imagined to have presided.

Scholars, among whom were A. Kuenen and W. R. Smith (Protestants), have shown that "the men of the Great Synagogue" was a fiction of the Scribes, and that it has no historical basis except in the assembly of the people which lasted eight days, described in the canonical book of Nehemias (II Esdras). After the destruction of Jerusalem, Scribes and Pharisees desired to build a massora or fence around the Hebrew text so as to preserve it. At the Council of Jamnia (90 A.D.), Scribes and Pharisees decided no book written outside of Palestine or after the time of Esdras belonged among the inspired Scriptures. They emphasized the activity of Esdras in collecting the books of the Bible. Elias Levita, at the time of Luther, advanced the theory that the men of the Great Synagogue assisted Esdras in closing the canon of the Scriptures.

The foundation for this legend is contained in chapters 8 and 9 of the book of Nehemias. Esdras, assisted by Nehemias, read to the assembled Jews the law of Moses every day for eight days. Since many of the returned exiles could not understand Hebrew, after the law was read in Hebrew a translator repeated it orally in Aramaic. The assembly (synagogue) was indeed a great one, and Esdras did promulgate anew the law of Moses; but he did not write or change or add to it. The translation was entirely oral. Esdras, indeed, wrote a book of his own or the two books that bear his name. It is noteworthy that the Talmud credits Nehemias with cooperating with him on the books of Chronicles (Paralipomenon).

The legend of Esdras' great literary activity was seized upon by Rationalists of the nineteenth century, and was used to lend plausibility to their theory of the natural evolution of the Hebrew Scriptures. But it is absurd to credit

Esdras with writing the law of Moses, upon which the whole history and religion of Israel had depended. Esdras and Nehemias had no purpose but to reeducate the returned exiles by reading to them the Law of Moses and interpreting it in Aramaic to make clear its meaning.[9]

In 132 B.C., when Sirach wrote a prologue to his grandfather's book, the canon of the Law and the Prophets had long been fixed; but this was not true of the Kethubim or other Writings. Sirach included his grandfather's book, written about 180 B.C., in the collection of Writings.

Christian Canon of the Old Testament

Many Hebrews never returned to Palestine after the exile. Some fled to Egypt, Asia Minor, and other places along the shores of the Mediterranean. These were called the *Diaspora:* i.e., dispersed Hebrews. They remained religiously and culturally dependent on Jerusalem; they paid the temple tax and returned for the great feasts as often as they could. After Alexander conquered the world, Greek became the common language of the countries bordering on the Mediterranean. A large and prosperous community of Jews in Alexandria learned to speak Greek, the language of the Ptolemies.

We have mentioned that when the exiles returned, many could no longer understand Hebrew, so that it was necessary for Esdras to make oral translations into Aramaic. Need for a written translation of the Law of Moses in Aramaic produced a number of written Targums, the most famous of which is the Targum of Onkelos. Rabbis, however, looked with disfavor on written Targums. They thought the law had been given into the custody of the tribe of Levi to be interpreted by the Levites for the people; and they feared private intrepretations of the law by persons not adequately educated in rabbinical tradition.

In Egypt the Jews continued to speak Aramaic until *koine* (common) became the language of business and social intercourse. Then they carried on their business and cultural life in the language of the new rulers. According to legend based on a letter of Aristeas (who says he was a member of the expedition which it describes), Ptolemy Philadelphus (285-247 B.C.) desired a Greek translation of the Hebrew Scriptures for his library. Accordingly, he sent an embassy to Jerusalem to tell the Jews of his plan. Not only was a copy of the Scriptures in Hebrew given him, but Eleazer, the high priest, sent with the manuscript seventy scholars well versed in Hebrew and Greek, to translate it. Because this translation was made by these seventy scholars, it received the name Septuagint (the seventy).

Whatever one may think of this legend, a Greek translation of the Torah was undoubtedly made in Egypt in the third century before Christ by Jews for their own use, with the consent and approval of the religious leaders in Jerusalem. Somewhat later, the Prophets were translated. By the time of Sirach (132 B.C.), the other Writings had also been translated. Sirach the Elder praises all the Prophets and many writings of the Kethubim in his panegyric on the great men of Israel (Sirach or Ecclesiasticus 48-49). From the time of Esdras, if not earlier, it had been the custom to read in the synagogue passages from the Law and the Prophets; from the (other) Writings nothing was read except the five Megilloth (rolls) and these were read only on special feasts: Canticle of Canticles on the Passover; Ruth on Pentecost; Lamentations on the anniversary of the destruction of Jerusalem (586 B.C.); Ecclesiastes on the feast of Tabernacles; and Esther on Purim. Since the other Hagiographa were not publicly read, the list is not easy to determine.

The Torah, or Law, was universally regarded by ancient Jews to be the work of Moses; no orthodox Jew entertained any doubt as to its inspired character. The same is true of Josue, Samuel, Isaias, Jeremias and the Twelve. Whatever disputes occurred among Jews before the time of Christ concerned Ezechiel, Song of Songs and Ecclesiastes, but objectors were overruled in Palestine, and their contentions never affected the Jews in Egypt. When the Hebrew Bible was translated into Greek, the arrangement into Law, Prophets and Writings appears to have been abandoned in favor of one based on chronological and logical classification. The Greek Bible paid less attention to order for liturgical use. Thus it came about that in the Greek Bible there were included a number of Scriptures (Kethubim) which were subsequently excluded from the canon of the Hebrew Bible by the rules laid down by Scribes and Pharisees at the Council of Jamnia (90 A.D.)

Christianity started before the Council of Jamnia, and the Apostles preached mainly in Greek. Thus the Greek Bible, known as the Septuagint, was the one the Christian Church received. In it are seven books excluded from the Hebrew canon: Tobias, Judith, Baruch (with the letter of Jeremias), Wisdom, Sirach (Ecclesiasticus), First and Second Machabees. Also excluded are parts of Esther (chapters 10-16) and of Daniel (verses 24-90 of chapter 3, and chapters 13 and 14). These books had been read by Jews in Palestine as well as in Egypt. For example, the book of Tobias existed in Aramaic, Hebrew and Syriac as well as in Greek, and was highly respected by all Jews. Scholars say Baruch and the Epistle of Jeremias were translated into Greek by the same person who translated Jeremias, indicating that when the Septuagint originated these three books were considered as one. Baruch was still read by the Jews in the Synagogues during the first two Christian centuries. There is nothing in any of these seven books that the Jews considered to be heretical. Even now they are regarded as excellent for private reading, and highly edifying. Unfortunately, however, these seven books have come to be classed by Jews and Protestants as *Apocrypha*. This is a term Catholics reserve for spurious books or pseudigrapha. In Catholic usage, these books are called *deuterocanonical,* to distinguish them from the protocanonical books: that is, books written before the time of Esdras, in Palestine, and in Hebrew.

The Septuagint was universally used in the Greek-speaking world evangelized by the Apostles. From it the first Latin translations of Scripture were made. The Christian Church accepted the Septuagint from the Apostles as the inspired word of God. Complete with all the books it contained, the Septuagint was part of the Apostolic Tradition. It was the only text read in the early Christian churches, East and West.

On the walls of the catacombs, one finds scenes from the deuterocanonical books such as the three boys in the fiery furnace, Daniel in the lions' den, Tobias, Raphael and the fish, Judith with the head of Holofernes, Judas Machabeus, and the mother of the Machabees with her seven martyred sons. No scenes from apocryphal books are found in the catacombs. Moreover, Christian writers quote from all the deuterocanonical books. After the time of Origen in the

East and after the time of Jerome in the West, some Fathers treated the deuterocanonical books as inferior; but their practice belied their theory because both quoted deutero-canonical books in their arguments as if they accepted them as inspired and authoritative. Origen, St. Athanasius, and St. Jerome did this, as well as other Fathers. Origen and St. Jerome, who studied under Jewish teachers, were in-fluenced by Jewish tradition which arose after the time of Christ, although they were perhaps unaware of the arbitrary rules adopted at Jamnia in 90 A.D. Of these rules, Stein-mueller writes:

> These four Pharisaical criteria, placing a limitation upon in-spiration and prophecy, are theologically indefensible, and yet they are of great importance in explaining the history of the formation of the Palestinian Canon. These artificial norms having been invented, only the proto-canonical books were recognized in the process of reexamining the Canon of the Old Testament. Since the deuterocanonical books and passages of the Alexandrian ver-sion did not meet the requirements of these four criteria, they were rejected. The Book of Baruch and the Epistle of Jeremias lacked Palestinian origin; the Book of Sirach and the First Book of Machabees were written after the time of Esdras; the Book of Tobias and the fragments of Daniel and of Esther were composed originally in Aramaic and probably also outside Palestine; the Book of Judith was probably written in Aramaic; and the Book of Wisdom and the Second Book of Machabees were written in Greek.[10]

Christian Bibles in Greek and Latin contained the deu-terocanonical books scattered among the protocanonical books. Tobias and Judith were associated with Job and Esther. Baruch remained with Jeremias and Lamentations. Wisdom and Ecclesiasticus (Sirach) logically belong with Proverbs and Ecclesiastes. First and Second Machabees, containing the latest history, conclude the Old Testament.

Modern Jews are not ungrateful to the Christian Church

for preserving these documents which reflect great glory on the Hebrew people but would have disappeared had it not been for the piety of Christians. Max Margolis, editor-in-chief of the American Jewish Bible, writes:

> If we today are in a position to read in the First Book of the Machabees, for instance, the exploits of Judas Machabaeus "who made Jacob glad with his acts, and his memorial is blessed forever," we owe a debt of gratitude to the Christian Church which, having received the Greek Scriptures at the hands of Greek-speaking Jews of the empire, with pious zeal kept them intact, and rescued from oblivion literary records of near-scriptural rank.[11]

The Council of Carthage (393 A.D.), under the influence of St. Augustine, canonized all the books we have today in Catholic Bibles. Pope Innocent I approved this action in a letter to Bishop Exsuperius in 405 A.D. The same canon was promulgated by the Council of Florence in 1441 A.D. for the Jacobites. The Greek Orthodox Churches remained faithful to this canon at three synods in the 17th century, declaring, against Protestant influence, their acceptance of the deuterocanonical books.

Among Reformers of the 16th century, Karlstadt called attention to St. Jerome's criticism of the deuterocanonical books. Luther's German Bible (1534 A.D.) placed them in an appendix, giving them the title *Apocrypha.* Some Protestants retained them; others opposed them, especially the Puritans of Scotland who insisted that they be kept out of their Bibles.

From the time of St. Augustine (430 A.D.) the canon of the Catholic Church was virtually closed, but not officially.

In 692 the Eastern Church, at the Council of Trullo, adopted the canon of the Council of Carthage (419 A.D.). In 1546, the Council of Trent declared all the books found in the Vulgate to be inspired by God and canonical. The definition of the Council of Trent was renewed at the Vatican Council (1870).

Apocrypha

Catholics distinguish between deuterocanonical books and apocrypha. Deuterocanonical books are accepted as canonical and divinely inspired; apocryphal books are writings of uncertain origin and authority. Not all of them are considered heretical or useless; they give interesting literary and historical sidelights on Hebrew theology and history. Some of them have the character of fiction, containing imaginary biographies of Henoch, Moses, Isaias, Jeremias, etc. Some were widely read as works of edification by Jews and Christians. A few were included in some manuscripts of Christian Bibles. The *Psalms of Solomon* (80-40 B.C.) express earnest longing for the coming of the Messias; the same longing is found in the *Fourth Book of Esdras*.[12] Among the best-known Old Testament apocrypha are the following:

Historical	Apocalyptic
Book of Jubilees	Book of Henoch
Third Book of Esdras	Assumption of Moses
Third Book of Machabees	Slavonic Henoch
Ascension of Isaias	Psalms of Solomon
	Fourth Book of Esdras
Moral	Apocalypse of Baruch
The Prayer of Manasses	Jewish Sibyls
Testaments of Twelve Patriarchs	
Fourth Book of Machabees	

Value of the Old Testament

The whole collection of books included in the canon in the Septuagint is acknowledged by the Catholic Church to be sacred and inspired. Inspired books have been carefully guarded. Only canonical books were considered appropriate for public reading. Some apocryphal books were recommended for private reading as edifying and instructive, but they were never regarded as authoritative sources of faith and morals. This does not mean that Synagogue or Church caused books to become inspired by canonizing them. Canonization means certification by Synagogue or Church that God is the author of a book. Hebrew religion, like Christianity, is founded on the truth of the witness of history as we have set it forth in this chapter.

We are here discussing the Bible not as an inspired book, but as a collection of historical documents. These belong not to Church or Synagogue, but to mankind. Hebrews and Christians, Catholics and Protestants, to the number of many millions have revered the Bible, and have relied on it to light them on their way to what they believed was their supernatural goal. This does not prove it true, but does give it tremendous historical value. Judged as a historical, literary monument, the Bible deserves profound respect. The idea that it is a product of natural evolution is fictional and historically unfounded. The doctrines it contains are superior to any doctrines found in the literature and annals of paganism, ancient or modern. "Hear, O Israel, the Lord our God is one Lord! Thou shalt love the Lord thy God with thy whole heart and with thy whole soul and with thy whole strength." This precept is nobler than any precept laid down in the writings of the pagans. The doctrine of the creation of the world out of nothing by the self-existent God is superior to the cosmogony of the Greeks, Romans, Egyptians or Babylonians. The Old Testament is a colossal historical fact. It must be reckoned with by anyone who tries seriously to explain the origin of Western culture and civilization. From the viewpoint of reason, all books of the Bible have historical value. They give evidence of the Messianic hope of the human race and of belief in divine revelation received by Abraham and his family. The central theme of the Old Testament is the vocation of man to the kingdom of God, the defection of man by sin, and the restoration of mankind to the friendship of God by the Messias.

NOTES FOR CHAPTER VI

1. "Bible," J. Hastings, *Dictionary of the Bible.*
2. *Against Apion,* I, 8.
3. Robert and Tricot, *Guide to the Bible,* Vol. I, p. 446, Translator's Note.
4. *Ibid.,* Vol. I, p. 34.
5. Max Margolis, *Hebrew Scriptures in the Making* (Philadelphia: Jewish Publication Society, 1922), pp. 87-91.
6. See Nehemias (II Esdras), chapter 8.
7. *Fourth Book of Esdras,* 14:45-46. See Robert and Tricot, *Guide to the Bible,* Vol. I, pp. 36-41.
8. *Baba Bathra,* ff. 14^b and 15^a, quoted in Steinmueller, *A Companion to Scripture Studies,* Volume I, pp. 73-74. Also see "Canon," Smith's *Dictionary of the Bible.*
9. See "Synagogue, The Great," Hastings, *Dictionary of the Bible;* also Robert and Tricot, *Guide to the Bible,* Vol. I, p. 41.
10. Steinmueller, *A Companion to Scripture Studies,* Vol. I, p. 81.
11. Max Margolis, *The Story of Bible Translations* (Philadelphia, 1917), p. 38.
12. A fuller discussion of the apocryphal books may be found in Steinmueller, *A Companion to Scripture Studies,* Vol. I, pp. 120-152. See also Robert and Tricot, *Guide to the Bible,* Vol. I, pp. 65-69.

CHAPTER VII

Texts of the Bible

According to Hebrew and Christian tradition, the oldest part of the Bible was written by Moses. Even at the time of Moses, writing had a long history. Several centuries earlier Abraham had come from Ur, on the site of which archaeologists have discovered inscriptions on temples and monuments. These inscriptions were the work of Sumerians, whose culture preceded that of Chaldeans, Assyrians and Babylonians. Scholars date some of them as early as 3500 B.C. In Egypt, too, inscriptions on tombs and other monuments are ascribed to 3500 B.C. or earlier. Assyriologists and Egyptologists disagree as to whether the valley of the Nile or the valley of the Tigris and Euphrates was the original home of handwriting.

The earliest writing is ideographic: in Mesopotamia it is cuneiform and in Egypt hieroglyphic. Ideographic writing is imitative, imaginative or representative, in contrast to alphabetical writing, which is symbolic. The Phoenicians are usually credited with inventing the alphabet—at least the Greeks borrowed it from them. Whether the alphabet originated among the Semites or in Egypt is disputed.

129

Flinders Petrie found Semitic inscriptions in alphabetical writing dating back to the nineteenth or eighteenth century B.C., in which the script appears to be based on Egyptian hieroglyphics, the Semitic language being a dialect closely related to the East Chanaanite. Some scholars believe these inscriptions to be the source of the Phoenician alphabet.[1]

The Hebrew Language

From the time they settled in the land of Chanaan until after the Babylonian exile, Hebrew was the language of the children of Israel. Abraham was called a Hebrew by the Chanaanites either because he was a descendent of Heber or because he came from beyond the flood (*'eber*), i.e., the Euphrates. Hebrew is a Semitic language, read from right to left instead of from left to right. Other Semitic languages are Arabic, Eastern and Western Aramaic, Moabite, and Phoenician. Hebrew was written in Phoenician or long script until the Babylonian Exile (586-536 B.C.). In Babylon the Jews learned to speak Aramaic. After the Exile, the Bible continued to be read publicly in Hebrew, but it began to be written in Chaldaic square script. Of this transition, we read in Robert and Tricot:

> A language which was spoken for more than ten centuries could not fail to have a history. . . . The Massoretic text really represents the late and perhaps arbitrary fixation of the Sacred Book, as it was read and chanted in the liturgy of the synagogue. We have definite indications of vocalic and consonantal changes which took place in the course of centuries. . . . In the land of Canaan Hebrew replaced the Canaanite language which is known to us by the glosses contained in the letters of Tell-el-Amarna (ca. 1400 B.C.), and which it closely resembles. During many centuries it was the only language of the country, and even after the Exile its position remained strong. But gradually another Semitic language, and one highly successful as a conqueror, established

itself in Palestine, first as a rival, then as sovereign. Long before
Our Lord, Hebrew was for the Jew a dead language which had
taken refuge in the schools. The common people understood the
Bible only in the translation which was made for them in their
own tongue, which was now Aramaic.[2]

Aramaic

The Arameans were a more or less nomadic people who
were widely diffused over the Middle East. They were never
dominant politically, but their language, more flexible than
other Semitic dialects, spread throughout Syria, Babylonia,
and the whole of Mesopotamia as a kind of universal
Semitic language until it was replaced in Syria and Egypt
by Greek, after the conquest of Alexander. Aramaic was
used by diplomats in Palestine before the Exile; afterwards
it became the language of the people. Hebrew remained
the language of the rabbis and the schools; but for the people the Scriptures had to be translated orally into Aramaic.
In Babylonia, Syria, and Egypt, Jews of the dispersion spoke
Aramaic, and it was also spoken in Galilee at the time of
Christ. Written translations, Targums, were made in Eastern
(Babylonian) and Western (Jerusalem) dialects. At the
present time Aramaic is spoken in only a few places. Hebrew,
on the other hand, is again a living language in modern
Israel. Traces of Aramaic are found in the New Testament
in words and phrases. St. Mark and St. John use Aramaic
sentence-structure. No doubt Jesus Christ preached in
Aramaic.

Greek

The original language of the Book of Wisdom, Second
Machabees, and the whole of the New Testament is Greek—

not the Greek of the classical writers but a simplified Greek called koine (common) which gradually became the universal language of the Near East after Alexander's conquest. Less flexible than Attic Greek, it was easier to learn and to use, having been considerably influenced by Aramaic in vocabulary and sentence-structure. Koine Greek, the language of Jews of the Diaspora, was the principal language used by St. Paul on his missionary journeys; it was also the language of St. Peter at Rome, as we see from the Gospel of St. Mark who wrote in Greek a resume of his sermons. Palestine itself appears to have been partially bilingual. Early writers like Papias say that Matthew wrote his Gospel in Palestine in Aramaic; but he soon translated it or someone else did, and it is in Greek that it has come down to posterity. The Greek translation of the Old Testament, that is, the Septuagint, was the one used by nearly all Christians in the first two centuries, although it is possible that the Old Testament had been translated into Syriac (Peshitta) before the time of Christ.

The Hebrew Text

All the protocanonical books of the Old Testament were written in Hebrew, with the exception of a few Aramaic passages. We should not lose sight of the fact, however, that printing was not invented until the fifteenth century of the Christian era. For all the centuries between Moses and 1524 A.D.—when Jacob ben Chayine's edition of the Bible was printed by Bomberg in Venice—the Hebrew Bible was transmitted in handwriting. The most enduring material for ancient books was parchment, skins of sheep and calves. But the custom of writing on parchment did not begin until the third or fourth century of the Christian era. Before that papyrus, a less durable material, was used. No manuscript antedating the use of papyrus has come down to us. The oldest complete manuscripts of the Bible are parchment codices, *Vaticanus* and *Sinaiticus,* both of the fourth century A.D. and both reproductions of the Septuagint (Greek) Bible, not of the Hebrew. For use in their synagogues, Jews still observe the custom of writing the Bible on parchment with pen and ink on rolls. Codices are not rolls, but manuscript-books. According to Tisserant, "For liturgical purposes the Jews still use only leather scrolls on which the text has been written by hand without vowel points."[3] The oldest complete manuscripts of the Hebrew Bible go back no farther than the tenth century of the Christian era. A manuscript of the prophets written in 895 A.D. is preserved at Aleppo. This served both at Cairo and at Jerusalem as a model for copyists. Recently a very old manuscript of the prophet Isaias was found in a cave near the Dead Sea.[4]

Most of the manuscripts of the Hebrew Bible now extant differ little from one another. This is due to the carefulness of Massoretes whose duty it was to build a fence, Massora, around the text of the Bible. The history of the Massoretes is obscure but the idea of building a fence around the Hebrew text can be traced as far back as the Council of Jamnia (90 A.D.). Before that time the Hebrew Bible had been written "as one word," that is, with consonants, without vowels, punctuation or spaces between words or sentences. Hebrew is a consonantal language and each generation of rabbis, priests and scribes learned to read the text by listening to their elders, i.e., by oral tradition. Only after the destruction of Jerusalem (70 A.D.), when the pronunciation of Hebrew words was in danger of being lost, did Jews invent a system of vowel points and other marks to indicate how words should be pronounced. Contact with Greek books showed the advantage of separating words and sentences by punctuation and spacing. When the Septuagint translation into Greek was made, beginning in the third century B.C., the Hebrew text was consonantal. This explains some variations between it and the Hebrew text of the Massoretes.

Two schools developed among the Jews after the destruction of Jerusalem, one in Palestine and one in Babylon. Neither school ever considered that writing was a substitute for oral instruction. Nevertheless, the Mishna was written embodying what had previously been oral tradition. The first expounders of the Mishna were called Tannites and the later commentators were called Amoraim. Vowel points were invented in Babylon and in Palestine and the difference between the two systems must be noted by students of textual criticism. Jewish scholars who devoted special attention to the text of the Bible were called Massoretes. According to Robert and Tricot, "One family played an important role in this fixation of the smallest details in the sacred text, namely, the family of Ben Aser, of which five generations are known from 800 to about 925 A.D."[5]

Seisenberger tells us:

> . . . As to the date when the present Hebrew text was definitely fixed, the following may be said: The Septuagint and the Samaritan Pentateuch are based upon older versions since they frequently differ from the Massoretic text. Onkelos and Jonathan (in the time of Christ) differ considerably from it; but on the other hand Aquilas, Theodotion and Symmachus (in the second century) show great resemblance to the Massoretic text, as do later Targumin. St. Jerome used a text that was almost identical with our own. We may assume, therefore, that the Jews fixed their text soon after the time of the Apostles.[6]

The Massoretes themselves placed variant readings in the margins. Although criticized by St. Justin and Origen for obscuring the Messianic prophecies, the Massora was highly regarded by St. Jerome. Monsignor Steinmueller, a reliable authority, says: "The Massoretic text is generally a *good critical text* and agrees substantially with the original text."⁷ This does not mean it is always to be preferred to the Septuagint; it means only that modern scholars, including Catholics, respect the Hebrew text and are grateful to the Massoretes for their reverent precautions to preserve it without alteration.

St. Jerome is largely responsible for the Protestant attitude toward the deuterocanonical books. He became deeply imbued with the Jewish point of view in regard to the canon of the Old Testament, and was apparently unaware that the Hebrew *veritas,* as he called the Massoretic text, did not have a fence built around it until long after the Septuagint translation had been made. The Greek translation was used by Jews of the Diaspora for approximately three centuries before the Council of Jamnia. Massoretes certainly had a different attitude toward Sirach, Tobias and Baruch than Jews who lived in Alexandria in 130 B.C. We should not assume that the Hebrew Bible is always to be preferred to the Septuagint; some Messianic prophecies are clearer in the Septuagint. While we grant that Christological interpretations should not be interpolated into the original text, we are also aware that Messianic prophecies might have been clouded in a text used in controversies with Christians. To us it appears that some Catholic scholars, in translating the Old Testament from what they speak of as the original Hebrew, are inclined to forget that the Massoretic text is not an autograph. The Septuagint was held in high regard by the Fathers of the Christian Church, and as we have noted, represents an older text than the Massoretic.

The Hebrew text through St. Jerome's Vulgate has been the basic text of Catholic Bibles. Nevertheless, the Fathers of the Church received the Septuagint from the Apostles, and from it the first Latin, Armenian, Ethiopic, Coptic, Georgian and Slavic translations were made. One fault of the Hebrew text is that it lacks seven books preserved in the Septuagint. Protestants adopted the Hebrew canon; thus their Bibles also lack these seven books. The history of the texts should be kept in mind.

We have no wish to weaken respect for the Hebrew text, or to encourage Catholics to criticize the Massoretic text or any good text of the Bible. On the contrary, we wish to correct the misapprehension that Catholics, Protestants, and Jews have entirely different Bibles. An admirable erudition has grown up around the Bible. Massoretes, Christian Fathers like Origen and Jerome, great Protestant scholars like Tischendorf, Westcott, Hort and Nestle, have devoted their lives to the study of the Bible. The Bible belongs to the whole human family. In no other field have Jews, Protestants and Catholics worked together with such honesty, intelligence, and energy. The history of textual criticism of the Bible from the Massoretes and Origen down through St. Jerome, Cervini, Sirleto, Hentense, Carafa, Tischendorf, Westcott, Hort, Nestle and Merk is a story of great intellectual achievement. The text of the Bible has been safeguarded and critically edited by the best scholars in the world. We thank God we are in possession of texts of both Old and New Testaments which competent scholars assure us are in substantial agreement with the autographs. A book copied so often, read so much in public assemblies, and annotated in margins by so many readers when clear distinction between printed page and marginal gloss was difficult, could not help but have variant readings. The wonder is that the text has been preserved so well.

The Septuagint

Through this translation of the Old Testament, made in Egypt by Jews before the time of Christ, knowledge of the Hebrew Scriptures was diffused among most of the peoples that first embraced Christianity. The Septuagint was used in Palestine by Greek-speaking Jews before Christ and was quoted by two of their eminent scholars, Philo and Josephus. At the time of Philo, a contemporary of Christ, this translation was honored by Jews with a feast; a century later the feast was turned into a day of mourning.

No fence (Massora) was built around the Septuagint. It was freely copied and widely used with the result that many variant readings crept into it. But in basic thought and substantial content, it remained in agreement with the Hebrew. Scholars say it was not all translated at the same time. The Torah, that is, the Pentateuch, was done first, and all authorities agree that in it a text older than the Massora was faithfully and accurately rendered. The same is said of the early prophets (historical books). The later prophets, they tell us, were not done so well. Basically and substantially, however, the prophets are intelligibly translated. The Septuagint is the best witness for an older and in some respects a better text than the one preserved in Hebrew manuscripts. When it was made, no disputes had arisen concerning Messianic passages.

Greek manuscripts are divided into papyri, uncials and

minuscules. Papyri are the oldest but consist of fragments. Uncials are manuscripts written in capitals, that is, in large, somewhat rounded letters, each one being separate as in printing. Uncials were used until the ninth century. Minuscules are cursive, that is, one letter is joined to another, making handwriting easier and swifter. This form of writing was used until the invention of printing. Minuscules are not so valuable as uncials, considered as textual witnesses. Among uncials three great parchment codices are famous: A, B, and S. A stands for *Alexandrinus,* dating from the fourth or fifth century, preserved in the British Museum. B stands for *Vaticanus,* in the Vatican Library; it comes down from the fourth century and contains nearly the whole of the Old and New Testaments. It may be one of fifty copies ordered by Constantine. *Sinaiticus* was named because it was discovered in the monastery of St. Catherine on Mount Sinai by the great Protestant scholar, Tischendorf, between 1844 and 1859. It is of the same material, form and age as *Vaticanus* and contains some passages absent from the latter. These are the most precious manuscripts in the world. They contain the text of the Septuagint used in the early Christian Church; and they contain also the New Testament. These manuscripts are supplemented by others almost as old, as well as by many quotations contained in writings of early Christian Fathers.

The Hexapla

Origen (185-254) used the Septuagint as his textbook. In arguing with Jews, he felt the need of verifying it, and with this in view he undertook a comparison of his Greek Bible with the Hebrew Bible and with other Greek translations. He wrote six texts in parallel columns on each page. First was the Hebrew text; second, the same text in Greek letters; third, Aquila; fourth, Symmachus; fifth, the Septuagint; and sixth, Theodotion. He had it in mind to note passages missing from the Hebrew and present in the Septuagint, passages missing from the Septuagint and present in the Hebrew, and differences occurring in words and phrases. Origen's Bible was called the Hexapla because of its six-columned pages. The Hexapla, being a very large book with thousands of pages, was not easily copied, but scholars could consult it in the library at Caesarea in Palestine until the Saracens conquered the country in the seventh century, and it disappeared.

The Hexapla was examined by St. Jerome in the fourth century and by Lucian, a priest of Antioch, who undertook earlier than Jerome to bring the text of the Septuagint closer to the Hebrew. Lucian's revision was adopted at Antioch, where St. John Chrysostom and other bishops of Constantinople used it. Although the Hexapla no longer exists, except for fragments, the fifth column of Origen's work was copied separately and had an influence on many manuscripts.

Old Latin Translations

Greek was the liturgical language in Rome until the third century. St. Paul wrote his Epistle to the Romans in Greek. St. Mark's Gospel, a summary of St. Peter's sermons to the Romans, was written in Greek. The first ecclesiastical writers of Latin were Africans: Tertullian (150-220 A.D.) and St. Cyprian (died 258 A.D.). Both were natives of Carthage, a district of Africa which had received its culture through the medium of Latin. Scholars tell us the first translations of the Bible into Latin were made in Africa and in Gaul. Both the African and the European translations are referred to as the Old Latin. Whether they were independent translations or whether the African was made first and the European was a revision of it is disputed. At the time of St. Cyprian the whole Bible certainly existed in Latin. Some manuscripts belong to the second half of the second century. They represent the Septuagint before its revision by Origen. The Old Latin is faithful to the Greek and is of value in enabling scholars to determine the text of the Septuagint read in the early churches. Since St. Jerome translated only two deuterocanonical books, Tobias and Judith, the Old Latin text survived, in the Vulgate, for Baruch, Wisdom, Ecclesiasticus, and First and Second Machabees.

The Vulgate

Eusebius Hieronymus (Jerome) was born in Dalmatia about 340 A.D. His father, ambitious to give his son a good education, sent him to Rome to study under the best grammarians and rhetoricians of that brilliant period. Jerome was so deeply impressed by Christianity that he determined to live as an ascetic in a desert near Antioch. But his love of learning moved him to attend lectures on theology by Apollinaris, and some years later to go to Constantinople to listen to St. Gregory Nazianzen. Jerome was an austere man who had prodigious energy, an insatiable thirst for knowledge, and a genius for languages. In 382 A.D. he attended a council in Rome where he met Pope Damasus. The Pope was so impressed by his knowledge of the Bible and his linguistic ability that he invited him to revise the text of the Psalms and the Gospels—books into which many variations had crept because they were so frequently copied. In the course of Jerome's life, he made three translations of the Psalms. For Pope Damasus, he revised the Old Latin from the Septuagint.

After the death of Damasus, Jerome retired to Palestine, took up residence at Bethlehem, and revised the psalter again according to the Septuagint as corrected by Origen. This has been called the Gallican psalter because it was much used in Gaul; it is the translation to be found in the Clementine Bible and, until recently, has been the psalter read in Catholic Bibles. During his residence in Palestine, Jerome learned Hebrew under Jewish masters; and after twelve years in Bethlehem he made a third translation of Psalms from the Hebrew. This is the psalter of Protestant Bibles.

St. Jerome began his translation of the Old Testament by revising Job, Proverbs, and several other books according to the Hexapla, Origen's text of the Septuagint, which was then available at Caesarea; but he did not continue this practice. Job is the only one of these translations that has come down to posterity. Although Jerome continued to consult and respect the Septuagint, he conceived great admiration for the Hebrew language and the Massoretic text. In his time Greek translations from the Hebrew made by Jews, Aquila, Theodotion, and Symmachus, were also extant.

Before his death in 420 A.D., Jerome translated from the Hebrew, in addition to the Psalms, all the protocanonical books of the Old Testament. He knew Hebrew well and was also a master of Latin. At once philologist, theologian and rhetorician, he understood the importance of rendering the meaning of the original text accurately, but not servilely.

The value of Jerome's translation is universally recognized. To him belongs the distinction of furnishing the Western Church with its commonly used translation, declared official for Catholics by the Council of Trent.

Jerome's translation was not received without criticism. Until his time the Septuagint had been the text of Christians; it was used by the Apostles and was considered inspired. Jerome minimized its authority. Even St. Augustine was not pleased. He thought a translation based on the Septuagint would have been better. In the course of time, however, the value of St. Jerome's translation became apparent to St. Augustine as it did to others.

History of the Vulgate

For several centuries St. Jerome's translation was used only as a supplement to the Old Latin. In the sixth century, Gregory the Great recognized it as of authority equal to the Old Latin. Cassiodorus promoted its diffusion in the sixth century, both in Italy and in Gaul. Cassiodorus deserves credit for the famous *Codex Amiatinus,* highly prized among manuscripts indicating the original text of the Vulgate. At the end of the eighth century Charlemagne made Jerome's translation authoritative in his domain. He commissioned Alcuin to edit a new edition from which were to be excluded passages from the Old Latin Bible resulting from the simultaneous use of both texts. Theodulf, Bishop of Orleans, also undertook, on his own authority, to restore the pure text of St. Jerome. The efforts of Cassiodorus, Alcuin, and Theodulf resulted in three families of manuscripts much copied before the Bible was first printed by Gutenberg about 1450 A.D.

The text of the first printed Bible was that adopted by

the University of Paris. It had been divided into chapters by Stephen Langdon, Archbishop of Canterbury. About one hundred and twenty editions of the Bible were printed between 1450 and 1520. The Paris Bible appears to have been based on Alcuin's text. In 1517 Cardinal Ximenes published the first polyglot Bible at the University of Alcala, in Spain. Robert Estienne printed nine editions of the Bible between 1528 and 1557. Estienne sought a text in conformity with the Hebrew for the Old Testament and the Greek for the New, thus departing from the custom of trying for the pure text of St. Jerome. Estienne's Bibles exercised much influence on Protestants.

So many editions of the Bible were printed by the Reformers, each of them manifesting words and passages colored to support unorthodox interpretations, that the Council of Trent judged it advisable to declare itself in favor of a standard text. On April 8, 1546, the following decree was issued:

> The same Sacred and Holy Synod, considering that it would be of no small advantage to the Church of God if it were clearly made known which of all the Latin editions of the Sacred Books in circulation is to be held authentic, hereby declares and enacts that the same well known Old Latin Vulgate edition, which has been approved by the long use of many centuries in the Church, is to be held as authentic in public readings, disputations, preaching and expositions and that no one shall dare or presume to reject it under any pretext whatsoever.

This was a decree designed to meet an existing situation. It was not intended to declare the Vulgate to be the perfect critical edition of the Bible, but to state that it conforms substantially to the original texts and is free from errors in faith and morals. The Council recommended that the Vulgate be printed as accurately as possible, and that the Pope himself undertake the task of collating or comparing the oldest and best manuscripts. The Benedictines of Monte Cassino had already done some of this work. Pius IV appointed one commission, and after his death, Pius V appointed another. Two great Biblical scholars, Cardinals Sirleto and Carafa, headed these commissions. The work progressed slowly because of differences in point of view.

Under Gregory XIII, Cardinal Perretti concentrated on an edition of the Old Testament in harmony with the Septuagint. Cardinal Perretti became Pope Sixtus V in 1585. He appointed Cardinal Carafa head of a new commission composed of the best scholars in Europe, including William Allen, who was responsible for the English Catholic Bible. These scholars had at their disposal many good manuscripts, some already collated by the Benedictines and Cardinal Sirleto. In 1589 they sent a copy of the corrections they proposed to Sixtus V. The Pope thought they were making too many changes. With the help of Francisco Toledo, a Jesuit, and Angelo Rocca, an Augustinian, Sixtus V published an edition of the Bible; but he died a few weeks later (in 1590) and the Cardinals stopped its sale. His successor, Gregory XIV, asked the commission to reconsider the recommendations of the Carafa Commission. Gregory reigned only a year and his successor, Innocent IX, only a few weeks; so the new edition of the Vulgate did not see the light until the pontificate of Clement VIII. At first it was called the Sixtine Bible, later Sixtine-Clementine, and now more commonly Clementine. It was adopted as the standard edition of the Catholic Church; no variants were printed in the margins.

On November 17, 1921, the Biblical Commission granted permission to publish editions of the Vulgate with critical apparatus: that is, with variant readings at the foot of each page. Pius XII, in his encyclical *Divino afflante Spiritu,* went further: "It is not forbidden by the decree of Trent to make translations into the vulgar tongue, even directly from the original texts themselves, for the use and benefit of the faithful." Pius XII confirmed what Catholic scholars always maintained: that the Council of Trent had no intention of setting the Vulgate text above the original Hebrew and Greek texts. Pius XII says: "The Vulgate's authenticity is not specified primarily as critical but as juridical." The Council of Trent did not mean to impugn the Septuagint, Massoretic text, or Greek manuscripts of the New Testament, for example, *Vaticanus,* B. The problem faced by the Council of Trent was a practical one—that of guaranteeing a Latin text as standard for public reading, argumentation and instruction. No one should overlook the fact that all autographs have perished. Critical scholars have to recover not only the pure text of the Latin Vulgate, but the pure text of the Septuagint and of the original Hebrew. The Massoretic text varies from the Septtuagint and from other older witnesses. At the same time, however, the Massoretic text, the Septuagint and the Vulgate are in substantial agreement with one another and with the autographs. This is evident to all scholars.

Two Anglicans, John Wordsworth and Henry White, made a noble effort to restore the pure text of the Vulgate. Their New Testament is highly respected by Catholic as well as non-Catholic scholars. In 1907 Pius X commissioned the Benedictines to undertake a thorough revision of the Vulgate, making use of the vast critical apparatus assembled during the nineteenth century. So far they have published Genesis, Exodus, Leviticus, Numbers, Deuteronomy, Josue,

Judges, Ruth, First and Second Samuel, First and Second Kings, and the sapiential books. The prophets and the New Testament remain to be completed.

English Translations

The Anglo-Saxon poet, Caedmon, translated or paraphrased parts of both Old and New Testaments about 670 A.D. Interlinear translations of Psalms were made in this early period. St. Bede (735 A.D.) is credited with having translated the whole Bible. The Psalter was frequently translated; King Alfred (900 A.D.) is said to have translated the psalms for his own use.

After the Norman Conquest, the New Testament, Psalms, and other parts of the Bible were done in a mixture of French and Anglo-Saxon. The activity of Wyclif (1384 A.D.) against organization and liturgy and in favor of Bible-reading and preaching made him so great a hero with Protestants that he received excessive credit for translating the Bible. Cardinal Gasquet, a Benedictine scholar of the early twentieth century, maintained that two versions of the Bible in English before the Reformation were not actually the work of Wyclif and his pupils, but of loyal Catholics. St. Thomas More wrote: "Myself have seen and can show bybles fayre and old written in Englyshe which have been knowen and seen by the bishop of the dyoces and left in laymen's hands, and women's too, such as he knew for good and catholike folks that used it with devotion and sobrenes."[8]

The controversy over Wyclif shows the danger lurking in the fact that any translation of the Bible may involve a certain amount of private interpretation. A translation made by a man like Wyclif can favor his erroneous opinions.

Wyclif, before Luther, opposed institutional Christianity and advocated the right of private interpretation. On the other hand, Catholic bishops recognized it to be their duty to interpret the Bible in conformity with Christian tradition. Wyclif, the "Morning Star of the Reformation," had much to do with arousing bitterness that has ever since prevailed between Protestants and Catholics over English translations of the Bible. He appealed to the Scriptures as having higher authority than the Church; and he taught that bishops, judged by the laity to be in mortal sin, are not entitled to obedience. He also held that transubstantiation is unscriptural and unphilosophical. These errors aroused fear in Catholics that his translation of the Bible might be dangerous.

William Tyndale (active between 1520-1536), was a partisan of Luther even before Henry VIII broke with the Church. He made a translation of the New Testament from Greek into English in 1525. England was slow with printing compared with Germany and the Netherlands where eighteen editions of the Bible in the vernacular had been printed before Luther's German Bible appeared. Tyndale's New Testament was set up in type at Cologne and Worms in Germany and was shipped secretly into England. In a preface, Tyndale made a vicious attack on the Catholic Church. Thomas More pointed out that his use of terms deliberately colored Greek words in favor of heresy. Besides the New Testament, Tyndale translated the Pentateuch (1530). Myles Coverdale, another Protestant, published a complete Bible in English, including Tyndale's New Testament and Pentateuch. This was printed in Switzerland in 1537.

Thomas Cromwell, successor to Wolsey, encouraged and

partly financed what was called the Great Bible (because of its size), bringing French printers to England with presses and type. Cromwell's Bible was based on Tyndale and Coverdale and became official in Anglican churches until the Bishops' Bible, edited by Matthew Parker, Archbishop of Canterbury, supplanted it in 1568. The Bishops' Bible, especially the New Testament, was more honest and scholarly, but too expensive for general use, each copy costing about $80. The most popular Protestant Bible of the period was the Geneva Bible made in Switzerland in 1560. It was Calvinist in inspiration, using Theodore Beza's Latin New Testament as its basic text. Convenient in size, moderate in price, it went through 140 editions before it yielded to the King James Bible. The Geneva Bible was also called the Puritan Bible because the preface and notes were Calvinistic.

King James (Authorized) Version

English translations, with preface and notes favoring one sect or another, caused strife among Protestants. When James I came to power in 1603, he desired a version of the Bible satisfactory to all Protestants. Calling a conference of scholars, he arranged for a new translation to be made by professors of Oxford and Cambridge, to be reviewed by the bishops and ratified by the privy council, with the king's approval.

Among rules laid down to guide the translators was this: no marginal notes were to be added to the text, except to explain the meaning of Hebrew or Greek words. The king desired that the Greek word for *Church* not be translated as *congregation;* that other terms not be colored or tendentious. The work was ready by 1611 and was a magnificent success. Its only rival was the Geneva Bible. Its "grave majestic English" has exercised a profound influence on the English language and is recognized universally as a classic of English style. Not all parts are equally well done, but this is always the case when many translators collaborate. The critical apparatus, especially for the New Testament, was not the best, and had to be revised in 1885 after the critical edition of Westcott and Hort had won acclaim. Although the King James Version was itself a revision of earlier English translations, it established itself as a model which has been imitated in subsequent English translations. In honesty as well as in literary excellence, it was a great improvement over previous Protestant translations. There is no solid basis for Catholics' fearing the King James Version. In it, terms are not deliberately colored in favor of heresy, as was the case in some of the earlier translations. Catholics in the United States should not try to keep the King James Bible out of public schools or hotels.

Catholic Bibles in English

An Oxford scholar named William Allen, who was driven out of England during the reign of Elizabeth, founded the English college of Douay, Flanders, in 1568. A number of Oxford scholars joined him and undertook to make an English translation of the Bible for Catholics, according to the Latin Vulgate. Gregory Martin, professor of Hebrew and Holy Scriptures at Oxford, translated both the Old and New Testaments. The others revised and annotated his work. For the New Testament, the notes were written by Dr. Worthington. The New Testament was published in 1582 at Rheims, where the scholars had moved temporarily because of political disturbances in Flanders. Due to lack of funds, the Old Testament could not be printed until 1609, when the scholars were back in Douay. The King James Bible was begun in 1604 and completed in 1611; the Rheims New Testament of 1582 was assiduously used by the makers of the King James Version. The Douay Old Testament, however, was published too late to have a like effect. Moulton says of the influence of the Rheims New Testament: "The Rheimish Testament was not even named in the instructions furnished to the translators, but it has left its mark on every page of their work."[9]

This scholarly achievement of Gregory Martin, William Allen, Richard Bristow and Dr. Worthington was recognized by Protestants. While it was not slavishly literal, it rendered faithfully the meaning of the Latin Vulgate, which Gregory Martin used as his basic text. For their New Testament, the King James translators depended on the *textus receptus* and Theodore Beza's text, but were influenced in the direction of the Vulgate by the Rheims translation. The Rheims New Testament was printed by Protestants a number of times in England and once in America (1834). It is regrettable that this translation is not available to Catholics in its original form.

Although all Catholic Bibles in English have been entitled "Douay-Rheims Version," the translation made by Martin with the notes of Allen, Worthington and Bristow was radically revised by Dr. Challoner in 1781. A Douay scholar and bishop of the London district (including the Catholic Church in the United States from 1758 to 1781), Challoner got rid of what he considered the excessive Latinity of Gregory Martin's style and adopted much of the phraseology and diction of the King James Version. Dr. Challoner further altered later editions. Challoner's Bible was itself revised in Ireland by Archbishop Troy and others and has been published in many editions in America (one hundred between 1790 and 1860). Challoner did well in phraseology and diction, but his notes were inferior to those of Allen, Bristow, and Worthington. Newman observed: "Challoner's version is even nearer to the Protestant than it is to the Douay, that is, in phraseology and diction."[10] Dr. Lingard, the English Catholic historian, made a translation of the four Gospels from the Greek in 1836. Archbishop Kenrick of Baltimore revised the whole Bible between 1849 and 1860. Father Spencer, a Dominican convert from Protestantism, translated the four Gospels from the Greek; his work was reprinted in 1940 by Macmillan. In England, between 1914 and 1935, the Westminster Version of the New Testament appeared, with abundant notes, under the general editorship of Father Cuthbert Lattey, S.J. Work on the Old Testament was interrupted by the second World War.

In the United States under the direction of the Episcopal Committee on Christian Doctrine, headed by Bishop O'Hara of Kansas City, a revision of the Challoner-Rheims Version, based on a critical edition of the Vulgate, was published in 1941. The Confraternity is now sponsoring a translation of the Old Testament based on Hebrew and Greek texts. So far the books from Genesis to Ruth, from Job to Sirach, and from Isaias to Malachias have appeared. In translating these books, the American scholars took advantage of Pius XII's permission given in 1943 (in *Divino afflante*) to translate directly from the Hebrew and Greek without feeling bound to reproduce the Vulgate.

Protestants published the English Revised Version and

the American Revised Version of the Bible in 1880-1890.
A Revised Standard Version of the New Testament was
published in 1946; of the Old Testament a few years later.
American Jews, under the general editorship of Max Margolis, published in 1917 a Hebrew revision of the King
James Old Testament, in conformity with the Massoretic
text. A Catholic translation by Father Ronald Knox, based
on the Vulgate with the help of the Hebrew and Greek,
appeared around 1950.

The Jerusalem Bible was published in 1966, translated
from a French edition which had been produced under
direction of the Ecole Biblique. In making the English
translation, the scholars consulted the original-language
manuscripts.

Respect for Non-Catholic Bibles

From this discussion of texts of the Bible, it is evident
that there is substantial agreement among textual experts,
Hebrew, Catholic, and Protestant, concerning the original
text of the Bible. Especially is this true of the New Testament. Apart from the exclusion of deuterocanonical books
by Protestants and Jews, there is substantial agreement in
respect to the Old Testament also. Catholic scholars have
high regard for the American Jewish translation as well as
for the King James Bible and some of its later revisions.
It is out of order for Catholics to criticize the text of the
Protestant Bible; certainly it is better for Americans to
read the King James Bible or its revisions than to remain
ignorant of divine revelation. In Rome itself, theological
students used Nestle's New Testament in Greek and Latin,
which was based on the work of Westcott and Hort, until

Merk, a Jesuit, produced a Catholic critical edition of comparable value.

Catholics who are not serious students of Holy Scripture or theology are still obliged by Canon Law to use editions of the Bible which have ecclesiastical approval; which have notes taken from the Fathers or written by Catholic scholars. But this does not mean that Catholics should oppose the use of Bibles that do not have Catholic notes in such places as schools and hotels, into which Bibles with Catholic notes have no chance to enter. The Bible is the great source of supernatural religion for non-Catholic believers. Catholics must realize that the Bible does not belong exclusively to them. The more widely it is read the better for the cause of supernatural religion which is based on divine revelation.

NOTES FOR CHAPTER VII

1. See Steinmueller, *A Companion to Scripture Studies,* Volume I, pp. 153-159 for further information on early writing.

2. Robert and Tricot, *Guide to the Bible,* Vol. I, pp. 75-76.

3. Tisserant, in Robert and Tricot's *Guide to the Bible,* Vol. I, p. 365.

4. Everyone has heard of Qumran, at the northwest corner of the Dead Sea, where an Essene community lived around 100-68 B.C. At this site, in caves, were found the Dead Sea Scrolls.

5. Robert and Tricot, *Guide to the Bible,* Vol. I, p. 365.

6. Seisenberger, *Practical Handbook for the Study of the Bible,* p. 223.

7. *A Companion to Scripture Studies,* Vol. I, p. 170.

8. See Robert and Tricot, *Guide to the Bible,* Vol. I, p. 430-38 (articles by P. W. Skehan).

9. W. F. Moulton, cited by Steinmueller, *A Companion to Scripture Studies,* Vol. I, p. 245.

10. Tracts, 416.

"There has arisen to the great detriment of religion, an inept method dignified by the name of 'higher criticism' which pretends to judge the origin, integrity and authority of each book from internal indications alone. It is clear that in historical questions, such as the origin and handing down of writings, the witness of history is of primary importance, and that historical investigation should be made with the utmost care; and that in this manner internal evidence is seldom of great value, except as confirmation. To look upon it in any other light will be to open the door to many evil consequences. It will make the enemies of religion much more bold and confident in attacking and mangling the sacred books; and this vaunted 'higher criticism' will resolve itself into the reflection of the bias and the prejudice of the critics."

—Pope Leo XIII
Providentissimus Deus

CHAPTER VIII

Modern Attack on the Bible

The substitution of the mechanical conception of the universe for a world governed by the Providence of God, assisted by angels, ushered in Naturalism. Naturalism demands total emancipation of reason from authority—even from divine authority. It denies that there is any conscious life higher than human life. The God of Naturalism is intelligent only in and through human intelligence. He is an impersonal God —immanent in nature, and identical with it. To compensate for the loss of Divine Providence, Naturalists derive optimism from the notion of world progress. "Civilization has moved, is moving, and will inevitably move in a desirable direction" is their credo. Naturalists worship the Cosmos or Nature out of whose immanent activity all things evolve— including minds, ideas, and religions. The spirit of pride that led men to rebel against the authority of the Church leads them to rebel against the authority of a personal God. The inspired Bible of traditional Protestants was challenged by men who deified humanity, and who regarded human reason as the sole, final arbiter of all religious questions.

155

They would not admit the possibility of divine revelation or the supernatural origin of Jesus Christ. For the Naturalist, there are no mysteries. The Bible is a natural book, written by men less highly developed than are modern scholars and critics. It can be analyzed and adequately explained according to the laws of Nature.

Religious Background of Naturalism

The first Protestants accepted the Bible as a book inspired by the Holy Ghost wherein God educated mankind to understand his plans for their redemption and salvation. The early Reformers exaggerated rather than minimized the supernatural. They had a low opinion of human reason and of human nature unaided by grace. Luther did not intend to set human reason above Sacred Scripture; quite the contrary. Miracles, prophecies, and mysteries related in the Bible were devoutly revered. Luther did not suspect the danger of the inspired Bible which lurked in his principle of private judgment. For him, the Bible was a book come down from heaven which recorded God's supernatural dealings with men. Inspiration signified, for almost all early Protestants, immediate divine influence on the mind and will of a writer to enable him to say what God wanted said and to avoid mixing error with the divine message. These inspired writings, men were morally bound to receive with reverential awe. Devout Protestants saw the Bible as an unimpeachable source of objective truth which no human mind could discover without the help of revelation, and they clung passionately to the Bible as the sole source of their hope of salvation.

But a wide variety of opinions arose as to the meaning

of the Bible. The seventeenth century was marked by disputes, divisions, and wars, and has been called "the wretched century of strife." Out of the conflict, leaders of Rationalism deduced the necessity of putting reason above the authority of the Bible. They said men are not saved by faith; what a man believes does not matter if only he cultivates piety toward God and purity of morals. Quakers and Pictists manifested this tendency. The essence of Christianity was claimed to be moral elevation and inner liberation; intellectual assent to creeds was minimized. Socinians went beyond the Pietists and Quakers, and attempted to find universal Christianity in the basic truths of naural religion. Only what is rational in the Bible is true, they argued. Reason should examine the Bible and separate what is rational from what is myth or superstition. Socinians rejected the Trinity and the Incarnation as irrational. Religion has nothing to do, they said, with faith in incomprehensible dogmas.

Philosophical Background of Rationalism

In the sixteenth century, the spirit of Rationalism began to manifest itself. Giordano Bruno (1548-1600) declared: "The conception of nature and of necessary production takes the place of a creator and free creation."[1] By unfolding himself, the infinite being produces the cosmical laws; he is in all things and all things are in him, because he is identical with all things. The God of Bruno is neither Creator nor First Mover; he is the soul of the world.

Descartes (1596-1650) "clearly and accurately expressed the ideals of modern thought; the downfall of traditional authorities in matters of knowledge and the autonomy of reason."[2] Thomas Hobbes, a contemporary of Descartes, laid down the principle: we ought to determine the date of composition of the books of the Bible from internal evidence. Using this principle, he concluded that Moses was not the author of the Pentateuch.[3] Spinoza (1632-1677), a Jew, turned from the God of Abraham and fashioned himself a pantheistic God which is Nature. For Spinoza, there is one substance; everything else is a mode or attribute of this one underlying being. God is neither Creator nor Father of the world; he is the world itself. Nature is the source and the sum of all. Thus, for Spinoza, the Bible could not be a book inspired by God, since there is no supernatural intellect; between the mind of man and the mind of God there is no essential difference. The books of the Bible represent a natural evolution of cosmic thinking. Spinoza concluded, following Hobbes' principle, that the history of Israel was not written until the time of Esdras.[4]

English Deists substituted natural religion for Christianity. True Christianity, they said, is nothing more than philosophical religion; the Bible must be expurgated of everything supernatural—mysteries, miracles, and prophecies. Only a bungling God would need to be continually interfering with Nature by answering prayers and working miracles. The laws of Nature, they proclaimed, were absolute. Their crusade was carried on chiefly by laymen, hostile to clericalism. They rationalized the Bible only to the point of discarding supernatural phenomena; they assumed that except for miracles, the documents were historical.[5]

Leibnitz (1646-1716), a great genius and a reverent Christian, dominated intellectual life in Germany during the early part of the eighteenth century. Realizing the perils to which Europe was exposed through loss of the common patrimony of the Christian faith, he tried to reconcile Protestants with Catholics. Failing in this, he did what he could to unite warring factions of Lutherans. He hoped to distill out of the conflicting creeds a creed on which all upright men could agree. He rationalized Christianity, but with great respect, admitting inspiration, mysteries, and miracles. He conceived the relation between natural religion and revealed religion as follows: "Revelation is above reason, but in harmony with reason; it is a necessary supplement to natural knowledge. That is revealed which the reason can not discover, but can understand as in harmony with itself after the revelation has taken place."[6]

Wolff, a disciple of Leibnitz, held that natural religion can be demonstrated, but not supernatural religion; the latter must be accepted by faith. He came to grief in trying to determine the proper attitude of reason toward the Bible, because the Lutherans of Halle suspected him of placing reason above the Bible and expelled him from their university. One of Wolff's disciples, Wilhelm Semler (1725-1791), frankly devoted himself to historical criticism of the Bible.

Kant (1724-1804) was educated in Pietism and in the philosophy of Leibnitz and Wolff. He set out to defend religion as he, a Pietist, saw it. Kant criticized human reason itself, arguing that it is not competent to arrive at objective truth, either natural or supernatural. Only when approached as Pietists approach it can the study of God and religion lead to knowledge and inner freedom. For Kant, religion was ethical conduct conceived as obedience to divine commands. Except for morality, religion may be resolved into subjective experience. Religious experience of exceptional souls has great influence. Followers of Kant looked for guidance to great souls whose experiences lighted the way for their fellowmen.

Hegel (1770-1831) taught that the common substance of God, the cosmos and human minds does not transcend but is identical with change or evolution. Reality is not being but becoming. Mind and matter are but successive modes of one absolute being; the absolute is the process itself. God does not transcend human reason, but becomes knowable in the very process of human thinking. Evolution is the law of mind. There can be no such thing as divine revelation in the sense of unchangeable dogmas or incomprehensible mysteries. The idea of a personal God, distinct from the world and free to create it or not, was abandoned in favor of the concept of immanency.

Scientific Background of Rationalism

The dispute between Aristotelian philosophers and Galileo unsettled the minds of many with regard to the inspiration of the Bible. In the book of Josue they read: "Move not, O sun, toward Gabaon, nor thou, O moon, toward the valley of Ajalon. And the sun stood still till the people revenged themselves of their enemies. Is not this written in the book of the just? So the sun stood still in the midst of heaven, and hastened not to go down the space of one day. There was not before or after so long a day, the Lord obeying the voice of a man and fighting for Israel" (Josue 10:12). Kepler, a great astronomer and a Protestant, called attention to the fact that astronomers themselves say the sun rises and sets, because it appears to. He held that Josue described a phenomenon, i.e., what appeared to his senses, just as all men do when they say the sun rises and sets. But unfortunately, many Aristotelians and Ptolemaists did not have the perception of Kepler. They insisted the Bible is opposed to the doctrine that the earth moves around the sun. Hence enemies of the Bible were put in a position to assert that the Bible and science are in contradiction.

The science of geology also raised difficulties. The crust of the earth consists in part of sedimentary rocks containing numerous fossils. Chalk and coal, for example, are made out of the remains of many generations of plants and animals. The crust of the earth, some geologists said, required millions of years for its formation. Scholars acquainted with the exegesis of Origen and St. Augustine realized that the word day *(yom)* need not be taken literally; but defenders of the Bible who relied on private judgment were nonplussed. Did geology contradict the Bible?

There was still more trouble to come. Cuvier found bones of elephants, rhinoceroses and reindeer in the vicinity of Paris; drawings on walls of caves, and sculptures in horn and bone suggested that men were contemporaries of these extinct animals. The climate of northern Europe must have undergone great changes. How long ago? Guessing as to the duration of ice ages and the intervals between them became a sport for zoologists and anthropologists. It appeared that more time for the development of animal life on earth was demanded than the Bible, as popularly interpreted, seemed to provide. The theory of biological evolution began to sweep over Europe like wildfire.

Some scientists took fiendish delight in ridiculing the Bible. They began to preach mechanistic evolution as the new gospel. As Canon Sheehan describes it: "All sacred things of religion—names that had so often brought comfort to the sorrowful, and sacred hopes that so long had their consecrated shrines in the human heart, are made the subject of derision. The scoff of the unbeliever has degraded in the eyes of thousands the purest and holiest revelations of Heaven."[7] Relying on the prestige they enjoyed as prophets of science, these wicked men audaciously scoffed at supernatural religion. Science, they said, has discovered there is no Creator, no souls, no life after death, no angels, no devils, no divine revelation. Religion, they said, had its origin in fetishism and ancestor-worship; the Bible is a book of myths and legends produced by a pre-scientific age. Rudolf Eucken wrote in 1904:

> There is probably more antipathy against religion today and a more widespread and popular denial of it than has ever been the case before. One regards it as an obstacle in the way of a clear understanding of life, another as a restriction of active force, a third as suppression of joyous vital feelings; in each case it appears to be a ruinous delusion demanding every effort for its removal.[8]

Sketch of Higher Criticism

Rationalism held that the Scriptures themselves, when correctly interpreted, corroborate Naturalism. Assuming the impossibility of the supernatural, Rationalism proposed to synthesize the Bible with modern philosophy and to rewrite the history of Israel. Schleiermacher (1768-1834), educated in the philosophy of Kant, placed the essence of religion neither in faith in dogmas nor in obedience to divine commands, but in a subjective feeling of absolute dependence. Religion, he held, cannot be classified as objective truth because one person finds contemplation of nature, another finds reading the Bible, and another interest in art the best means of arousing the feeling of dependence. As a matter of fact, most persons, according to Schleiermacher, become religious through contact with great personalities who have had extraordinary religious experiences. Evolution is the law of all religion; the Bible cannot possibly be its last word. The old-fashioned idea of revelation, proposing for men's beliefs objective, changeless truths, must yield to the new notion of revelation through inner experience. It is unreasonable to suppose the Apostles surpassed all other men in the depth and sublimity of their religious experiences.

The principle of determining the date of composition of the books of the Bible by internal evidence bore fruit luxuriantly in the nineteenth century. In 1753 Jean d'Astruc, a French physician, published several articles in which he attempted to show that the use of two names for God, Elohim and Yahweh, indicate that Moses used two documents in composing the first chapters of Genesis. Somewhat later, Doderlein, a German theologian, held that Isaias 40-66 was not written by the same author as Isaias 1-39. Soon afterwards, Alexander Geddes (1737-1802), a Scotsman, suggested that the book of Genesis is a compilation of many fragments.

These eighteenth century theories gave rise to a more highly developed *documentary theory* in the nineteenth century. Johannes Eichhorn (1752-1827) wrote an *Introduction to the Old Testament* in which he gathered the results of earlier criticism of the Bible according to the principle of internal evidence, and, as his personal contribution, argued in favor of a later date for Daniel, Ecclesiastes, and Esther. He favored the theory of documents proposed by Astruc for the composition of Genesis. So successful was his *Introduction* that it set the fashion for a parade of Old Testament introductions which criticized various books in accordance with the criterion of internal evidence. Philological study of Semitic languages, and research into history and archaeology of Bible lands, were invoked in support of late dates of composition, and proved effective in silencing protests from defenders of Hebrew and Christian tradition.

Karl Ilgen (1763-1834) succeeded Eichhorn at Jena. He sensed the presence of a second Elohist in Genesis, which meant there must be three documents: the Yahwist, the First Elohist and the Second Elohist. DeWette (1780-1843) invented the theory of *pious fraud,* according to which Helcias, the high priest, wrote the book of Deuteronomy and pretended to the young king Josias that he had discovered it in the wall of the temple. Josias was so moved when he heard the book read that he instituted a great religious reform. According to DeWette, Helcias wrote the book of Deuteronomy about 623 B.C.

Heinrich Ewald (1803-1875), who had defended the Mosaic authorship of the Pentateuch, was converted to the documentary theory and applied it to the five books of Moses. He thought he had discovered four documents: the First Elohist, the Yahwist, their Organizer, and the Deuteronomist. In 1853, a hundred years after the publication of Astruc's documentary theory, Hupfeld published a book on the *Sources of Genesis,* in which he defended the theory of four documents so convincingly that a number of outstanding scholars—such as Franz Delitzsch and August Dillman—were won over to it. Hupfeld classified the documents as the First Elohist (P), the Yahwist (J), the Second Elohist (E), and the Deuteronomist (D). Even this did not satisfy radical evolutionists. According to the law of evolution, P should come last. Laws regulating sacrifices and priestly duties, as found in Leviticus, represent the highest development of Hebrew religion: therefore, Leviticus must have been written last. Reuss, Graf, Kosters and Kayser argued this point so well that the documents were arranged into what has proved to be a more or less final form: J, E, D and P. Thus the documentary theory overcame fragmentary and interpolation theories. In 1870 Abraham Kuenen, a Dutch scholar and a leader among conservative Protestants, announced his acceptance of the late date for the Priestly Code (P). His capitulation weakened the conservative Protestant front against Higher Criticism.

Wellhausen

In 1876 Julius Wellhausen (1844-1918) published a series of articles on the *Composition of the Hexateuch* (by this time the Critics were talking about the Hexateuch instead of the Pentateuch, because they had found that their documentary theory could be applied to the book of Josue, as well as to the five books of Moses). A few years later he published his *History of Israel,* and in 1883 his *Introduction to the History of Israel.* He then resigned his chair of theology at the Lutheran University of Greifswold "freely and in the conviction that he could no longer adhere to the Evangelical church or even to Protestantism."[9]

Of Wellhausen's influence, Professor Coppens writes:

> The critical program of Wellhausen aroused vehement protests from conservative exegetes.... Nevertheless Wellhausen carried the day in German university circles. The brilliance of his writings—their engaging and convincing tone, fine exposition of the problems, clever and orderly presentation of arguments—

assured that. . . . It may be added that Wellhausen very skillfully and successfully set up his critico-literary conclusions in the framework of a new history of the Jewish religion, and indeed insinuated them into a comprehensive history of religion in the ancient East. It is well known . . . that he used the popular traditions of pre-Islamic Arabia as a guide in his interpretation.

From 1878 onward, Wellhausen's critical principles steadily conquered one country after another.[10]

Wellhausen was an accomplished synthesizer, and welded the theories of his predecessors into attractive philosophical form. His critical system was accepted in England, Holland, and the United States as the classical expression of scientific criticism of the Bible.

Even some old-fashioned Protestant theologians and professors of Scriptural exegesis were carried off their feet by the erudition of Wellhausen and other German Rationalists. Higher Criticism made use of the *argumentum ad verecundiam,* i.e., opponents were put to shame because they did not know the Oriental languages and had not studied the archaeology of Egypt, Babylon, and other countries of the ancient world. The Wellhausen theories found a place in almost all non-Catholic introductions to the Old Testament. Protestant writers began to talk about the Hexateuch, and to assume that it was compiled from J, E, D and P. While they refused to "lop Christology off of religion," most Protestant professors of Bible-science taught the new literary criticism as affecting the Hexateuch, Isaias, the Psalms and many other books.

In his book *Rebuilding a Lost Faith,* John L. Stoddard gives a picture of the demoralizing influence Higher Criticism of the Bible had upon the seminary in which he was studying for the ministry. Obscure American teachers needed great courage to hold out against the showy erudition of German scholars. The following quotation from a leading Protestant in 1934 shows how the Wellhausen theory became entrenched in England:

> The triumph of the theory of Wellhausen may be said to have been gained in England with the publication of Sanday's Bampton lectures on *Inspiration,* delivered in Oxford in 1892, following Driver's *Introduction to the Literature of the Old Testament* (first edition 1891). Since then there has been no serious opposition in quarters where opposition was likely to count for much; and all subsequent Old Testament study, far from shaking the theory, has found that it could only proceed by making the Wellhausen view its starting point and presupposition. . . . Indeed, the Wellhausen position may well be called orthodox. . . . Outside the Wellhausen proposition, any view of the history (to say nothing of the evolution) of Old Testament literature is so uncertain that no conception of the evolution of religion can be founded on it.[11]

Evolution was the fashionable system of thought at the end of the nineteenth century. Anyone attempting to explain the Bible was expected to rely upon the philosophy of evolution, which did not tolerate the idea of a Creator or the possibility of supernatural events.

Fundamental Principle of Higher Criticism

"Underlying all these exegetical schools," notes Robert and Tricot, "is an undemonstrated and undemonstrable postulate, but admitted as a principle that is not even discussed, namely, the non-existence of the supernatural."[12] Catholic professors of Holy Scripture, like conservative Protestants, were slow to realize that German Higher Criticism, in spite of its gorgeous show of erudition and its profession of scientific method, was fundamentally a deduction from a philosophy utterly inconsistent with the existence of a supernatural, personal God. The only God recognized by the Higher Critics was Nature: an immanent, unknowable force moving endlessly from chaos to cosmos and from cosmos to chaos, according to necessary laws.

Nature is not a God that can work miracles, answer prayers, send inspired prophets or elevate men to a higher order of knowledge and love. Since there is no supernatural God there can be no supernatural religion. Old and New Testaments can be no more than records of progressive religious experiences. Consequently, the Jewish and Christian tradition that the law of Moses was given at Mount Sinai by a personal God, and that monotheism was fully developed at the very beginning of human history, must be classed as myth or legend. Higher Criticism is founded on Naturalism, and Naturalism is inconsistent with the historical origin of supernatural religion as it is related in the Bible.

Hebrew and Christian tradition always considered the books of Moses the oldest part of the Bible. For the first eleven chapters of Genesis, Moses may have inherited oral and written traditions brought by Abraham from Ur. Of what is related in the other four books, Moses was an eyewitness and was, moreover, ordered by God to write as he did. Marginal glosses may have crept in, and revisions may have been made from time to time to adapt the books to changes of language.[13] Nevertheless, the whole Torah was inspired by God and protected by his special providence from errors at variance with divine truth. The theocracy founded by Moses is the rule of God and is inconceivable without divine revelation, divine guidance, and inspired prophets.

Rationalist critics claim the Law as a whole was not

promulgated until the time of Esdras (450 B.C.), after the Babylonian Exile. They admit some ancient documents, J and E, used by later redactors. According to these critics, at the time of Moses, Yahweh was only a tribal god and the Hebrews only a nomadic people of inferior culture. They learned much from the highly cultured Chanaanites. Hebrew prophets of the ninth and eighth centuries were the real founders of monotheism; they are the geniuses to whom credit is due for what is intellectually superior in the culture of Israel. The prophets, these critics say, are the oldest authentic books of the Bible. Isaias, greatest of the prophetical books, was not written by one man; Deutero-Isaias wrote chapters 40 to 66, after the Exile. (Some more ambitious critics have now discovered a "Trito-Isaias"). The historical King David wrote few psalms. A daring literary fraud by Helcias, the high priest, in 623 B.C., succeeded in making the young King Josias and the ignorant people believe that Moses received the Law from Yahweh at Mount Sinai. It evolved gradually, reaching its final form with the publication of Leviticus (P) after the Exile.

The Higher Critics expurgate from the Bible all supernatural events. They recognize an objective core of facts, but eliminate what they consider to be subjective elements: that is, the judgment of the ancient writers that these events had a supernatural cause. Where they concede that the facts are true, they declare the interpretation to be false. All these critics are advocates of an evolutionist philosophy. They are determined by *a priori* judgments to discover that Hebrew religion developed along naturalistic lines, parallel to the religious development of Babylonia, Egypt, and Persia.

Consequences

The results of this criticism of the Old Testament are summed up by Seisenberger, one of the first to reply to the critics, in an introduction to the Bible written from the Catholic point of view. This book appeared in 1909, and was soon afterward translated into English.

> If these theories are correct, then we must conclude:
>
> 1. That the Israelite priests who (IV Kings xxii.8 etc.) in 623 B.C. under King Josias ... are said to have compiled the Law of Moses, ... and especially Helcias, the high-priest, who "found" it in the temple and pointed it out to the king as the work of Moses, were all liars and forgers. Josias, the king, and the whole nation would in that case have been deceived by a very clumsy forgery, quite easy of detection;
>
> 2. That Esdras and Nehemias, who, after the Captivity, strove to revive the national spirit on the ground of the Mosaic Law "which the Lord God had given to Israel" were likewise liars and forgers ..., and the Israelites of that time were deceived, as a recently composed work was read to them and expounded as the Law of Moses, and they were credulous enough to accept it without question;
>
> 3. That the whole of Judaism and Christianity based upon it are the outcome of repeated acts of deception and not of divine revelation;
>
> 4. That Jesus Christ Himself, who speaks of Abraham as the founder of the race, of Moses as a writer, and of David as a Psalmist was Himself ignorant, and therefore could not be God.[14]

The Wellhausen school, *per se,* has now been almost entirely discredited by later critics.[15] "Form criticism," however, which is heir to its general principles, holds a prominent position in critical circles, and produces much the same results as the earlier and more openly radical "source criticism."

NOTES FOR CHAPTER VIII

1. Alfred Weber and Ralph Barton Perry, *History of Philosophy* (New York: Scribner's, 1925), p. 230.

2. *Ibid.*, p. 254.

3. *Leviathan III*, 33.

4. *The Theologico-Political Treatise.*

5. Robertson, *A History of Free-Thought* (New York: G. P. Putnam's Sons, 1930), Vol. I, p. 133.

6. Wilhelm Windleband, *A History of Philosophy* (New York: Harper & Row, 1958), p. 487.

7. Canon Patrick Sheehan, *Early Essays and Lectures* (New York: Longmans, Green & Company, 1906), p. 57.

8. Rudolf Eucken, *Main Currents of Modern Thought* (London: T. F. Unwin, 1912), p. 466.

9. J. Coppens, *The Old Testament and the Critics* (Paterson, N. J.: St. Anthony Guild Press, 1942), pp. 18-19. This book gives a good account of Higher Criticism of the Bible.

10. *Ibid.*, p. 19.

11. W. F. Lofthouse, "The Evolution of Religion in the Old Testament," *The Modern Churchman*, Vol. XXVI (1934), quoted by J. Coppens, *The Old Testament and the Critics*, p. 49.

12. Robert and Tricot, *Guide to the Bible*, Vol. I, pp. 478-79.

13. This is further spelled out in the Biblical Commission's letter to Cardinal Suhard, 1948.

14. Seisenberger, *Practical Handbook for the Study of the Bible*, pp. 41-42.

15. See *The Jerusalem Bible*, p. 7.

"The progressive exploration of the antiquities of the East, . . . the more accurate examination of the original text itself, the more extensive and exact knowledge of languages both biblical and oriental, have with the help of God, happily provided the solution of not a few of those questions which . . . were raised by critics outside or hostile to the Church against the authenticity, antiquity, integrity and historical value of the Sacred Books. . . .

"Thus has it come about that confidence in the authority and historical value of the Bible, somewhat shaken in the case of some by so many attacks, today among Catholics is completely restored; moreover there are not wanting even non-Catholic writers who by serious and calm inquiry have been led to abandon modern opinion and to return, at least in some points, to the more ancient ideas."

—Pope Pius XII
Divino afflante Spiritu

CHAPTER IX

Reaction to the Higher Criticism

Higher Critics armed themselves with knowledge of Hebrew and other Semitic languages, as well as with Greek and Latin. They familiarized themselves with the findings of excavations in Babylon, Egypt, and other Biblical lands; they developed a vast apparatus of literary criticism; they were supported by an army of biologists, geologists, anthropologists and pre-historians who were evolutionists and anti-creationists. Obviously, defense against such a host called for a disciplined army. Pope Leo XIII, in his encyclical *Providentissimus Deus* (November 18, 1893), said: "Nothing is more necessary than that Truth should find defenders more powerful and more numerous than the enemies it has to face." Only experts in Oriental languages could combat experts in Oriental languages. Scientists who were atheists must be opposed by scientists loyal to God and to the supernatural order. An organized army of attackers must be met by an organized army of defenders.

Even before the encyclical *Providentissimus Deus,* the French Dominicans, appraising the danger, founded the

173

Ecole Biblique in Jerusalem in 1890. In 1902 Leo XIII established the Pontifical Biblical Commission, composed of Cardinals and learned consultors. Pius X, in 1909, set up the Biblical Institute in Rome, directed by the Jesuits, for advanced study of the Bible. All popes after Leo XIII have endeavored to carry out his program of providing a copious supply of scholars thoroughly prepared to deal with problems arising from scientific, literary, and historical criticism of the Bible.

Leo XIII quotes St. John Chrysostom as one well aware of the need of competent scholars to defend the Bible:

> We must use every endeavor that the "Word of God may dwell in us abundantly." Not merely for one kind of fight must we be prepared—for the contest is many sided and the enemy is of every sort; and they do not all use the same weapons nor make their onset in the same way. Wherefore it is needful that the man who has to contend against all should be acquainted with the engines and arts of all—that he should be at once archer and slinger, commander and subordinate, general and private soldier, skilled in sea-fight and siege; for unless he knows every trick and turn of war, and the devil is well able, if only a single door be left open, to get in his fierce bands and carry off the sheep.[1]

Conservative Protestants

Good defensive work was done by Protestants, especially in the field of textual or "lower" criticism. With incredible labor, Tischendorf, Tregelles, Westcott, Hort, Nestle, and many others demonstrated that we are in possession of the text of the Bible substantially as it was written. The hundreds of thousands of variants in manuscripts of the Bible with which Higher Critics frightened timid professors in theological seminaries were shown to be inconsequential from the point of view of the substantial text of the Bible.

Many Protestants loved Jesus Christ and revered the Bible as a book inspired by the Holy Ghost, free from errors. They defended supernatural revelation with courage and learning. But Protestant ministers and seminary professors were often weak in systematic theology and defenseless against nominalism and agnosticism. They labored under the handicap of free thought and evolutionism into which private interpretation had degenerated. Consequently they found themselves hard put to defend the inerrancy of the Bible against critics who invoked their right of free thought and interpretation to insist that there is no absolute truth in the Bible—or indeed anywhere.

Amateurs and tyros rushed to the defense of the Bible; but they were no match for the erudite professionals they encountered. Personal insight and religious experience did not furnish the erudition necessary to meet scientific, historical and literary criticism. The flashy brilliance of the Wellhausen school overawed unorganized ministers and seminary professors. Disturbance and confusion resulted. The Bible, the fortress of Protestantism, was under fire. In 1892 Charles Briggs, professor of exegesis at the Union Theological Seminary in New York, was excommunicated by the Presbyterian Church for Liberalism (i.e., Wellhausenism). The Presbyterians in the United States split into Liberal and Fundamentalist factions. The latter demanded that preachers stand on a platform of principles in defense of the supernatural inspiration and inerrancy of the Bible. The Anglican Church divided into three parties: High, Low, and Broad. The High Church declared for the faith of the early Christians, thus drawing nearer to tradition and the position of the Catholic Church. The Low Church entrenched itself behind Luther and Calvin. The Broad Church was agnostic and rationalistic.

Among Lutherans, many leaders in Germany, the Scandinavian countries and the United States ignored the Higher Critics and continued to treat the Bible as the inspired word of God, free from all errors. Chicago University, founded by the Baptists, under the presidency of William Rainey Harper, undertook to organize an elaborate school of Oriental languages and archaeology, sponsoring exploring expeditions to Bible countries. Many Protestants who surrendered the Old Testament to Rationalistic criticism continued to defend the Gospels and the Epistles of St. Paul as inspired books. They denied all other miracles, yet continued to confess the miracles of Christ.

The greatest trouble was that many Protestant leaders did not clearly grasp the essence of Christianity; they did not distinguish between the natural order and the supernatural order. Under pressure from those who had espoused the fashionable doctrine of evolution, they ceased to preach original sin and redemption through Christ to grace and supernatural life; they compromised by preaching Christ the social reformer, the friend of mankind, the herald of democracy. Not too sure that man had not evolved from a monkey, they concentrated on the moral doctrine of Christ, his peerless example, and his doctrine of brotherly love.

Catholic Reaction

Providentissimus Deus was a clarion call to Catholic scholars, clerical and lay, to recognize the seriousness of the attack on the Bible and the need of organized effort

to defend it. Leo XIII directed attention to the insolence
of critics who, in spite of impious utterances against God
and supernatural religion, pretended to be Christians, theologians, and men of the Gospel. He noted that scientists
were in many cases cooperating with Higher Critics. He
scored the unfairness of skepticism toward the venerable
documents of Hebrew tradition and slavish credulity toward every scrap of recently unearthed information from
Egypt, Babylon and Persia. Obviously the campaign was
directed against the very existence of supernatural religion.
Leo XIII declared:

> They deny there is any such thing as revelation or inspiration
> or Holy Scripture at all; they see, instead, only the forgeries and
> falsehoods of men; they set down the Scripture narratives as
> stupid fables and lying stories: the prophecies and oracles of
> God are to them either predictions made up after the event or
> forecasts formed by the light of nature; the miracles and won-
> ders of God's power are not what they are said to be, but the
> startling effects of natural law, or else mere tricks and myths; and
> the apostolic Gospels and writings are not the work of the Apostles
> at all.[2]

Catholic defenders of the Bible were warned "not to
make rash statements or to assert as known what is
not known." Originally the advice of St. Augustine, it was
repeated by Leo XIII. God does not need lies to defend
the truth of his words. Scientific difficulties of one generation have a tendency to disappear and to be replaced by
scientific difficulties of another generation. What is asserted
as a fact by one school of scientists often turns out to be
false conjecture when exposed by better scientists. Facts
and theories should not be confused. On the other hand,
ancient exegetes did not know everything. Texts must be
examined with care and considered in the light of new
knowledge. If there is apparent conflict between the Bible

and science, all sides should practice patience, recalling that many seeming contradictions in the past have disappeared with the advance of knowledge. The Bible was written to be understood by ordinary people, and it describes phenomena as they appear—as we describe the rising and setting of the sun. The senses do not lie, nor do they penetrate to causes.

Leo XIII was respected by the learned world. He pointed the way for a sound defense of the Bible; he roused bishops to provide capable teachers of Holy Scripture for their seminaries, and specialists to write introductions to the Bible for general enlightenment.

Pius X was obliged to condemn the errors which certain Catholics had assimilated from false philosophies and from the Higher Critics. He termed this synthesis of errors Modernism. On July 3, 1907, he condemned sixty-five specific errors in the syllabus *Lamentabili Sane;* and on September 8 of that year he issued the encyclical *Pascendi Dominici Gregis,* pointing out that these errors were derived from the psychology and metaphysics of Rationalists and agnostics. He showed clearly that there can be no compromise between the atheistic and the theistic points of view. While the source of Modernism was its philosophical assumptions, it is also involved with Scriptural interpretation, and we will summarize the points that were made by Pius X, as they do much to reveal the sources of modern intellectual confusion.

Agnosticism

At the root of Modernism, said Pius X, is the doctrine that the human mind is limited to a knowledge of phenomena: "that is to say, to things which are perceptible by the senses and in the manner in which they are perceptible. Hence it is incapable of lifting itself up to God and of recognizing His existence even by means of visible things." Consequently, both natural theology and revelation are swept aside. In both science and history, there is room for nothing but phenomena; "God and all that is divine are utterly excluded."

Vital Immanence

Religion, to the Modernist, is a subjective experience— an interior sense which originates in a need of the divine. This need, although only a sentiment of the heart, implies the existence of its object. In this sense, there is not only faith but revelation; the immanent God manifests himself directly to the human heart.

Faith and History

This sentiment of the heart, which is the beginning of faith and revelation, does not present itself as something isolated, say the Modernists; it appears in conjuction with something in the phenomenal world. This something may be a fact of nature, or it may be a man whose deeds and words cannot be reconciled with the ordinary laws of history—for example, Jesus Christ. In the Person of Christ, they say, science and history find nothing that is not human; therefore, whatever in his history that suggests the divine must be rejected. Faith has transfigured and disfigured the historical Christ, as it has transfigured and disfigured all other prophets and religious geniuses. Modern science must distinguish between the historical facts in the life of Jesus and their elaborations by the religious consciousness of his followers. For example, in the Gospel of John we have not the Christ of history, but the mystical elaboration of the historical Christ in the consciousness of the early Christian community.

Dogmas

Religion begins for the Modernist, as we have said, as a sentiment of the heart, an irrational experience in response to a subconscious need. But a new need arises: to rationalize the experience and to communicate it to others. The religious man ponders his faith; endeavors to express in intellectual judgments what the sentiment of his heart signifies. In doing so, he states propositions and draws inferences. Modernists recognize the possibility of mystical experience of God, which infuses a sense of God's existence; but the God who is the object of such experience has an infinite number of aspects, and the intellectual judgments drawn from religious experiences are of the nature of working hypotheses. As long as they serve to keep religious experience alive they are useful; when they have outlasted this function they should be discarded.

The Church

The Church, in the Modernist view, is a vital emanation of the collectivity of consciences. The individual who has had a religious experience feels the need of communicating it to others. The group feels the need of an organization to safeguard and propagate the common good. Every society needs authority. But this authority does not come, as was formerly thought, directly from Christ to the head of the Church, but from the members to the head. Authority has its source in the religious consciousness of the members of the society whose instrument the person in authority is. Liberty has reached a fuller development than of old, and the Church must take on a more democratic form under penalty of becoming obsolete.

Evolution of Dogma

Dogmas of the Christian religion, as the Modernist sees it, do not express absolute truth. They are rather symbols of truth—approximations or working hypotheses which may and should evolve, finding better expression with the refinement of intellectual and moral life. As the individual consciousness passes through various phases in the attempt to rationalize religious experiences, so, too, does divine revelation. Authority is naturally conservative and must be stimulated by individuals to whom religion is a living experience. Conflicts arise, but in the end a compromise is effected; this is the law of progress. Tradition is not unchangeable; it is merely the communication of religious experience. Dogmas are not truths which have fallen down from heaven. They are interpretations of religious facts, and can always find more suitable expression. "Divine revelation is, therefore, imperfect and subject to continued and indefinite progress, corresponding to the progress of human reason."

Faith and Science

Since faith is concerned with something which science declares unknowable, faith and science exist on different planes, and, as long as each confines itself to its own field, there would seem to be no chance of conflict. Nevertheless, the Modernist claims, the religious experience of faith is always connected with individual men and women who live in the phenomenal world and whose words and deeds belong to the domain of science. Science, therefore, has the right to superintend religious experiences and to keep them within the boundaries of law and reason. Science has the right to criticize religion as a psychological phenomenon, purify it of superstitions, and harmonize it with the modern view of the universe. Although science is completely independent of faith, faith is subject to science in its phenomenal manifestations. Science, for example, has a right to declare that miracles do not occur; therefore, the miracles recorded in the Bible are legendary. Considered from the point of view of psychology, however, they may be looked upon as interesting phenomena in the subjective world of religious experiences.

The Holy Scripture

The Bible is regarded by the Modernist as a collection of remarkable religious experiences. God speaks in these books, as he speaks in the intimate religious experience of every man, only the experiences preserved in the Bible are experiences of prophets, men of religious genius. They were inspired as poets are inspired, or indeed as all utterance is inspired. Nevertheless, looked at scientifically, the Bible is a human book, written by men for men. Those who believe God is really its author in the sense of having formed the judgments it contains display excessive simplicity or ignorance. The Hebrew Scriptures have evolved and reflect gradual progress of human consciousness; their inspiration consists in the fact that the Israelite writers have handed down doctrines under a peculiar aspect, little or not at all known to the Gentiles.

Rewriting the History of Israel

Modernist critics of the Bible felt obliged to rewrite the history of Israel. Only by this procedure could they separate the residue of fact from subjective elaborations of faith. The history of Israel, as we have it in the Bible, they held, attributes to the real world of scientific fact much that has occurred only in the consciousness of religious minds. It is thus the duty of the scientific historian to recover the Moses of history, the Isaias of history, and the Christ of history.

It requires an expert trained in modern historical methods, the Modernist is convinced, to detect in the various books of the Bible what occurred in the world of reality and what has been added by the subjective consciousness of a later age. The modern critic regards himself as uniquely equipped to tell, from reading an ancient document, just how much of it is objectively true and how much has been interpolated from the thinking of later generations.

The history and the criticism of the Modernists, Pius X points out, are saturated with their philosophy, however loudly they claim to be purely objective. In the case of Christ, in particular, they argue from principles which are entirely subjective. They put themselves in his position and attribute to him what *they* would have done in like circumstances.

From this analysis, it should be apparent that Modernists, like Rationalists, embraced a philosophy of divine immanence which is indistinguishable from agnosticism and pantheism. Their mutilation of Bible history is based on their *a priori* philosophic principles.

The Pontifical Biblical Institute

Pius X, to provide an adequate supply of qualified teachers, instituted the academic degrees of licentiate and doctorate in Sacred Scripture to be conferred upon Biblical scholars. In 1909 he founded the Pontifical Biblical Institute in Rome and entrusted it to the Jesuits, desiring that it be equipped "with a superior professional staff and every facility for biblical research." He also invited the Benedictines to edit the best possible edition of the Vulgate.

Benedict XV, on the anniversary of the death of St. Jerome, issued an encyclical, *Spiritus Paraclitus* (September 15, 1920), in which he urged Catholics to imitate St. Jerome in intense study of the Bible recognizing its superiority to all other books. He confirmed the program begun by Leo XIII and continued by Pius X. Addressing the bishops of the world, he said:

> It is your duty to train as many really fit defenders of this holiest of causes as you can. They must be ready to combat not not only those who deny the existence of the Supernatural Order altogether, and are thus led to deny the existence of any divine revelation or inspiration, but those, too, who—through an itching desire for novelty—venture to interpret the sacred books as though they were of purely human origin; those, too, who scoff at opinions held of old in the Church, or who through contempt of its teaching office, either reck little or silently disregard, or at least obstinately endeavor to adapt to their own views, the Constitutions of the Apostolic See or the decisions of the Pontifical Biblical Commisssion.

Three classes of enemies are distinguished: (1) those

who deny the existence of a supernatural order, that is, the possibility of divine revelation; (2) those who think Synagogue and Church canonized books written by human authors whose doctrines they approved; (3) those who deny the competence of the Church to proscribe errors of interpretation. Benedict XV repeated what Leo and Pius had said: the Church can, when necessary, determine by dogmatic definition the genuine sense of Holy Scripture.

Problem for Psychologists

Before descending to details, we wish to contrast the irreverence of Higher Critics toward the Bible with the reverence of Gamaliel, St. Paul, St. Ambrose, St. Augustine, St. Jerome, St. Thomas, Dante, Erasmus, Thomas More, Shakespeare, Pascal, Leibnitz, Bossuet, Newman, and the long line of Christian thinkers and scholars, Protestant and Catholic, who acknowledged the supernatural character of the Bible. To Rationalists the Bible was not a mysterious book; to Christians it was. Has the Bible been thoroughly analyzed and mastered in modern times? Have Rationalists succeeded in taking the mysteries, as well as the miracles, out of Scripture? Every Rationalist who has attempted to write a life of Christ has been forced to confess that Jesus Christ is incomprehensible; that he cannot be measured by the categories of human thought; that he transcends them. We shall deal with this further when we come to study Christ. Here we merely call attention to what is well known to scholars who have attempted to write lives of Christ. Christ manifests the warning of Isaias: "For as the heavens are exalted above the earth, so are my ways exalted above your ways and my thoughts above your thoughts" (Isaias 55:9).

Rationalists maintain the Bible is not mysterious; that modern scientific scholars can psychoanalyze the authors of its various books, determine their degree of culture, indicate the time they wrote and the contributions made by redactors, always assuming their own intellectual superiority. They are skeptical about the authenticity of almost all the books of the Bible. They think that one who believes God is the author of these books displays excessive simplicity and ignorance.

Few persons of sound mind would assert the superiority of modern Bible critics to Augustine, Jerome, Dante, Pascal, Leibnitz, Bossuet and Newman. Who can doubt that these great Christians deserve the reverence and respect Christian tradition has shown them? Their thoughts were higher than the thoughts of Rationalist critics because they found in the Bible objects to think about which the critics denied because of philosophical prejudice. Rationalism fails to get out of the Bible what is in it; therefore it is inferior— a system of thought which is dwarfed in comparison with Christianity. It does not solve the problems of deepest concern to human beings; it regales itself with the shallow delights of skepticism.

Why has the Bible remained a perennial classic, translated into every language? Why does it continue to outsell other books? Why has it had more effect on literature, art, culture and civilization than any other book? Have men been so generally deceived by a book which turns out (as the Higher Critics would have it) to be a product of nomadic culture, foisted upon the Jews by forgers?

Scientific method requires that every hypothesis be adequate to explain its facts. If the Bible is not mysterious, how is it that so many great minds have found it so? Most modern critics are specialists. They have vast erudition in one field of knowledge, along with barbaric ignorance of Christian philosophy and theology. This is particularly frequent in the case of scientists who have been educated without attention to the Christian synthesis of Greek philosophy with supernatural revelation. They do not understand the spiritual nature of man's intellect and its obediential power to receive divine communications. They do not recognize that intellect, by its nature, has power to know universal, absolute truths; or that it has obediential capacity for divine revelation. Although men cannot wholly understand the mysteries of the Bible, they can learn about them from a divine teacher.

The mysterious realm beyond the horizon of natural knowledge is of great interest to men. Homer and Virgil delighted their readers with descriptions of the world inhabited by disembodied human souls. Skepticism cannot quench interest in the possibility of life after death. No pagan poet ever treated of life after death so well as did Dante, who derived many of his thoughts from the Bible. Serious minds have always turned to the Bible for information about life after death.

The First Eleven Chapters of Genesis

Everyone should read the first eleven chapters of the Bible, if for no other reason than to become aware of how briefly the Bible treats of the origin of the universe, the sun, moon, stars, planets, earth, and its inhabitants, including man; and man's primitive history down to about

2000 B.C. Obviously such brevity makes it impossible for the Bible to teach astronomy, geology, physics, chemistry, biology and pre-history. All dates before Abraham are uncertain. How old are the stars, the sun, the oceans, the crust of the earth? How many centuries elapsed between the creation of Adam and the flood? How many of Adam's descendants found their way to Africa and Europe before the flood? The Bible does not answer all these questions. But it *does* answer some.

The Bible definitely asserts that God created the universe, including the earth and its inhabitants. It teaches that Adam and Eve were the first man and woman; that all men belong to the family of Adam and Eve; that all needed to be saved by the Messias. The Bible leaves no doubt that Adam knew how to talk, that he had respect for his wife and for marriage; that Cain and Abel possessed domestic animals, cultivated the fields, made fires, and offered sacrifice. It does not deny that some men may have wandered to Europe, encountered hairy elephants, woolly rhinoceroses and sabre-toothed tigers, and lived in caves; but they never ceased to belong to the human species; they never became irrational animals. They continued, wherever they went, to be endowed with the power of abstract thought, freedom of will, and hope for life after death.

Neither science nor history is able to contradict the positive teaching, reasonably interpreted, of these first eleven chapters. Scientists still say the sun rises and sets; for the same reason, the Bible describes natural phenomena as they appeared to the observer. The flood, for example, was universal so far as Noe and his sons could observe.[3] Early Semites did not write history in the same way that

Greek and Roman historians did; nevertheless, they wrote history, not myths. There is a hard core of history in the first eleven chapters of Genesis; and they are, moreover, of great consequence to the Christian religion. Rationalists allege that original sin is a myth; that the notion of a snake that talked is childish. And here the lines between Naturalism and Christianity are firmly drawn. The doctrine of the elevation and fall of the first man and woman is indispensable to the doctrine of the redemption of the human race by the Messias. Christ came to atone for Adam's sin and to restore Adam's fallen family to the friendship of his Heavenly Father.

The Biblical Commission, set up in 1902 by Leo XIII, issued a decision of great importance on June 30, 1909. Eight questions were asked concerning the historical character of the first three chapters of Genesis. We quote the answer to the third question.

> Question 3: Whether, in particular, we may call in question the literal and historical meaning where, in these chapters, there is question of the narration of facts which touch on fundamental teachings of the Christian religion, as, for example, the creation of man, the formation of the first woman from man, the unity of the human race, the original happiness of our first parents in a state of justice, integrity and immortality, the divine command laid upon man to prove his obedience, the transgressing of that divine command at the instigation of the devil under the form of a serpent, the fall of our first parents from their primitive state of innocence, and the promise of a future Redeemer.
> Answer: In the negative.[4]

Documentary Hypothesis

Father Cuthbert Lattey, S.J., wrote some twenty years ago:

> The modern study of the Old Testament outside the Church

may be said to be founded on what is known as the Documentary Hypothesis. It is a theory which is built to a considerable extent upon an analysis of the Pentateuch into supposed sources; but the analysis would not of itself be so momentous in its consequences, were it not for the dates assigned to the several sources, and especially to one of them. For these sources are supposed to correspond to the stages of religious evolution to be traced in the historical books other than the Pentateuch, stages which in their turn are supposed to be confirmed by the Pentateuch sources themselves. The whole is a marvelous *tour de force,* depending for the most part on the Old Testament itself for its justification and evidence, and yet resulting in conclusions which imply that no small portion of the Old Testament is illusion and fraud.[5]

The document referred to as of special importance is P, that is, the Priestly Code, chiefly Leviticus. This part of the Mosaic Law is dated as late as the Exile, out of deference to the theory of natural evolution of the Bible. Rationalists envisioned an evolution of Hebrew religion in which a gradual movement reached its highest point of development in the organized liturgy of sacrifices offered in the temple at Jerusalem by a priesthood trained according to precise rules of priestly procedure.

Hegelian pantheism inspired Higher Critics with a desire to rewrite the history of Israel in accordance with their philosophical principles. For this purpose, they decided to belittle Hebrew and Christian tradition as being of no historical importance and to rely on the criterion of internal evidence. The postulate that modern critics are qualified to discover who wrote an ancient book and its probable date of composition from internal evidence is false. Historical evidence consists primarily of objective testimony by contemporaries, preserved by tradition.

The first to lay down the principle that the authenticity of the books of the Bible can be determined by internal evidence rather than by Hebrew and Christian tradition were the philosophers, Hobbes and Spinoza, one a materialist and the other a pantheist. They were deducers, not inducers. Neither of them admitted the existence of a supernatural God. Observe carefully that this principle of determining authenticity by internal evidence was not the outcome of scientific study of the Bible or legitimate development of historical method. It was the hypothesis of philosophers in search of a method to justify their ambition to expurgate the Bible of everything supernatural. History is not a deductive science; it depends on the testimony of those who witnessed actual facts. We cannot reasonably assume that Wellhausen, who depends on pre-Islamite legends of Arabia to concoct his version of the history of Israel, knew as much of what happened during the march of the Israelites through the Arabian desert as did Moses. How could he? History is a record of past events by eye-witnesses who are no longer living. What modern writers tell us of ancient history is mere fiction when they depart from the witnesses. Moses testified that God appeared to him at the burning bush, and again at Mount Sinai. Wellhausen denies these facts. How could Wellhausen know what happened except by inference from his pantheistic philosophy?

Leo XIII challenges this idea in *Providentissimus Deus:*

> There has arisen, to the great detriment of religion, an inept method, dignified by the name of the "higher criticism," which pretends to judge the origin, integrity and authority of each book from internal indications alone. It is clear, on the other hand, that in historical questions, such as the origin and handing down of writings, the witness of history is of primary importance, and that historical investigation should be made with the utmost care; and that in this matter internal evidence is seldom of any great value, except as confirmation. To look upon it in any other light will be to open the door to many evil consequences. It will make the enemies of religion much more bold and confident in attacking and mangling the sacred books; and this vaunted "higher criti-

cism" will resolve itself into the reflection of the bias and the prejudice of the critics. It will not throw on the Scripture the light which is sought, or prove of any advantage to doctrine; it will only give rise to disagreement and dissension, those sure notes of error which the critics in question so plentifully exhibit in their own persons; and seeing that most of them are tainted with false philosophy and Rationalism, it must lead to the elimination from the sacred writings of all prophecy and miracle, and of everything else that is outside the natural order.

Historical Criticism Distinguished from Literary Criticism

In the Robert and Tricot *Guide to the Bible,* Father M. J. Lagrange, one of the outstanding Biblical scholars of the twentieth century, is quoted as distinguishing between historical and literary problems proposed by modern criticism of the Bible, and of allowing that some kind of documentary theory of the literary origin of the Pentateuch is not incompatible with the inspiration and inerrancy of the Bible. Of course, he does not mean to countenance denial of historical facts recorded in Genesis, but only to admit a literary problem arising from possible re-editing of the books before and at the time of Esdras. The author of this part of the *Guide,* A. Vincent, says: "Until the last quarter of the nineteenth century, Catholics did not become interested in the literary problem (as distinguished from the historical problem) connected with the Sacred Books. All such questions had been considered until then as being incompatible *a priori* with Catholic doctrine." Father Arbez, the translator, is careful to note that a modern Jewish scholar, Umberto Cassuto, defends the unitary character of Genesis, as Hebrews and Catholics have hitherto felt to be their duty.[6]

No one denies, as Leo XIII himself says, that internal evidence deserves consideration and should be carefully weighed. But the method used in this kind of literary criticism is full of danger. A critic can interpret according to his own wishful thinking. We cannot be too cautious in accepting any part of a theory which has been used by enemies of supernatural religion to weaken respect for the historical sources of Christian faith.

On June 27, 1906, the Biblical Commission replied to four questions concerning the Mosaic authorship of the Pentateuch. The only concession made to the documentary idea was an affirmative answer to the following question:

> Question 4: Whether, granted the substantial Mosaic authenticity and integrity of the Pentateuch, it may be admitted that in the long course of centuries some modifications have been introduced into the work, such as additions after the death of Moses, either appended by an inspired author or inserted into the text as glosses or explanations; certain words and forms translated from the ancient language to more recent language, and finally, faulty readings to be ascribed to the error of amanuenses, concerning which it is lawful to investigate and judge according to the laws of criticism.

On September 30, 1943, Pius XII published the encyclical *Divino afflante Spiritu,* in which he took stock of what had been accomplished by Catholic Biblical scholars in defense of the Bible during the fifty years since Leo XIII had published *Providentissimus Deus.* He expressed satisfaction that the challenge of Higher Criticism had been met by his predecessors, Leo XIII, Pius X, Benedict XV and Pius XI. He congratulated the scholars of the Biblical Institute on providing the Church with a copious supply of capable Biblical scholars. He encouraged all Biblical scholars to continue their arduous labors, assuring them academic freedom. He recognized the fact that while many difficulties have vanished in the light of research, others remain to keep scholars humble.

On January 16, 1948, the Biblical Commission sent a letter to Cardinal Suhard of Paris, in which it discussed the state of literary criticism of the Pentateuch and the literary form of the first eleven chapters of Genesis in the light of *Divino Afflante Spiritu,* and assured Catholic Biblical scholars freedom to grapple with problems raised by historical and literary criticism. So long as they respect the traditional teaching of the Church in regard to the inerrancy of the Sacred Scriptures, the pope had said that "these resolute laborers of the vineyard of the Lord should be judged not only with equity and justice, but with the greatest charity."

Referring to the questions answered in 1906, in which it was granted that Moses may have used written documents or oral traditions in his work, the letter to Cardinal Suhard states:

> There is no one today who doubts the existence of these sources (i.e., written documents and oral traditions used by Moses), or refuses to admit a progressive development of Mosaic laws due to social and religious conditions of later times, a development which is also manifest in the historical narratives.

The letter stresses, however, "the great part and deep influence exercised by Moses as author and law-giver." It calls attention to progress made during the previous forty years in studying "the literary processes of the early Oriental peoples, their psychology and their way of expressing themselves and their notion of historical truth."

In his encyclical *Humani Generis* (August 12, 1950), Pius XII refers to the aforementioned letter and warns that it must not be believed to countenance

> too free interpretation of the historical books of the Old Testament. . . . The first eleven chapters of Genesis, although properly speaking not conforming to the method of Greek and Latin historians, or to the historical style of modern authors, do record

historical facts and need to be studied further in the light of what has been learned of literary genres of ancient times.

It is worthy of note that a number of capable Protestant scholars have, in the last few decades, produced excellent works which defend the historicity of Scripture, uphold the Mosaic authorship of the Pentateuch, and present cogent reasons for their rejection of the documentary theory.[7]

Conclusion

It has not been our purpose, in this chapter, to establish the authenticity of the Pentateuch, but to tell the story of the attack on the Old Testament on the part of Rationalist scholars, and to indicate what has been done by organized Christianity to defend the inspiration and inerrancy of the Bible. To combat the army of professional scholars that attacked the Bible, it was necessary to train another army of scholars similarly equipped with knowledge of Oriental languages, archaeology, comparative religion, textual criticism and natural science. This Pope Leo attempted to do; and his successors have tried to carry out his plan.

While many excellent books and articles have come from the pens of Catholic Biblical scholars, the result has not been entirely what was hoped for. Some Catholic scholars were so deeply influenced by the erudition and sophistication of Rationalists and Modernists that they were themselves led to minimize the supernatural authorship and to magnify the influence of natural evolution in the sacred documents. They became too much addicted to the study of "genres," with the result that they called into question the inerrancy of the Bible and its total divine inspiration.

In this book, we are treating the Bible as a source of history—not establishing its divine inspiration and inerrancy.

As a historical document, we believe it to be entirely true and reliable, as the great Fathers of the Church have taught. Jesus Christ and his Apostles, we must remember, regarded the Old Testament as the inspired word of God. In the New Testament there are about three hundred quotations from the Old Testament. And Moses, David, and Isaias are referred to as the authors of the books attributed to them.

It is shocking to find some Catholic Biblical scholars taking their stand beside Rationalist critics and pantheistic philosophers; to find them treating the Holy Scriptures like fallible human documents. What they term "the modern approach" to the Bible is no more than the erroneous approach of the Higher Critics of the nineteenth century.

NOTES FOR CHAPTER IX

1. *On the Priesthood,* IV, 4.
2. This quotation is from *Providentissumus Deus,* issued November 18, 1893. This encyclical may be found, together with Pius X's condemnation of Modernism (1907), Benedict XV's *Spiritus Paraclitus* (September 15, 1920), and Pius XII's *Divini Afflante Spiritu* (September 30, 1943) and *Humani Generis* (August 12, 1950), at the end of Monsignor Steinmueller's *Companion to Scripture Studies,* Volume I; in Father Seisenberger's *Practical Handbook;* and in *Rome and the Study of Scripture.*
3. The extent of the flood is not certain; but there has been much archaeological and geological evidence presented in late years for an extensive deluge. See Father Patrick O'Connell's *Science of Today and the Problems of Genesis* (St. Paul: Radio Replies Press, 1964) and *The Origin and Early History of Man* (Houston: Lumen Christi Press, 1968).
4. This decision is quoted in *The Church Teaches,* a very useful collection of the Church's official teachings compiled by Jesuit Fathers of St. Mary's College, Kansas (St. Louis: B. Herder Book Company, 1955), pp. 153-54. It is also given, along with other decisions of the Biblical Commission, at the end of Robert and Tricot's *Guide to the Bible,* and in *Rome and the Study of Scripture.*
5. Lattey, *Back to the Bible,* p. 56.
6. Another Jewish scholar has published a convincing and much more recent defense of the unitary character of the entire Pentateuch. See M. H. Segal, "The Composition of the Pentateuch, a Fresh Examination," *Scripta Hierosolymitana,* V. VIII, *Studies in the Bible,* edited by Chaim Rabin (Jerusalem: Hebrew University, 1964), pp. 68-114.
7. One of these books which is particularly recommendable is Dr. Oswald T. Allis' *The Five Books of Moses* (Nutley, N. J.: Presbyterian and Reformed Publishing Company, third edition, 1964). Also worthy of attention are Dr. Allis' *The Unity of Isaiah* (Presbyterian and Reformed Publishing Company, 1952); and Rachel Margalioth's *The Indivisible Isaiah* (New York: Yeshiva University, 1964).

"What can we say of men who in expounding the very Gospels so whittle away the human trust we should repose in it as to overturn Divine faith in it? They refuse to allow that the things Christ said or did have come down to us unchanged and entire through witnesses who carefully committed to writing what they themselves had seen or heard. They maintain—and particularly in their treatment of the Fourth Gospel—that much is due of course to the Evangelists—who, however, added much from their own imaginations; but much, too, is due to narratives compiled by the faithful at other periods, the result, of course, being that the twin streams now flowing in the same channel cannot be distinguished from one another.

"Not thus did Jerome and Augustine and the other Doctors of the Church understand the historical trustworthiness of the Gospels . . . St. Jerome . . . says of the Canonical Scriptures: 'None can doubt but that what is written took place.' "

—Pope Benedict XV
Spiritus Paraclitus

CHAPTER X

Attack on the Authenticity of the New Testament

One of the most dangerous and destructive attacks ever made against Christianity was aimed at the historical value of the four canonical Gospels. Enemies of supernatural religion made a determined attempt to prove that these main sources of knowledge of the life of Christ were not written by eye-witnesses and their immediate disciples. Deists in England and France began the attack by denying the possibility of miracles and prophecies; but neither Deists nor the Voltaire school were capable of learned Biblical criticism. This was left for German Rationalists, backed by certain scientists. Reimarus (1694-1768) claimed the whole Gospel was based on deliberate deception by Christ and his Apostles. Paulus (1761-1851), while conceding the good faith of the Evangelists, vigorously denied all supernatural facts and attempted to give them naturalistic explanations. Reimarus and Paulus were precursors of Hegel (1770-1831), who furnished an evolutionary conception of history that proved

199

an inspiration to all who wished to reduce the Gospels to the level of mere human documents. According to him, history is a natural evolution determined by necessary laws. Because there is no God except the God immanent in and identical with Nature, there can be no miracles, no revelation, no supernatural order. David Strauss (1808-1874) and Ferdinand Baur (1792-1860) applied Hegel's idea of history to the historical sources of Christianity. In his *Life of Christ* written in 1834, Strauss explained the miracles of Christ as folklore developed by hero worship during the century following the death of Christ. Consequently, he insisted upon a late date for the writing of the Gospels.

Ferdinand Christian Baur conceived the evolution of Christianity to have occurred according to Hegel's law of thesis, antithesis and synthesis. He discovered the thesis and antithesis in a struggle between Peter and Paul, or between Judaizing and Hellenizing Christians. Baur occupied an influential position as head of the school of divinity at the University of Tubingen. Although he was in reality a Hegelian rather than a Christian, he was influential enough to keep his position as head of this prominent Lutheran school of theology and to introduce into Protestant Germany a serious doubt concerning the value of the Gospels as truthful records of the life of Jesus.

The erudition of German Bible critics intimidated many professors in Protestant seminaries throughout Europe and America. The latter were unprepared to judge how much of what the German professors said was based on fact and how much of it was inference drawn from Hegelian philosophy. The situation was thus described by Vigouroux, a French Biblical scholar:

> One cause of the influence exercised by negative criticism is the tone of assurance with which it draws its conclusions. . . . In setting forth their views these unbelievers say with an air of great confidence: "Science proves, criticism demonstrates," and this assertion frequently takes the place of proof and demonstration. As though science were incarnate in their person! As though criticism did not exist outside the hypotheses invented by their imagination![1]

The underlying purpose of the Rationalist attack on the authenticity of the Gospels was to deliver Europe from what French deists and German pantheists described as medieval superstition. The Gospels must be proved to be a collection of myths or legends, invented or embellished by popular consciousness during the two centuries after the birth of Christ. At all costs, miracles must be given a purely natural explanation. The idea that the account of Christ's life in the Gospels was a product of collective thinking—the thought of the Christian community—was substituted for the traditional belief that the Gospels were written by eyewitnesses, Matthew and John, and disciples of eyewitnesses, Mark and Luke. Paul and John were said to be philosophers to whom the Christian synthesis owed more than it did to Christ. For a time, Baur's theory that the Christian synthesis evolved from a struggle between Peter and Paul over abrogation of the Mosaic law received much attention.

On the heels of Baur of the Tubingen school came Bruno Bauer (1809-1882), a left-wing Hegelian and a disciple of Feuerbach, who went further in the direction of skepticism by questioning the very historical existence of Jesus. Bauer was supported by the "Dutch School": Pierson, Naber, van Manen, et al. Adolf von Harnack of Berlin (1851-1930) realized that such skepticism was absurd from the point of view of scientific historical criticism. Harnack was the greatest historian of the Liberal School of Higher Criticism founded by Ritschl (1822-1889). He affirmed that the Synoptic Gospels, as well as the Epistles of St. Paul and the Acts of the Apostles, were written in the first century (as had been traditionally believed). He recognized that Christ was the genius of Christianity; he did not concede his divinity, but conjectured that the essence of Christianity is its admirable moral system, the kingdom of God preached by Christ being no more than the reign of natural justice. Harnack and the Liberal School were as unwilling to acknowledge the historical truth of the miracles of Christ as were Strauss and Baur. They, too, were embarrassed by the presence in the Gospels of supernatural phenomena. The Gospels, they believed, are indeed historical documents of the most precious kind; nevertheless they are human writings in which facts are explained according to the prevailing superstitions of the time. These Liberal theologians believed the demonical possessions recorded in the Synoptics could be explained as epilepsy, or as various kinds of psychoses and neuroses.

The Eschatologists tried to prove that Jesus was a religious fanatic, proclaiming the imminent end of the world and his own second coming to judge mankind during the lifetime of some of his contemporaries. Along with many prominent Germans such as Weiss and Schweitzer, the French Abbe Loisy espoused this theory. To support it, the Eschatologists placed emphasis on such passages as Mark 13:30 and First Thessalonians 4:17. They were hard pressed between the desire to treat Christ with respect and the determination to deprive him of supernatural dignity. All of these schools were alike in that they assumed the natural evolution of Christianity.

A further development of Naturalism led to the school of Syncretists, who sought to discover the essence of Christianity in a synthesis of Jewish, Oriental, and Hellenic mystery-religions. After the Syncretists came the Form Critics, who were bent upon discerning in the Gospels layers of documents, edited, re-edited, and redacted until the sayings and doings of Christ became exaggerated and legendary.[2]

Higher Critics, whether they called themselves Rationalists, Hegelians, Liberal Protestants, Eschatologists, Form Critics, Liberal Theologians or Liberal Christians, were in agreement in denying the divinity of Christ and the existence of a supernatural order. They attempted to make Jesus of Nazareth personally as inaccessible as possible to historical research. They distinguished between the "Jesus of history" and the "Christ of faith"; between objective facts and pious glorification of Jesus in the subjective thinking of his followers. Christ's miracles, according to them, were embellishments due to the myth-making propensities of early disciples. Fillion writes,

> "Rationalists," strictly speaking, "critics," "modern theologians," Liberal Christians": at bottom these are only denominational variations, for all agree in rejecting the supernatural and in acknowledging no authority but reason.[3]

This audacious attempt to explain the origin of Christianity as a product of natural evolution concentrated attention during the latter part of the nineteenth century and the early part of the twentieth on the history of Jesus of Nazareth was the center of religious controversy. Was Jesus personally the author of Christianity, or was it a product of the times in which he lived? Many critics held chairs of theology in universities, some even in seminaries; some belonged to the clergy. The strategy employed by hard-core atheists was to take advantage of the supposed conflict between natural science and Scripture; between the new knowledge furnished by archaeology and Oriental research and the supposed naivete of Christians in past centuries; and to claim that Jesus of Nazareth was a legendary figure. Just as Higher Critics had challenged the Mosaic authorship of the Pentateuch, so now they challenged the authenticity of the First and Fourth Gospels, attempting at the same time to minimize the witness of Mark and Luke by claiming that these Gospels had been frequently re-edited until the time of the closing of the New Testament canon.

Harnack and the Liberals had too much historical sense to deny that the Synoptic Gospels, Acts, and the Epistles of Paul were writen in the first century. Experts were obliged to concede that the longer Epistles of Paul were written before 63 A.D. It was impossible for anyone to dispute the fact that before the end of the second century Matthew, Mark, Luke and John were regarded as authors of the four canonical Gospels. Although great effort was made to dethrone Jesus of Nazareth as the founder of a supernatural religion, his historical existence and influence could not be disputed. Matthew and John were eyewitnesses. Their testimony became the special object of attack by enemies of the supernatural.

Papias, Bishop of Hieropolis

In 1866, Constantine von Tischendorf, a famous textual scholar whose special field was examining manuscript-sources of the New Testament, wrote a little work on the *Origin of the Four Gospels,* against Higher Critics, Rationalists, and Liberal theologians who were making dishonest use of the Bishop Papias concerning the origin of Matthew's Gospel. Papias, Bishop of Hieropolis in Asia Minor in 130 A.D., was an obscure person whose memory was preserved by Eusebius. Higher Critics found him useful "to open to the freest play of conjecture all our investigations respecting the origin and mutual relations of our three Synoptic Gospels."[4]

Papias had written five books in which he gathered and commented on sayings of Apostles and other hearers of Christ. He was not—according to Eusebius—a man of strong intellect or sound judgment. This is evidenced by the fact that he reported sayings of Jesus which were extremely doubtful.

Irenaeus himself was misled by Papias into believing Christ promised an earthly kingdom which would endure for a thousand years, before or after his second coming. Irenaeus quotes Papias as follows:

> Then shall come the days in which vinestocks shall appear and each one putting forth ten thousand branches, each branch ten thousand shoots, each shoot ten thousand clusters of grapes, and each cluster twenty-five measures of wine; and if one of the saints should try to take hold of one of the clusters, another cluster will cry: I am better, lay hold of me, and praise the Lord for me; in like manner, an ear of corn will bring forth ten thousand ears, and each ear ten thousand grains, etc.[5]

Because of the fantastic nature of this and some other sayings which Papias attributed to disciples of Apostles, Eusebius (260-340 A.D.) judged Papias to be a man of limited understanding, whose writings were far from reliable. Eusebius quoted him, however, to show what an early ecclesiastical writer had to say about the origin of the books of the New Testament, since during the lifetime of Eusebius, there was dispute concerning the books belonging to the canon. Spoken against were James, II Peter, Jude, II and III John, Hebrews, and Apocalypse. The four Gospels, thirteen epistles of Paul, I Peter, I John and the Acts were not disputed. Eusebius quotes Papias concerning the origin of the Gospel of Mark:

> Mark, the interpreter of Peter, wrote down carefully all that he recollected, but not according to the order of Christ's speaking or working; for he neither heard Christ, nor was a direct follower of him, but of Peter, as already intimated, who always held his discourses as circumstances made it expedient, but did not seek to arrange the sayings of the Lord in any regular order. Mark accomplished all that he purposed in writing what he had to record just as he remembered it. There was one thing, however, which he did keep in mind: that was not to omit anything he had heard, or to falsify anything which he set down.[6]

Eusebius also quotes Papias concerning the origin of Matthew's Gospel: "Matthew recorded in the Hebrew language the *Sayings (Logia) of the Lord,* and everyone translated them as best he could." These obscure words furnished Higher Critics with the suggestion that the original Gospel of Matthew, written in Aramaic, contained only sayings (Logia) of Jesus, and nothing about miracles. Although Papias entitled his own books *Exegesis of the Sayings of the Lord,* in them he dealt with what Christ did as well as with what he said. The Higher Critics nevertheless insisted that Papias declared the original Matthew contained only *sayings* of the Lord, and gave no account of miracles.

Because Papias mentioned nothing about the origin of the Gospel of John, the critics inferred from his silence that he could not have been acquainted with that Gospel, and therefore, that it did not exist in 130 A.D. They held that if Papias had known the Gospel of John, he would certainly have mentioned it. If it had existed, he should have known

it, Hieropolis being in the neighborhood of Ephesus. Eusebius quotes nothing from Papias about the origin of the
Gospel of Luke or of the Epistles of Paul; but the critics,
strangely enough, did not conclude from this fact that they
had not yet been written. Their animosity toward the Gospel
of John made them fasten on Papias' silence about it as
strong evidence against its existence.

Fillion says of the critics' reasoning:

> This argumentation has no foundation in fact. That in Papias'
> mind the *Logia* of St. Matthew did not contain exclusively sayings,
> but also related events, is proved by the fact that in his "Explana-
> tions of the Sayings of the Lord," the same author inserted ac-
> counts of miracles and other incidents, as appears from the frag-
> ments quoted by Eusebius. Moreover, just before speaking of St.
> Matthew, Papias mentions the Gospel of St. Mark, affirms that
> it contains "words and deeds" of Christ, and designates it as a
> collection of *Logia:* whence it conclusively follows that this word,
> in Papias' use of it, stood for deeds as well as sayings.[7]

Irenaeus (140-202 A.D.) had access to the testimony of
Polycarp (115 A.D.) who was a disciple of St. John. Therefore, he was not obliged to rely on the testimony of Papias.
He was not ignorant of Justin, who wrote his first apology
in 139 A.D., or of Ignatius (107 A.D.) and Clement (95
A.D.). Higher Critics make light of the fact that the Gospels
were translated into Latin in the second century; that they
were used in Latin by Tertullian before the end of the second
century; that Tatian, disciple of Justin, wrote a harmony
of the four Gospels in that century.

Why is Papias—a relatively inconsequential person—so
important to Rationalist critics? Obviously, because his
words provide them with a hypothesis: that is, that the
original Matthew knew nothing about the miracles of
Christ. The critics claim, furthermore, that Papias was
acquainted with John the Elder, Bishop of Ephesus, but

knew nothing of John the Fisherman, the Apostle (who died, they would like to think, with his brother James in the persecution of Herod). If these critics can prove that Matthew the Apostle said nothing about miracles, and that John the Elder rather than John the Apostle wrote the fourth Gospel, they go far toward discrediting the testimony of two eyewitnesses concerning the life of Christ. They try to gain credence for their theories by insisting that the Greek Gospel we attribute to Matthew is only partially the work of Matthew the Apostle; that its stories of miracles originated as popular legends and were later incorporated into the Greek Matthew by a redactor. They gain support for their theories if they can convince us that the Gospel of John was not really the work of John the Apostle. They ignore the testimony of Irenaeus, which is rooted in that of Polycarp, Ignatius, Justin, and the whole tradition of the Oriental Church.

The Synoptic Problem

Although they were forced by indisputable evidence to admit that the Gospels of Matthew, Mark, and Luke were written in the first century (It is clear that their authors knew Palestine as it was before the destruction of Jerusalem in 70 A.D.), many Higher Critics still insisted that these Gospels are not the work of eyewitnesses, but a reflection of the collective consciousness of the Church. These three are called the "Synoptic Gospels," because they treat of Christ's life from the same point of view. The "Synoptic problem" has to do with their presumed dependence on one another.

Comparative study of the Gospels of Matthew, Mark, and Luke reveals remarkable resemblances and differences.

What is related by Mark is found also in Matthew and Luke; in parts of Matthew and Luke which treat of subjects not found in Mark, there are parallel passages. There is relationship in sentence structure, surprising in authors who display such distinctive literary qualities in other passages. These resemblances cannot be attributed to chance. The most simple hypothesis is that the three used a common source. Their differences are no less noteworthy than their resemblances. Mark gives no account of Jesus' infancy or his hidden life; Matthew and Luke apparently derived their information from different sources. Some parables occur only in Matthew, others only in Luke; Mark recounts one not found in either of the others. Matthew tells of Christ's walking on the water, of his cures at Genesareth, of his journey to Phoenicia, of the cure of the deaf mute, and of a second multiplication of loaves. These are not mentioned by Luke. On the other hand, much of the content of chapters 9 to 18 of Luke is not found in Matthew. Luke alone relates the raising to life of the widow's son at Naim and the parables of the Good Samaritan and the Prodigal Son; and he tells about appearances of the risen Christ which are omitted by Matthew. Such differences seem to indicate that Matthew and Luke each had sources of his own.

Most modern critics have adopted what is called the Two-Source theory to solve the Synoptic problem. Matthew and Luke, according to this theory, used an original Mark and a document called *Q*, which stands for the German *Quelle* (source). *Q* no longer exists, according to the theory, except as it is incorporated in the Gospels of Matthew and Luke. Various guesses have been advanced as to the origin of *Q*, which is assumed to be the most important source of the life of Christ. Some say that Papias refers to *Q* when he says that Matthew recorded the *Logia of the Lord;* that is, that the original Matthew, written in Aramaic, was identical with *Q.* The Gospel which now bears the name of Matthew, the theory goes, is the result of a redaction by an anonymous author who combined these *Logia* or sayings with legends of miracles taken from Mark. In other words, whereas all Christian churches of East and West have considered the Gospel of Matthew as it has come down to us in Greek to be substantially identical with the original, Higher Critics assert that it is a compilation made from two sources by an anonymous redactor. Besides *Q,* the redactor probably used Mark in a primitive form; and he must have consulted other sources as well, since these two do not account for the infancy narratives and geneologies which are in both Matthew and Luke.

At first, Higher Critics placed the composition of Mark after the fall of Jerusalem (70 A.D.) because it contains a prophecy of the destruction of that city. They now see advantages, however, in placing it at about 65 A.D., since Mark is supposed to have been a source for Luke, who probably wrote the Acts before 65 A.D. However, in Mark they find "doublets," which means that they think he gives two accounts of the same event (e.g., two multiplications of loaves). From this they conclude that the present Mark is not the original Mark, but a document compiled by an unknown redactor who used several sources. They concede that Peter's preaching probably had an influence. Mark's Gospel, then, a combination of several older documents, is the oldest of the Gospels, and served, together with *Q,* as the groundwork of Matthew and Luke. This in outline is the Two-Source theory.

The critics gain certain advantages by making the Greek

Matthew a later work. For one thing, in Matthew 16:18 Peter's jurisdiction over the Church is proclaimed. Rationalists suppose that this did not occur until after the power of James in Jerusalem and Paul in Ephesus had declined. By the time Matthew reached its present form, they say, the international organization of the Church needed unified authority. The Greek Matthew evolved in a cosmopolitan city, perhaps in Antioch, where Peter could safely be credited with having received from Christ the power of the keys. Since the Greek Matthew has absorbed the universalism of Paul and the Hellenic wing of early Christians, the redactor puts in the mouth of Christ a commission to preach the Gospel to all nations. Luke, too, the critics contend, shows signs of an evolution of original sources; for example, he manifests a neutral attitude toward the differences between Paul and Peter. They allow that besides Q and Mark, Luke no doubt questioned Johanna, the wife of Chusa, Herod's steward, and Manahen, Herod's foster brother.

Historical Value of Q

In a book that was published in London in the 50's, Thomas Henshaw undertakes "to acquaint the reader with the light which modern scholarship throws on the literature of the New Testament." His reverence for Q is profound; he regards it as the only primitive source of knowledge of the historical Jesus. He writes:

> The document Q is of great historical value. Forgotten as an independent record when once it had been incorporated in the larger works of Matthew and Luke, and reconstructed in recent times, it is now a priceless heritage of the Christian Church. It has preserved for all time the teaching of Jesus which has changed the whole course of human history. Its early compilation, combined with the inherent nature of the material composing it, con-

vinces us that we have the authentic words of Jesus. It was written a few years after the Crucifixion when the original witnesses were yet alive and memories were still undimmed. The teaching which it enshrines is the noblest ever given to mankind, while the profundity of thought, prophetic fervour, and deep understanding of human nature which characterizes the utterances, bear the unmistakable signs of being the work of a great religious genius.[8]

This is quite a tribute to an anonymous document which has no place in history or tradition.

Protestants are inclined to forget that the Gospel was preached orally for twenty years or more before it was recorded in writing. The oral Gospel long preceded the written one, and left its impress upon it. Apostolic tradition overflowed the written Gospels. Each Apostle, each disciple, taught substantially the same doctrine, but each used his own words and adapted his discourse to his audience and his environment. No deviation from substantial truth was tolerated, but there was no insistence upon verbal uniformity. Christ's words were reported as accurately as possible, but different memories used different phraseology. To suppose that a hypothetical Q was the only original source of the life of Christ, when the Apostles were still preaching in various countries, is unreasonable. Christian catechists and preachers did not learn the words of Christ by translating as best they could from Matthew's Aramaic Gospel. Jewish educational method was oral instruction and memorizing, not reading books. The effect of oral preaching, catechizing and memorizing is evident in the Synoptic Gospels, and goes a long way toward providing a solution for the Synoptic problem.

St. John's Gospel

Matthew, Mark, and Luke present the history of Jesus as it was preached by Matthew, Peter, and Paul. Matthew and Luke also give some information about his birth and his hidden life. John, who outlived the other Apostles, wrote his Gospel as a supplement to the other three, bringing more clearly into relief Christ's consciousness of his divinity, manifested in arguments with priests, Scribes, and Pharisees at Jerusalem. The Synoptic Gospels deal chiefly with his preaching and his miracles in Galilee. John records a long, intimate discourse with his Apostles after the last supper.

If Jesus of Nazareth really said the things attributed to him by the writer of the fourth Gospel, he unquestionably thought he was God. Reimarus' suggestion that Jesus was a wilful deceiver never proved attractive; and later Rationalists preferred to deny the historical value of the fourth Gospel. They claimed it was not written by John, the beloved disciple, eye-witness and companion of Christ, but by John the Elder, a contemplative philosopher of Ephesus. Christian tradition, they said, had confused the two Johns; the fourth Gospel is a development of thought carried beyond the popular preaching of the historical Jesus.

John, son of Zebedee, brother of James, a fisherman of Galilee, was one of the three disciples admitted to closest intimacy with Jesus. He and Andrew were the first of John the Baptist's disciples to follow Jesus, after John the Baptist pointed him out as the lamb of God. Jesus called John and his brother James *Boanerges,* Sons of Thunder; John was "the disciple whom Jesus loved." With Peter and James he witnessed the raising of Jairus' daughter, the transfiguration, and the agony in the garden. It was he who leaned on the Lord's bosom at the last supper, brought Peter into the court of the high priest, beheld the crucifixion, and ran with Peter to verify the emptiness of the tomb. To John's care the dying Christ committed his mother. Of all the

Apostles he was most closely associated with Jesus. An early Christian tradition, unchallenged before the nineteenth century, asserted that John became Bishop of Ephesus after the death of Paul; that he was forced into exile on Patmos, but returned to Ephesus and died there at an advanced age.

Against this tradition, Rationalists maintain:

1. John, the Apostle, was martyred with his brother James in Jerusalem fourteen years after the death of Christ. They say Christ himself predicted that both would be baptized with death. Papias is invoked in favor of this opinion:

> In a seventh- and eighth-century Epitome of the History of Philip of Side, a Church historian of the fifth century (c. A.D. 410), we read: "Papias in his second book says that John the Divine and James his brother were killed by the Jews." George Hamartolus, a ninth century chronographer, quoted Papias as saying that John "was killed by the Jews, thus plainfully fulfilling along with his brother the prophecy of Christ concerning them."[9]

2. The tradition that John, the Apostle, ever lived at Ephesus has no foundation in fact. The *Acts of the Apostles* makes no mention of John's being in Ephesus; Paul refers to evil days in store for Ephesus after his departure, and Ignatius, in a letter to the Ephesians, speaks of their indebtedness to Paul but says nothing about John. Irenaeus, Clement, and others who testified that John the Apostle presided over the Church of Ephesus after Paul's departure were confusing John the Elder with the Apostle.

3. Ignatius, Polycarp, and Justin do indeed show by references to it that the fourth Gospel was in existence in the first half of the second century, but they do not formally ascribe it to John the Apostle. Such a formal ascription does not occur until about 170 A.D. in the Muratorian Fragment.

4. Mark's Gospel presents John as a Galilean fisherman. How could he have had such intimate knowledge of Jerusalem and its environs as the writer of the fourth Gospel exhibits?

After stating the foregoing arguments, Henshaw concludes:

> There is today a wide acceptance of the view that the Gospel was written by John the Elder of Ephesus. It is practically certain that the three Epistles of John are written by the same author. In the second and third Epistles the author calls himself the "Elder." Irenaeus tells us that in his youth he used to listen to Polycarp, Bishop of Smyrna, who described his relations with "John and others who had seen the Lord." Irenaeus identifies John with the Apostle, and states that he survived in Ephesus until after the accession of the Emperor Trajan (A.D. 98). It is thought that he confused John the Elder, who wrote the Gospel, with the Apostle, and that this mistake accounts for the early Church tradition.[10]

Henshaw himself, who professes great reverence for the fourth Gospel as a valuable historical document, is "inclined to the view that it (the fourth Gospel) was written by John the Elder, a disciple of John, or by a group of disciples at Ephesus."[11]

Catholic Position

Catholic reaction to the attempts to deny the authenticity of the Gospels of Matthew and John may be seen in the decisions of the Biblical Commission published between 1905 and 1941.[12] According to these decisions, the first Gospel to be written was that of Matthew, and the Greek translation is held to be substantially identical with the Aramaic. Mark's Gospel is in reality the preaching of Peter written down by Mark, his companion and secretary. Some Catholic exegetes believe that by the time Matthew's Gospel was translated into Greek, Mark's was available as a help to the translator, but this opinion is not the same as that which asserts that Matthew and Luke are dependent on Mark and Q, in such wise that they are only secondary sources of apostolic tradition. The Biblical Commission holds that "the Apostle John and no other must be acknowledged as the Author of the Fourth Gospel, and the reasons to the contrary brought forward by the critics in no wise weaken this tradition."

Neither Matthew, Mark, nor Luke had any intention of displaying his religious genius by writing an original work. Luke says in his prelude that his aim is to write "according as they have delivered them unto ups who from the beginning were eye-witnesses and ministers of the word." After the Gospel had been preached orally for twenty-five or thirty years, the Church having spread and the Apostles growing old, there was need to preserve the preaching of the original witnesses in writing. The Evangelists intended to write as they preached, not to contribute toward the evolution of a new system of thought. A brief summary of the synoptic Gospels is already evident in Peter's sermon to the household of Cornelius:

> You know what took place throughout Judea; for he began in Galilee after the baptism preached by John: how God anointed Jesus of Nazareth with the Holy Spirit and with power, and he went about doing good and healing all who were in the power of the devil; for God was with him. And we are witnesses of all that he did in the country of the Jews and in Jerusalem; and yet they killed him, hanging him on a tree. But God raised him on the third day and caused him to be plainly seen, not by all the people, but by witnesses designated beforehand by God, that it, by us, who ate and drank with him after he had risen from the dead. And he charged us to preach to the people and to testify that he it is who has been appointed by God to be judge of the living and of the dead. (Acts 10:37-42)

The Christian religion is founded upon the preaching of

the Twelve. Any effort to substitute Q or proto-Mark for the eye-witnesses must be resisted firmly. The first preachers of Christianity were companions of Jesus from his baptism by John until his ascension into heaven. Among these were Matthew, the tax-gatherer, and John, the son of Zebedee. Mark's Gospel is a summary of Peter's preaching. All ancient authorities testify that Mark wrote what Peter preached. Luke, a physician of Antioch, heard Paul preach the Gospel, and in addition informed himself from many sources then available. He was a historian, not a novelist. He wrote the Gospel preached by Paul, who had conferred with Peter, John and James, the first Bishop of Jerusalem; he probably consulted the mother of Jesus concerning events of the hidden life, and Cleophas, who was one of the disciples he describes as talking with the risen Christ on the way to Emmaus. Cleophas lived a short distance from Caesarea, where Luke resided for two years while Paul was detained there in prison. Lebreton writes, in his *Life of Christ:*

> From the first days of the Church, Peter, chief of the Twelve appears as their mouthpiece, thus filling a place of first importance in the formation of the evangelical tradition. In S. Mark's Gospel especially, his personality is prominent both in the vivid freshness of the Galilean narrative and in the reserve which characterized all reference to himself. In the Fourth Gospel, similar characteristics, but still more pronounced, betray the 'disciple whom Jesus loved,' for although S. John never names himself, . . . he sets down his memories with incomparable vitality of style which reveals his authorship on every page.[13]

Oral teaching, preaching, and catechetical instruction have left their imprint upon the synoptic Gospels. Oral teaching was the traditional method of education among the Hebrews; they were adept in providing aids to memory. Obliged to depend on memory because there were no printed books and few manuscripts, the disciples were accustomed to carrying in their minds what they had been taught. The Gospels were written to preserve the apostolic catechesis. This should go far toward accounting for the similarities and differences between the three synoptics. Men who deny the divinity of Christ, his miracles, and the very existence of a supernatural order seek to obscure the sources of historical Christianity. Those who defend the divinity of Christ and the truth of supernatural revelation are deeply concerned with showing that the story of Christ has been told by eye-witnesses and the disciples of eye-witnesses. Christianity stands or falls on historical facts.

The great scholar, Tischendorf, expresses this position when he says:

> The person of Jesus is the cornerstone on which the Church bases its foundations; to it the doctrine of Jesus and his disciples always and with the utmost distinctness points; with the person of Jesus Christianity stands or falls. . . . Whence do we derive our knowledge of the life of Jesus? Almost exclusively from our four Gospels, in which the divine person of Jesus, the center of Christion beliefs, and the main object too of all attacks upon it, is presented in essentially the same light as in the Epistles of Paul, unquestionably the oldest of all the apostolic documents.[14]

To defend divine revelation and supernatural religion, we must defend the historical truth of the records which inform us about the life of Christ. Proof for the divinity of Christ is not derived, as is proof for God's existence, from the world around us and from our own psychology. Christianity is a historical religion, founded on positive facts. The existence of Jesus of Nazareth, crucified by Pontius Pilate, is unquestionable. We know it not only from the Gospels but from pagan and Jewish sources. Even modern Rationalists do not deny his reality as a historical person. The four Gospels are our principal sources of information concerning his life, and no intelligent defender of the Christian faith can shirk the duty of upholding their authenticity, integrity, and veracity.

Disagreement Among Critics

In our sketch of the schools of criticism, we have observed that Rationalists are not in agreement on any of the theories they have proposed to account for the origin of Christianity. Reimarus said Christ and his Apostles were deceivers; Paulus attempted natural explanations of Christ's miracles; Strauss saw the miracles as products of second century folklore; Baur found in Christianity a working out of the Hegelian principle of thesis, antithesis, and synthesis; Bruno Bauer and the Dutch School thought the only logical course was to deny the existence of Jesus; Liberal Protestants led by Harnack saw that this was ridiculous, but still attempted to get rid of the supernatural; Eschatologists viewed Jesus as a fanatic who expected the world to end in the lifetime of his contemporaries; Syncretists looked for the distinctive dogmas of Christianity in Hellenic-Oriental mystery religions; Form Critics found, in the Gospels, various documents which were changed by several generations of editors and redactors.

In an article on "New Testament Problems" in the *Encyclopedia Americana*, William Benjamin Smith, late of Tulane University, declares the net result of the mountainous labor engaged in by the critics to be only the ridiculous mouse of complete skepticism. The trouble with critics, he says, has been their willingness to assume that Jesus of Nazareth originated Christianity; and they will continue to fail until they realize that Jesus contributed little or nothing to the movement that bears his name.[15] What, then, is Smith's conclusion? That the Jesus of history is of no consequence to Christianity; that ninety-nine percent of what has been attributed to him is derived from Judaeo-pagan sources. Almost the whole of Christian doctrine and practice, he insists, can be derived from the religions of the time; Bruno Bauer and the Dutch School had "extraordinary glimpses of the truth."

Critics, says Smith, must cease to regard the historical Jesus as the source of Christianity, and must look on it as a syncretic religion: a product of the evolution of the century before and the century after the beginning of our era. In this, he affirms, he is supported by the most advanced school of critics in Europe: the Syncretists Gunkel, Pfleiderer, Bousset, Zimmern, Jeremias, et al. According to his theory, the synoptic Gospels do not give an accurate account of the life of the historical Jesus; they are filled with chronological displacements, inaccuracies, and alternations in statements attributed to Jesus.

We can agree with Smith on one thing: that skepticism is the most logical result of a Rationalism. Rationalists, Liberals, and critics of similar schools who speak glibly of the essence of Christianity do not really try to comprehend the nature of Christian faith. They profess to find it in the moral teaching of Jesus, but they overlook the fact that Jesus demanded faith in his authority. He does not argue with his disciples; he tells them mysteries, and they are expected to believe. He takes for granted that he has established his authority by his miracles. Let us examine one instance.

The day after Jesus had fed five thousand men with five loaves and two fishes, he was greeted by an enthusiastic multitude in the synagogue at Capharnaum. He told his listeners not to labor for food that perishes, but to seek food that will nourish them unto eternal life. This food is his teaching and his presence among them. Beyond that, he told them, he would give them his body to eat and his blood to drink. His audience was dumbfounded. This was a hard saying: who could believe it? Jesus repeated: "Unless you eat my flesh and drink my blood you shall not have life in you" (John 6:54). At that, many left him; he did not call them back. On the contrary, he turned to his most intimate followers and asked whether they, too, wished to go away. Peter replied that although what Christ said was mysterious, he believed him because he believed he spoke with the authority of God. This is the test to which every true Christian must submit. He must accept the word of the Master, no matter how mysterious. Faith in Christ is essential; if you do not believe, you cannot be his disciple. "You call me Master and Lord, and you say well, for so I am." (John 13:13).

Instruction Concerning the Historical Truth of the Gospels

The Biblical Commission issued, in 1964, an "Instruction Concerning the Historical Truth of the Gospels." The Church, it reminds us, has always defended Sacred Scripture from every sort of false interpretation. Biblical Scholarship should be encouraged; but the impression should never be given that truths of revelation and divine traditions are being called into question. Catholic exegetes should indeed work today more than ever to counteract those writings which question the truth of the Gospels.

The Commission insists upon certain points that exegetes

must respect. First of all, they should profit from "all that early interpreters, especially the holy Fathers and Doctors of the Church, have contributed to the understanding of the sacred text." To shed more light on the Gospels, they should employ such available aids as textual criticism, literary criticism, and study of languages; they should study the manner of expression used by the sacred writer; they should seek to learn all that they can about the religious life of the early churches, and to probe apostolic tradition.

As occasion warrants, the instruction continues, scholars may examine such reasonable elements as are contained in the "form critical" method; but at this point they should be wary, because

> quite inadmissible philosophical and theological principles have often come to be mixed with this method, which not uncommonly have vitiated the method itself as well as the conclusions in the literary area. For some proponents of this method have been led astray by the prejudiced views of rationalism. They refuse to admit the existence of a supernatural order and the intervention of a personal God in the world through strict revelation, and the possibility and existence of miracles and prophecies. Others begin with a false idea of faith, as if it had nothing to do with historical truth—or rather were incompatible with it. Others deny the historical value and nature of the documents of revelation almost *a priori*. Finally, others make light of the authority of the apostles as witnesses to Christ, and of their task and influence in the primitive community, extolling rather the creative power of that community. All such views are not only opposed to Catholic doctrine, *but are also devoid of scientific basis and alien to the correct principles of historical method.*

Christ's chosen disciples, the instruction insists, saw his deeds, heard his words, and were well equipped to be witnesses to his life and doctrine. "These men understood the miracles and other events of the life of Jesus correctly. . . . They faithfully explained his life and words." Their faith rested precisely upon what Jesus did and taught. There is no reason to deny that they passed on to their listeners what Jesus really said—the more so, because of their fuller understanding which came from their being "instructed by the glorious events of the Christ and taught by the light of the Spirit of Truth."

The truth of the Gospels is not at all affected, says the Commission, by the fact that their authors relate words and deeds in different ways. As St. Augustine says: "It is quite probable that each Evangelist believed it to have been his duty to recount what he had to in that order in which it pleased God to suggest it to his memory."

Let the exegete never forget, the Commission insists, "that the Gospels were written under the inspiration of the Holy Spirit, who preserved their authors from all error." When dealing with Biblical events, "let them not add all imaginative details which are not consonant with the truth." Let them avoid innovations and "trial solutions."

NOTES FOR CHAPTER X

1. Vigouroux, *Les Livres Saints et la Critique Rationalists,* 5th ed., II, 651, quoted by Fillion, *Life of Christ,* Vol. I, p. ix.
2. For a short history of these schools of criticism see Robert and Tricot, Guide to the Bible, Volume I, pp. 479-86; Steinmueller's *Companion to Scripture Studies,* Vol. III, introduction; Giuseppe Ricciotti, *The Life of Christ,* unabridged edition (Milwaukee: Bruce Publishing Company, 1947), pp. 179-216.
3. Fillion, *Life of Christ,* Vol. I, p. 477, footnote.
4. Constantine von Tischendorf, *Origin of the Four Gospels* (London, 1868), p. 181. An American edition of this book was also printed by the American Tract Society, Boston.
5. Quoted by Eusebius, *Historia Ecclesiastica,* III, 39.5.
6. Eusebius, *Historica, Ecclesiastica,* III, 39, 16.
7. Fillion, *Life of Christ,* Vol. I pp. 484-85.
8. Thomas Henshaw, *New Testament Literature in the Light of Modern Scholarship* (London: Allen and Unwin, 1952), p. 72.
9. *Ibid,* p. 148
10. *Ibid,* p. 151.
11. *Ibid.,* p. 152.
12. See *Rome and the Study of Scripture.*
13. Jules Lebreton, *Life of Christ* (New York: The MacMillan Company, 1950, 1957), p. xiv.
14. Tischendorf, *Origin of the Four Gospels,* p. 23.
15. *The Encyclopedia Americana* (1943 edition), Vol. 20.

"It is clear that in historical questions, such as the origin and handing down of writings, the witness of history is of primary importance; and that historical investigation should be made with the utmost care; and that in this matter internal evidence is seldom of great value except as confirmation. To look upon it in any other light will be to open the door to many evil consequences. It will make the enemies of religion much more bold and confident in attacking and mangling the sacred books; and this vaunted 'higher criticism' will resolve itself into the reflection of the bias and the prejudice of the critic."

Leo XIII, *Providentissimus Deus*

CHAPTER XI

Authenticity of the Gospels

Historical books are tested for authenticity, integrity and veracity. A book is authentic if written by the author to whom it has been traditionally ascribed. If Matthew and John, companions and Apostles of Christ, and Mark and Luke, disciples of Apostles, wrote our four Gospels they are authentic. The integrity of a book refers to the purity of its text. Has it been changed by editors and redactors? Has it been interpolated by persons who wished to slant it in the direction of their opinions? Does the modern text agree with the original? Where changes have crept in through frequent copying, have these changes substantially altered the facts about the historical Jesus? Even if we know who wrote a book and possess the genuine text, we have yet to inquire whether the author was competent and honest; whether he was an eye-witness of the things he records; whether he would be disposed to report events as they happened, or to relate as true what was fictitious.

The question of the veracity of the Gospels is involved in their authenticity. If Matthew and John, Apostles, and

225

Mark and Luke, disciples of Apostles, recorded the sayings and doings of Jesus of Nazareth, we can be sure we possess a reliable history of his life and ministry. These four men stood in such close relation to Jesus and were held in such high regard by their contemporaries that no reasonable grounds can be adduced for doubting their competence or honesty. They knew the facts and had nothing to gain by lying. What they wrote was of such concern to their contemporaries that they could not misrepresent the facts without exciting controversy that would have left its impress on history. Soon after the Gospels were written they were read in the churches. No one could have tampered with the text without protests from the churches. Because it was so frequently copied, the integrity of the text necessarily suffered accidental changes; but for that same reason substantial changes were impossible. The fundamental historical problem, therefore, is authenticity. We must show that from the earliest times the churches possessed records of the words and deeds of Christ written by eyewitnesses and immediate disciples of eyewitnesses; that these records are our Gospels; that they were jealously guarded by the Apostolic churches as being truthful accounts.

During the lifetime of the Twelve, the oral Gospel determined the faith of Christians. When they departed for other countries or died, need for a written record of what they preached was evident. Apostolic authority is the source of Christian faith, the necessary standard for the preaching of all who were not eyewitnesses. Reading the Scriptures in synagogues was a prominent part of Hebrew liturgy. The educational value of this custom was evident to Christians, and they adopted the custom of reading in their churches, along with the Law and the Prophets, the four

Gospels and the Epistles of St. Paul. The oral Gospel, as remembered by hearers of Apostles, enabled them, at the end of the first and beginning of the second century, to discriminate between what was apocryphal and what genuine in written documents.

If the Gospels related only natural events, no historian would challenge their authenticity, because they have been carefully guarded and universally used by churches from the time of the Apostles. Since the second century, they have been in the possession of Christian churches in Greek, Latin, and Syriac. They were publicly read, carefully studied and harmonized. The real difficulty for modern critics is not historical but philosophical. The Gospels relate supernatural events, and Rationalist critics do not believe in supernatural events nor, indeed, in a supernatural God. Consequently, they are obliged by their loyalty to Naturalism to deny the historical truth of books which narrate, as objective facts, that Jesus of Nazareth changed water into wine, fed thousands with a few loaves and fishes, gave sight to the blind, cured leprosy, raised the dead. According to these critics such happenings could not have been objectively true; they must have been subjective interpretations of natural occurrences.

Philosophers who denied that the world was created by a personal God and governed with a view to the salvation of men's immortal souls found it reasonable to theorize that the New Testament is based on subjective thinking of early Christians. Consequently, they tried to show that the "Jesus of history" is not identical with the "Jesus of faith"; that the Gospels are products of community thinking; that Christianity does not owe its origin to a unique individual.

Christians, on the contrary, have always regarded the

Gospels as a fourfold summary of the preaching of the Apostles, who were commissioned by Christ to relate what they had seen and heard. The Apostles all preached the same Gospel; during their lifetime it spread to many lands. There was no time for its "evolution" under influence of local thinking or pagan mystery religions. The Evangelists set down in writing what had been everywhere preached. Bishops who presided over churches would not have accepted innovations; the standard of orthodoxy was the oral Gospel to which accounts had to conform.

The oldest manuscripts do not use the title "Gospel of Mattthew" but "Gospel *according to* Matthew." That is, Matthew was not the original thinker; he set down what he saw the historical Jesus do and what he heard him say. Mark wrote what Peter preached; Luke what he had learned from "those who from the beginning were eyewitnesses and ministers of the word" (Luke 1:2). John wrote later and supplied from his own experience what the others had omitted. All the Apostles and Evangelists looked upon Jesus as the Messias, the Son of God. They would have considered it blasphemous to add to his message, or to subtract from it. They reported what they heard Christ say and what they saw him do. They revered him as God's Son.

The Witness of History

We intend to set forth the witness of history which is called, by modern scholars, external evidence. Leo XIII says: "In historical questions, such as the origin and handing down of writings, the witness of history is of primary importance and historical investigation should be made with the utmost care."[1] In other words, according to Leo, external evidence is of greater value than is internal evidence. The method of modern literary criticism is to minimize the testimony of tradition, i.e., the witness of history, and to decide everything on the basis of internal evidence, as though literary critics were clairvoyants, able to tell after the lapse of twenty centuries what Matthew, Mark, Luke and John might, could, would, or should have written. Tischendorf agrees with Leo XIII that it is the serious duty of those who defend the authenticity of the Gospels to make "a most careful investigation into the most ancient sources of testimony respecting the existence and recognized credibility of the records of the life of Jesus."[2]

We present the case for the authenticity of the Gospels as we have received it from the great scholars of ancient times. The experts grant that from 180 A.D., when Irenaeus wrote his work *Against Heretics,* the four Gospels were universally received as authentic by the apostolic churches. This fourfold record of the life of Jesus was canonized by the time of Origen (254 A.D.) in the sense that four Gospels, and four only, were read publicly in the churches and revered as Scripture on a par with the Law and the Prophets. Strictly speaking, there is no need to argue about the witness of history after the time of Irenaeus, Tertullian, Clement of Alexandria and Origen.

St. Jerome and St. Augustine in the fourth century faced the problem of the authenticity of the documents that comprise the New Testament. They were obliged to assure themselves of the security of the historical foundations of the Christian faith, and they did so by examining the witness of history, the testimony of apostolic churches, and of writers, orthodox and heretical, who preceded them. In the third century, Origen, Clement of Alexandria and Tertullian dealt with the same problem. All these great men were as much concerned as we are with ascertaining whether in the Gospels they possessed authentic, reliable records of the sayings and doings of Jesus of Nazareth.

Prescription

Prescription is a process by which a right is acquired through long use. It is important for a lawyer to show a court on which side of a case lies the burden of proof. Now it is an undisputed fact that Matthew, Mark, Luke and John have been credited with being the authors of the Gospels since the last quarter of the second century. Apocryphal gospels attributed to Peter, James, Thomas and others were rejected by the same critical process that canonized our Gospels. The burden of proof is definitely on any modern scholar who contradicts this ancient tradition. Irenaeus, Clement of Alexandria, Origen, Tertullian, John Chrysostom, Jerome and Augustine were no less intelligent than modern critics; and they were not ignorant—as some modern critics would have us think—of ancient languages and genres. The historical truth of the Gospels was as important to them as it is to us.

Tertullian and Clement of Alexandria, active at the beginning of the third century, formally discuss the question of the origin of the Gospels and assert without hesitation that Matthew, Mark, Luke and John were their authors. Tertullian and Clement of Alexandria were highly capable scholars, in touch with sources of information that are not available now. They were far more favorably situated to find out the facts concerning the origin of the Gospels than were critics seventeen hundred years later. If the Gospels were products of community thinking rather than a record of divine revelation, it is certain the great, earnest scholars of the early centuries would have found it out, for the authenticity of these records was a matter of great concern to them. The law of parsimony obliges us to explain facts by the simplest hypothesis. In this case, the simplest hypothesis is to suppose that men like Jerome, Augustine, Chrysostom, Basil, Athanasius, and Gregory Nazianzen were in possession of the truth.

The argument from prescription is clearly stated by Tischendorf:

> By what logicians call the method of rejection it is shown successively that the Gospels which were admitted as canonical in the fourth century could not have been written so late as the third century after Christ. Then in the same way the testimony of the third century carries us up to the second. Again the writers of the second century not only refer to the Gospels as commonly received parts of Sacred Scripture but also refer their origin to a date not later than the end of the first century. The induction is complete, that these writings which the earliest of the apostolic fathers refer to and quote as apostolic writings must have had their origin in apostolic times. Thus we see that of all theories the most irrational is that of the Rationalists who have so often maintained that St. John's Gospel was not written before the middle of the second century by a writer who palmed himself off as the Apostle John. We are at a loss to understand how the Church of the second century could have been so simple as not to detect the forgery—as it did in the case of the so-called Apocryphal Gospels.[3]

Born about 85 A.D., Marcion came from Sinope, on the Black Sea, to Rome in 138 A.D. where he preached his own version of Christ's doctrine, minimizing the role of the Jews in divine revelation and blaspheming the God of the Old Testament. To support his anti-Jewish view of Christianity he cited especially the Epistle of Paul to the Galatians and approved nine other Epistles of Paul, but only one Gospel: that of Luke. The other Gospels he considered too favorable to the Jews. Tertullian (160-240 A.D.), a powerful advocate, defended the historical value of the four Gospels in a book *Against Marcion*. He asks who this "gnawing mouse" from Pontus thinks he is to change the Gospels, approving and rejecting as he pleases. The question of the authority of the Gospels is settled not by the will of Marcion but the testimony of witnesses. The churches founded by the Apostles are the authentic witnesses. Tertullian wrote, with regard to the four Gospels:

> Among the Apostles, John and Matthew communicate the faith to us; among Apostolic men, Luke and Mark renew it. . . . The authority of the Apostolic churches . . . takes the Gospels under its protection; whence it follows that we have the Gospels by those churches and according to them.[4]

How could the churches founded by the Apostles have been mistaken in regard to the authenticity of documents on whose truth their very existence depended? Tertullian speaks as a witness to historical tradition at the beginning of the third century. He was fully aware of the importance of the Gospels as historical records.

Fathers of the Fourth Century

In 303 A.D. Diocletian ordered the Christian Scriptures to be burned. In 313 A.D. Constantine granted full liberty to Christians and, at his own expense, had fifty Bibles copied on parchment. The new freedom stimulated scholars and promoted discussion of the canon of the Bible in both East and West. In 324 A.D. Eusebius summed up the state of the canon of the New Testament in the East, naming three classes of books: homolegoumena, antilegomena, and a third class which included books edifying and absurd.[5] The first class, received by all, consisted of the four Gospels, fourteen Epistles of Paul, I Peter and I John, and, with some hesitation, the Apocalypse. The second class, books "questioned, but generally received," was made up of James, Jude, II Peter and II and III John. The third class, books useful for private reading but not sanctioned for public use: the Shepherd of Hermas, Epistle of Barnabas, Didache, Acts of Paul, Apocalypse of Peter; and last of all were listed books "entirely absurd and impious," written by heretics.

Every bishop who presided over a church had to decide what books were to be read publicly. The four Gospels were universally approved. None of the bishops hesitated as to the authenticity of any of them; they were attributed to Matthew, Mark, Luke and John, while on the other hand, a large number of apocryphal gospels were firmly rejected.

With regard to the establishment of the New Testament canon as a whole, we read in Robert and Tricot:

> In the second half of the fourth century, St. Cyril of Jerusalem, the Council of Laodicea, St. Gregory Nazianzen, and St. Amphilochius, have the same canon [the twenty-six books mentioned by Eusebius] without the Apocalypse; likewise S. Basil, St. Gregory of Nyssa and St. Epiphanius, but with the Apocalypse. St. Athanasius in 367, in his XXXIXth Pascal Letter lists the twenty-seven books, and he declares that all are apostolic and canonical. ... We may say the canon is fixed among the Greeks from this period.[6]

In the West, that is, among the Latins, there was no question as to the authenticity of the four Gospels. The only dispute related to the authenticity of Hebrews, James, Jude, II Peter, and II and III John. Under the influence of St. Augustine, the Council of Carthage (419 A.D.) declared twenty-seven books canonical. This decision reflected the tradition of the churches of the West. St. Augustine, without deciding on the authenticity of Hebrews, II Peter, and II and III John, held that all the books of the New Testament unerringly reflected the teaching of the Apostles. St. Jerome (340-420 A.D.) taught the same doctrine. He wrote commentaries on the four Gospels and entertained no doubt about their authenticity. Since the whole life of this great scholar was devoted to study of the Scriptures, his teaching is not merely his own, but reflects the scholarly tradition that preceded him. St. Ambrose (397 A.D.), St. Hilary (367 A.D.) and St. Cyprian (258 A.D.) cited the four Gospels as books written by Matthew, Mark, Luke and John. These men were intellectual giants, occupied for years with expounding the Christian faith, and seriously concerned that the sources they relied upon should be truthful. They were not men to be imposed upon by spurious documents which exploited myths and legends. And it cannot be too strongly emphasized that the scholars of the early centuries had access to sources of information that later scholars and critics did not.

Fathers of the Third Century

Outstanding defenders of the authenticity of the four Gospels in the third century are Origen (185-254 A.D.), Clement of Alexandria (150-216 A.D.) and Tertullian (160-240 A.D.). Clement and Tertullian were active in the last decade of the second as well as in the third century. Origen, born in 185, was active during the first half of the second.

The Hexapla was evidence of the immense labor Origen undertook to secure a reliable text of the Old Testament. The Bible was his textbook. He left no stone unturned to guarantee its integrity. In his *Commentary on St. Matthew* (Book I), he says: "Four Gospels alone have been received without opposition." Again, with regard to Luke *(First Homily on St. Luke)* he writes: "The Church of God approves only four Gospels." According to Eusebius, Origen gathered from sources available in his time that Matthew's Gospel was the first one written, then the Gospel of Mark "who had followed Peter and whom Peter himself recognizes in his catholic epistle as his son—'My son Mark greeteth you.' The third was Luke's, defended by Paul, and prepared for use of those converted from heathenism. All these were followed by the one which bears the name of John."[7]

Clement of Alexandria

Clement of Alexandria was a converted pagan philosopher, an admirer of Plato. He travelled through southern Italy, Greece, Syria, Palestine and Egypt, everywhere inquiring about the sayings and doings of Jesus, the preaching of the Apostles and the recollections of the presbyters. He was disposed to include among inspired works the *Epistle of Barnabas,* the *Shepherd of Hermas,* the *First Letter of Clement,* and the *Kerygma Petri.* His testimony carries us back to the last decade of the second century. He says clearly that the four Gospels were transmitted faithfully in the churches from the time of the Apostles and therefore are entitled to confidence and respect.[8] Eusebius quotes from Clement's *Hypotyposes:*

> While Peter was publicly preaching the word of God at Rome
> and expounding the Gospel under the inspiration of the Spirit,
> his numerous hearers besought Mark (as a man who had long
> accompanied Peter and remembered his teaching) to put in
> writing what the latter had said. Mark did so and gave the
> Gospel to those who begged for it.[9]

Tertullian

We have already given Tertullian's argument from prescription. The passage cited was from his book *Against
Marcion,* written about 207 A.D. He had written *Apolo-
geticum* and *De Praescriptione,* in 197 A.D. and 200 A.D.
respectively. In his work on *Prescription* he reviews the
century elapsed since the death of John and traces the faith
of the African church to the church of Rome "where Peter
and Paul poured out their blood, as well as their doctrine,"
and "where John was plunged into boiling oil but came
out unharmed." He asks heretics "to show us the origin
of your churches; enumerate the succession of your bishops
from the beginning, in such a way that the first bishop had
as his predecessor one of the Apostles." The Gospels belong
to the churches; they are their custodians. Tertullian protests to those who would distort Christian teaching:

> As they are not Christians, heretics have no right to Christian
> books, and we may justly say to them: "Who are you? When
> and whence do you come? What are you doing with my things,
> seeing you do not belong to me? By what right, O Marcion, are
> you cutting down wood in my forest? What right have you, O
> Valentine, to change the course of my streams? Who authorizes
> you, O Apelles, to remove my landmarks? This domain belongs
> to me, I have long possessed it, it was mine before your time.
> I have authentic documents, emanating from the owners them-
> selves to whom the property belonged. I myself am the heir of
> the Apostles.[10]

This review of the first hundred years of the Church's history has great force. How could the apostolic churches have been deceived in regard to the history of their origin and the authenticity of the documents on which they relied?

Heretics of the Second Century

Tertullian refers to Marcion, Valentine, and Apelles as heretics of the second century. Gnosticism was assimilated to Christianity early in that century under the leadership of Basilides and Valentine. Basilides lived in Alexandria during the reign of Hadrian (117-138 A.D.) and Valentine at Rome (136-165 A.D.). Valentine's disciples, Ptolemy and Heracleon, commented on the first chapter of St. John's Gospel; Heracleon also commented on the discourse of Christ with the Samaritan woman (John IV). Basilides, in the first half of the second century, according to Eusebius and Clement of Alexandria, composed a commentary on the Gospels. In the fragments that remain are found allusions to the Gospels of Matthew, Luke, and John.[11]

Valentine admitted revelation as a source of religious knowledge, but did not recognize the Church as its custodian. He spoke of the four Gospels and appears in the beginning to have belonged to the Church. Tertullian says he was offended because he was not made a bishop. In any case, before the middle of the second century, he endeavored to unite the speculative doctrines of Gnosticism with the teachings of the Gospel. The letter of Valentine's disciple Ptolemy to Flora was preserved by St. Epiphanius; his interpretation of the first chapter of John, by St. Irenaeus. Ptolemy was of the same generation as Valentine; they both used St. John's Gospel before the middle of the second century. The fact that Heracleon commented on that Gospel is known from quotations in the writings of Origen. Clement cites a commentary of Heracleon on the Gospel of St. Luke.[12]

St. Irenaeus (135-202 A.D.)

St. Irenaeus is a star-witness because he is the first to name the authors of the four Gospels, to explain the occasion of their composition, and to quote from them so extensively that his writings provide us with a considerable part of their text. Tischendorf says that St. Irenaeus quotes four hundred passages from the Gospels, eighty of them from John.[13]

St. Irenaeus represents not the isolated tradition of the Church of Lyons, but the tradition of Asia Minor where he was born and educated. In Asia Minor the faith is the same as in Gaul. Irenaeus points to doctrinal unity in all Christian churches. This unity is preserved by agreement with the apostolic churches among which the Church of Rome which was founded by Peter and Paul is preeminent. If anyone complains that he cannot follow the succession of bishops in other churches, he cannot so complain about the exact succession of the bishops of Rome; for Irenaeus gives a catalogue of them from Peter to Eleutherius.

To a Gnostic who had grown up with him in Asia Minor and listened with him to Polycarp when the latter told of conversations with the Apostle John, Irenaeus writes: "All this Polycarp had gathered from those who had seen the Word of Life, and he related all, in conformity with the Scriptures. I carefully listened to all these things then, by the grace of God given me, I have kept them in memory."[14] Irenaeus also wrote:

Matthew published a Gospel, writing among the Hebrews in their tongue, at the time when Peter and Paul were announcing their glad tidings at Rome and were founding the Church. After their departure, Mark, the disciple and interpreter of Peter, delivered to us in writing what had been preached by Peter. Luke, Paul's companion, recorded in a book the Gospel preached by Paul. Then John, the disciple of the Lord, who reclined on his breast, also published the Gospel, whilst staying at Ephesus in Asia.[15]

The lives of John and Polycarp completely bridge the interval between Irenaeus and the age of the Apostles. John the Apostle lived at Ephesus; Polycarp met him there. Irenaeus listened to Polycarp, Bishop of Smyrna, disciple of John the Apostle; he asserts that John the Apostle lived at Ephesus and that he wrote the fourth Gospel. It is preposterous to say that Irenaeus confused John the Apostle with John the Elder, a shadowy, obscure person who would certainly have emerged from obscurity had he done anything so important as to write the fourth Gospel. For Irenaeus, the four Gospels are the four pillars on which the Church rests as she covers the whole world. The Church faithfully echoes the teaching of the Apostles; bishops have guarded this teaching, conscious of their responsibility for the purity of the deposit of faith.

Justin (100-165 A.D.)

Justin was born of pagan parents near Sichem, in Palestine. He studied philosophy under a Stoic, Peripatetic and Platonist; when about thirty years of age, convinced that philosophy could not sufficiently enlighten him concerning God, he sought the instruction of prophets. He envied the intellectual peace of Christians, and was impressed by their courage and patience under persecution and their asceticism. Three of his works are recognized as authentic: First and *Second Apology,* and *Dialogue with Trypho.* They contain many quotations from Old and New Testaments. Since Justin was active in the middle of the second century, his use of the Gospels has been carefully studied. Justin refers to them as *Memoirs of the Apostles.* He does not name their authors, but employs the word "gospel" in the phrase: "the Apostles in their memoirs that are called gospels."[16] Justin also speaks of these Memoirs as Scripture. He says they are read in the assemblies of Christians along with the Prophets;[17] that they were composed by Apostles and by those who followed them.[18]

The custom of the time was to quote freely, and the quotations of Justin differ somewhat from our text; hence some have held that Justin was quoting earlier versions. Tischendorf considers this inadmissible, because quoting from memory was the custom in Justin's time, and many of the quotations closely resemble our text. Lebreton says: "It is quite probable that Justin used a concordance, or harmony, in which were united the three synoptic Gospels, and it seems the text of this concordance resembled in more than one point the so-called Western text of the Gospels."[19]

Tatian, converted about 150 A.D., "a hearer of Justin," composed a harmony of the four Gospels. This book, known as the *Diatessaron,* was written in Greek and translated into Syriac when Tatian returned to Edessa in 172 A.D. The existence of the four Gospels in this harmonized form in the second century is strong evidence that the four had been in use before the time of Justin. If Tatian united them into one continuous narrative before 172 A.D., a comparative study must have been made of them by Justin, who was active in the middle of the second cecntury. The *Dia-*

tessaron was used in Eastern Syria for two centuries after the death of Tatian.

Justin does not quote from John as often as he does from the synoptics; but he evidently depended on John for his concept of the Word of God. Lebreton says: "Justin's dependence on John is indisputably established by the facts which he takes from him. *I Apol.* 61-4 and 5; *Dial.* 69 and 88)."[20] Tischendorf cites the following text from Justin: "Unless ye are born again, ye cannot enter the kingdom of heaven. It is manifest to everyone that those who have been born once cannot enter again into their mother's womb."[21] This was evidently prompted by John 3:3-5. The idea and its expression are so unusual as to leave no doubt that Justin derived them from John.

Polycarp (69-155 A.D.)

While the apostolic age in the West ended in 67 A.D. with the martydom of Peter and Paul, and the sub-apostolic age about 101 with Clement, "who had seen and conversed with the blessed apostles," in Asia Minor, it is worthy of note, the apostolic age lasted until the death of John and the sub-apostolic age until the martyrdom of Polycarp in 155 A.D. Polycarp was eighty-six years old when he died a martyr. The long lives of John and Polycarp span the century and a quarter between the death of Christ and the time of Irenaeus. Moreover, Polycarp, Bishop of Smyrna, was a friend of Ignatius of Antioch who addressed a letter to him and refers to him in two others. The *Epistle of Polycarp to the Philippians* is an authentic document written shortly after the martyrdom of Ignatius. There is also an account of Polycarp's martyrdom, preserved in a letter of the church of Smyrna to the church of Philomelium.[22]

Fillion says: "The Letter of Polycarp contains eleven quotations of allusions, eight of which refer to St. Matthew, one to St. Mark, and two to St. Luke.[23]

Steinmueller says: "St. Polycarp . . . quotes from the four canonical Gospels, the Acts and the following Epistles: Romans, 1 and 2 Corinthians, Galatians, Ephesians, Philippians, Colossians, 1 Thessalonians, 1 and 2 Timothy, 1 Peter and 1 John."[24]

Tischendorf insists that Polycarp quotes from or alludes to I John in the following: "For everyone who does not confess that Jesus Christ is come in the flesh is anti-Christ" (Chapter VII of Polycarp's letter). I John 4:3 reads as follows: "Every spirit which does not confess Jesus is not of God. And this is Antichrist of whom you have heard that he is coming." Since critics agree that the first Epistle of John and the fourth Gospel were writtten by the same person, this quotation is significant.

Ignatius (107 A.D.)

According to Eusebius, Ignatius, Bishop of Antioch, was condemned to die in Rome in 107 A.D. On his way he wrote seven letters to the churches of Ephesus, Magnesia, Tralles, Rome, Troas, Philadelphia, and Smyrna. A direct disciple of St. John, Ignatius is a spokesman for the tradition of the last decades of the first century and the first years of the second. His letters were collected during the lifetime of St. Polycarp.

Although Ignatius does not name the authors of the Gospels, he uses the word "Gospel" (Evangel) and treats it as Scripture.[25] Steinmueller says: "Ignatius, Martyr of Antioch, quotes from the Gospels of St. Matthew, St. Luke and St. John, the Acts and from the following Epistles: Romans, 1 and 2 Corinthians, Ephesians, Colossians and 1 Thessalonians."[26] Tischendorf quotes from Ignatius' Letter to the Romans: "For what doth it profit a man if he gain the whole world and lose his own soul?" This is evidently from Matthew 16:26. In the same Letter to the Romans, Ignatius says: "I want the bread of God, the bread of heaven, the bread of life which is the body of Jesus Christ, the Son of God; ... and I want the draught of God, the blood of Jesus, which is imperishable love and eternal life." This certainly contains an allusion to the sixth chapter of John. To the Philadelphians he writes: "What if some wished to lead me astray after the flesh? But the Spirit is not enticed; he is from God; he knows whither he cometh and whither he goeth."[27] This was inspired by John 3:8.

If we bear in mind that Ignatius was writing about ten years after St. John's death, these references cannot fail to impress us. They cannot have come into use later than the last years of the first century or the first years of the second. Lebreton and Zeiller note that in Ignatius' theology, the influence of St. Paul and St. John is evident, especially that of St. John.[28]

Early Translations

The Gospels were translated into Latin and Syriac before the end of the second century. Both Tertullian and the Latin translator of Irenaeus, writing at the beginning of the third century, quote the Old Latin text. This implies that the Gospels were translated into Latin in the second century. In the year 172 Tatian, having retired to Adiabene in Eastern Syria, translated the four Gospels into Syriac. A Syriac version of the "separate" Gospels was made about 200 A.D., but did not supplant the *Diatessaron*.[29]

Muratorian Canon

The Muratorian Canon is a list of books approved by the Roman Church in the second century, consisting of eighty-five lines of Latin, discovered by Muratori in the library of Milan in 1740. Scholars recognize it to be a genuine catalogue of books accepted by the Church of Rome as Scripture about 180 A.D. The list begins with Luke, which is called the third book of the Gospel; it calls John the fourth. Evidently Matthew and Mark were first and second. This list shows that the four Gospels were being read as Scripture by the Roman church in the middle of the second century. It is incredible that at that time, in the church founded by Peter and Paul, any records of the life of Christ should have been read that did not faithfully reflect the doctrine of the Apostles.

Epistle of Barnabas, Didache, St. Clement

The Epistle of Barnabas was written during the reign of Nerva (96-98 A.D.). It is directed against converts from Judaism who tried to make Christians observe the Jewish laws. The author cites several texts from Matthew and in one instance uses the solemn phrase "as it is written," showing that he considered the Gospel of Matthew Scripture. "Let us pay attention lest perhaps, as it is written, many are called but few are chosen, may be applied to us." The phrase "as it is written" applied to a text of Matthew by a writer of that period is indeed impressive. The expression is found not only in the Latin translation but in the Greek text of the Sinaitic Bible.[30]

The *Didache* was composed between 70 and 90 A.D. This little treatise deals with morality, liturgy, and the relations between laity and hierarchy. According to Fillion, "the *Didache* several times designates the Gospel as a definite, well-known book, and quotes about twenty passages from St. Matthew and two from St. Mark, and perhaps contains allusions to St. John."[31]

The Letter of Clement to the Corinthians, consisting of sixty-five chapters, is a historical document of the first century. According to Irenaeus, Clement was the fourth Bishop of Rome. He may have been the Clement Paul mentions in Philippians 4:3; in any case he was one of the first four popes. His letter to the Corinthians was written about 96 A.D. to put down agitation against the authority of bishops. Fillion says, "in the Epistle of Clement have been found twenty-four passages containing Gospel Reminiscences."[32] Steinmueller observes that Clement quotes from the Gospels of Matthew and Luke.[33]

Conclusion

We have examined the witness of history concerning the authenticity of our four Gospels, and have found that from 180 A.D., the tradition that Matthew and John, Apostles, and Mark and Luke, disciples of Apostles, wrote the four Gospels was solidly established. In 180 A.D. Irenaeus stated plainly that Matthew, Mark, Luke and John wrote the Gospels. Irenaeus had listened to Polycarp, who had listened to John the Apostle. Twenty years later Tertullian affirmed that the apostolic churches—in particular, the church of Rome which was founded by Peter and Paul —authoritatively taught that the four Gospels were written by the men to whom we attribute them. During the first century of its existence, the Church of Christ had spread so rapidly that those who presided over local churches were obliged to treasure written records of what the Apostles preached concerning Our Lord. It is fundamental that written records of what the Apostles taught were indispensable to bishops. Apostolic churches in the time of Irenaeus and Tertullian recognized four Gospels, and only four, as authentic sources of the life of Christ.

Quotations from the Gospels in the writings of Justin, Polycarp, Ignatius and Clement, and in the Epistle of Barnabas and the *Didache,* are made freely after the manner of the time, but objective scholars recognize the fact that these authors held the same respect for the words of the Apostles as they did for the writings of the Hebrew prophets. Doubts raised by modern skeptics have been met by scholars of all Christian churches. No labor has been spared in investigation of the historical origins of Christianity; and negative criticism has been shown to rest upon conjectures and inferences drawn from pantheistic philosophy, whereas Chrisian tradition is firmly supported by facts. The historical sources of the life of Christ are unimpeachable. As Tischendorf says: "There are few instances in the collective literature of antiquity of so general and commanding assent being given to works of a historical character as to our four Gospels."[34]

NOTES FOR CHAPTER XI

1. *Providentissimus Deus.*
2. Tischendorf, *Origin of the Four Gospels,* p. 33.
3. *Ibid.,* Introduction.
4. Tertullian, *Adversus Marcion,* IV; 2-5, quoted by Fillion, *The Life of Christ,* III, p. 39.
5. *Historia Ecclesiastica,* III, 25.
6. Robert and Tricot, *Guide to the Bible,* Vol. I, p. 57.
7. Eusebius, *Historia Ecclesiastica,* VI, 35, quoted by Tischendorf, *Origin of the Four Gospels,* p. 195.
8. *Stromata,* IV, 41.
9. Eusebius, *Historia Ecclesiastica,* VI, 14, 1.
10. *De Prescriptione,* XXXVII, 3-4.
11. See Fillion, *The Life of Christ,* Vol. I, p. 46, and Tischendorf, *Origin of the Four Gospels,* p. 94.
12. Jules Lebreton and Jacques Zeiller, *History of the Primitive Church* (New York: The MacMillan Company, 1944), Vol. II, p. 636.
13. Tischendorf, *Origin of the Four Gospels,* p. 102.
14. From letter to Florinus preserved by Eusebius, *Historia Ecclesiastica,* V. 20.
15. *Adversus Haeraeses,* III, 1, 2.
16. *I Apology,* 66, 3.
17. *I Apology,* 67, 3; also *Dialogue with Trypho,* 49.
18. *Dialogue,* 103.
19. Jules Lebreton, article on St. Justin in *Catholic Encyclopedia,* Vol. VIII.
20. *Ibid.*
21. Tischendorf, *Origin of the Four Gospels,* p. 70.
22. Lebreton and Zeiller, *History of the Primitive Church,* Vol. I, p. 396.
23. Fillion, *The Life of Christ,* Vol. I, p. 44.
24. Steinmueller, *Companion to Scripture Studies,* Vol. I, p. 104, footnote.
25. Robert and Tricot, *Guide to the Bible,* Vol. I., p. 50.
26. Steinmueller, *Companion to Scripture Studies,* Vol. I, p. 104, footnote.
27. Tischendorf, *Origin of the Four Gospels,* p. 56.
28. Lebreton and Zeiller, *History of the Primitive Church,* Vol. I, p. 431.
29. Robert and Tricot, *Guide to the Bible,* Vol. p. 61.
30. See Tischendorf, *Origin of the Four Gospels,* p. 156.
31. Fillion, *The Life of Christ,* Vol. I, p. 43.
32. *Ibid.,* p. 44.
33 Steinmueller, *A Companion to Scripture Studies,* Vol. I, p. 104, footnote.
34. Tischendorf, *Origin of the Four Gospels,* p. 218.

CHAPTER XII

Internal Evidence

Leo XIII warned scholars that in determining the authenticity of ancient books, the witness of history is of more weight than is internal evidence, which can confirm but not establish authorship. The publication of a book is a fact learned, like other facts of history, from contemporary witnesses. Modern critics, following the lead of Hobbes and Spinoza, attempt to reverse this judgment. They claim they can tell who wrote a book, when it was written, whether it has been interpolated and re-edited, and the sources used by a careful, critical examination of its contents. The witness of history asserts that the Gospels were written by Matthew, Mark, Luke and John. Rationalistic critics deny that the first and fourth Gospels were written by Matthew and John, disregarding the testimony of Irenaeus, Clement of Alexandria, Tertullian, Origen, Jerome and Augustine.

Early Rationalists such as Strauss and Baur went further, denying the authenticity of Mark and Luke as well. They imagined they could distinguish a "proto-Mark." Baur claimed that Luke was written in the second century. In regard to the second and third Gospels, however, Rationalists were forced by internal evidence to execute what Harnack aptly named "a retrograde movement." The homely honesty, artless simplicity and unsophisticated realism of Mark's Gospel point unmistakably to the recollections of Peter. No good reason can be given why Mark should have been credited with its authorship if he were not really the author. The literary style and picturesque charm of the third Gospel and Acts captivated modern critics, many of whom echo Renan's judgment that the Gospel of Luke is one of the most beautiful books ever written. Since Mark and Luke were not eye-witnesses, enemies of the supernatural are better disposed toward them than they are toward Matthew and John.

Primitive Character of the Four Gospels

In the year 70 A.D., a catastrophe occurred which wiped out the political, social and religious institutions under which Jesus of Nazareth and his original disciples lived and labored. Jerusalem ceased to be the center of Jewish worship and culture; the great pilgrimages of dispersed Jews from Egypt, Babylon, Syria and Asia Minor were abandoned; the temple-tax was no longer paid; the government of Palestine as it had existed was abolished; the home of the people of Israel had disappeared.

The destruction of Jerusalem, with the dispersion of the Jews, marks the end of a period. Writers who had not experienced the Jerusalem, Judea and Galilee of Jesus and His Apostles would betray themselves in trying to reconstruct it. Intent on discovering blunders in chronology, topography, ceremonies, customs, historical persons, political conditions, languages, coinage, et cetera, modern critics made a pitiless scrutiny of the Gospels. But the Gospels triumphed. Philo, Josephus, the Talmud and the Septuagint corroborate them. In the environment of Palestine as it was in the first century, the four Evangelists move unerringly. Events are dated, office-holders are named, customs are cited: buildings, pools, fountains, gardens and distances are described with familiar accuracy. Tiberius was emperor, Pontius Pilate was governor of Judea, Herod was tetrarch of Galilee, Annas and Caiphas were high priests, when Jesus of Nazareth announced himself as the long-expected Messias of Israel. The Evangelists describe Herod, Pilate, Annas, Caiphas, Peter, John and Judas with artless precision. They understand the casuistry of the Pharisees, the subserviency of the Herodians, the avarice of the Sadducees, the narrow-mindedness of the Scribes, the restlessness of the Galileans. They know Palestine as it was between the death of Herod the Great and the destruction of the holy city.

Harnack testifies that Rationalists like himself were obliged to give up the hypothesis of Strauss, Baur, and Renan of the late origin of the Synoptic Gospels. He writes:

> Sixty years ago David Frederic Strauss thought he had deprived the first three Gospels of almost all their value, but the historical and critical labor of two generations has succeeded in restoring it to them in great measure. . . . The Gospels . . . belong, in their essentials, to the primitive, Judaic period of Christianity . . . . The absolutely unique character of the Gospels is today universally recognized by critics. . . . That in them we are, for all essentials, face to face with primitive tradition is incontestable.[1]

Internal evidence confirms the witness of history. The Synoptic Gospels were written by men who knew Jerusalem, Galilee, and Palestine before Titus conquered the

Jews in the war that lasted from 65 to 70 A.D. The author of the fourth Gospel, also, knew Jerusalem well, as he did Galilee.

Style

With regard to the manner of writing, Grandmaison observes:

> From the literary point of view, the Gospels are for the greater part of their contents (I mean not merely in their Aramaic sources, but in their actual Greek form) much more Hebraic than Hellenic. They were composed by Jews or by men whom the assiduous reading of the Septuagint had imbued, as in the case of Luke, with Jewish ways of thinking and expressing themselves.[2]

The language of the New Testament is the Greek spoken in countries conquered by Alexander, having an Attic base but bearing the impress of Semitic words and Semitic sentence-structure. Aramaic words are mixed with Greek words and Greek words sometimes have Semitic meanings. This was the language of the Jews of the dispersion and to some extent of Palestine itself when the Gospel was first preached. Luke, who was the only literary artist among the four, possessed the rare gift of being able to vary his style, sometimes using polished Attic Greek, as in the first sentence of his Gospel, more often the common Greek, and occasionally the archaic Greek of the Septuagint. The Gospels of Mark and John especially exhibit Semitic habits of thought and Semitic sentence-structure. Matthew uses poetic parallelism, contrast, and mnemonic devices, according to the genius of the Hebrews who relied on oral teaching, with memorizing, rather than on reading and writing.

Literary critics realize the style of the Gospels, as well as their content, furnishes internal evidence that they were written in the first century by Palestinian Jews; and against their inclinations they have been compelled by this evidence to recognize the Gospels' unique character. Certainly they would have dated them in the second century if internal evidence had permitted. Scholars like Harnack, although they denied the possibility of miracles and other supernatural phenomena, were conscientious enough to affirm that the Gospels "belong, in their essentials, to the primitive, Judaic period of Christianity."

The Gospel According to St. Matthew

According to the testimony of Christian tradition, the first Gospel was written by Matthew, one of the Twelve, who had been a tax-collector. He is also called Levi by Mark and Luke. This historical tradition, transmitted by apostolic churches and early Fathers, was undisputed until the rise of Rationalistic criticism in the nineteenth century. Origen and Eusebius say that Matthew was the first to write a Gospel. According to Irenaeus, Matthew wrote for the Jews of Palestine, both those who accepted and those who rejected Jesus of Nazareth as their Messias. Papias, Jerome, and other Fathers say that Matthew wrote originally in Hebrew (Aramaic). Eusebius relates that Pantaenus, founder of the catechetical school of Alexandria, brought back a copy of this Gospel from lower Arabia in the second century, whither the Apostle Bartholomew is said to have carried it. Although there is some obscurity about its translation into Greek, the early Fathers quote the Greek Gospel as having the authority of an original The Greek Gospel alone has been preserved by the churches, and Christians have always regarded it as an inspired book, the work of Matthew the Apostle. St. Jerome, who was an enthusiast for Hebrew documents, found in a library in Caesarea a copy of what appeared to be Matthew's Gospel in Hebrew. After he made a translation of it, however, he realized the manuscript had been adapted by the Nazarenes to their errors. The disappearance of the Aramaic original is explained by the fact that the reading public of the first century read Greek and not Aramaic. Those who spoke Aramaic were accustomed to learn by hearing rather than by reading. Matthew himself was bilingual, and may have written in both languages. Tischendorf and Lagrange do not think the Greek Matthew reads like a translation. The Greek Gospel is quoted even by Fathers like Origen who understood Hebrew. There is no evidence to show that there is any substantial difference between the Aramaic and the Greek Matthew.

Rationalists, Modernists, and some other critics challenge tradition, asserting that Matthew the Apostle did not compose a complete Gospel but merely a collection of sayings of Christ. The narrative of the birth, the flight into Egypt, the miracles, Passion, and Resurrection, they say, were added by an anonymous translator who used Mark's Gospel as a source for the miracles and other sources for the story of the birth of Christ. The *Logia,* as we have noted, they call *Q*. These critics admit that the compiler of the Greek Gospel had a wonderful talent for conflating different documents, giving them the appearance of literary unity. Nevertheless they think they have discovered contradictions in the Greek Gospel which arise from the use of a third source called *M*, a Judaizer who makes Christ a stickler for the Law of Moses, in saying that not one jot or tittle of the Law shall pass. They think, too, that they have discovered still a fourth document (incorporated after the Church had become a world-wide organization) in which Peter was made the rock on which Christ built, and the mission of the Apostles was broadened to include all nations.

Henshaw, under the following headings, summarizes the case against the authenticity of the first Gospel:

(1) One of the twelve apostles would not have used as his main source the Gospel of Mark, who was not an eyewitness of the ministry of Jesus.

(2) The parts peculiar to Matthew do not suggest personal recollections of an eyewitness.

(3) Matthew, a converted publican, could not have had the rabbinic training necessary to codify the preaching of Jesus into a complete system of morality.

(4) The book Jerome translated was probably the apocryphal Gospel according to the Hebrews.

(5) The term *Logia* used by Papias probably did not refer to the Gospel but to a collection of sayings identical with Q.

(6) The sayings: "Wherefore that field was called the field of blood unto this day" (27:8) and "This saying was spread abroad among the Jews and continueth until this day" (28:15) suggest a long time between the occurrence of the events and the writing of the Gospel.

(7) The allusion to Peter as the rock on which Christ built his Church suggests the latter part of the century.

(8) There is a contradiction between a Judaizing Matthew who has Christ say the law of Moses must be observed in every detail and the cosmopolitan Matthew who puts into the mouth of Christ a commission to his apostles to preach the Gospel to the whole world.[3]

We reply to these arguments as follows:

(1) The relationship of Matthew to Mark is an enigma which literary critics have not solved. The "Two-Source Theory" is merely a conjecture. The Ur-Marcus Theory and the Four Document Theory contend with the Two-Source Theory. All critics are obliged to take into consideration the influence on the written Gospels of the oral Gospel preached

for some fifteen years before Matthew's Gospel was written, and the part played by memorizing in Oriental learning. St. Augustine believed that Mark was dependent on Matthew. Christian tradition teaches that Matthew's Gospel was written first; and that there is no substantial difference between the Aramaic text and the Greek. Since the Gospel was preached for years before either Matthew or Mark wrote, we should expect them both to incorporate some of the phraseology of the preachers. Peter's sermon to the household of Cornelius, recorded in the tenth chapter of Acts, outlined the general plan of the three synoptic Gospels. Even those who advocate the theory that the Greek Gospel according to Matthew is a compilation must admit that Mark and Q cannot account for it all; they must postulate other sources to explain the first two chapters and the Judaizing and catholic tendencies of the author. The Gospel of Matthew is more complete than that of Luke; in the early Church it was more frequently quoted than any other.

(2) Matthew's style is not so vivid as Mark's; he was not so artless as Peter, an extrovert, unsophisticated and candid to a fault, whose sermons Mark recorded. Matthew is more detached, restrained, and businesslike. His Gospel has unity of plan and is carefully executed. Matthew wrote for Jews who knew the Law and the Prophets. He put into his Gospel what Jews needed to know about their Messias; how Jesus of Nazareth fulfilled the prophecies, and how his coming had affected the fortunes of the house of Israel. Matthew's Gospel is the best balanced of the synoptics. It contains five connected discourses, relates twenty miracles, and has two chapters on Jesus' birth and infancy. Prejudice alone prevents critics from recognizing Matthew's account of the confession of Peter (16:13) to be testimony of an

eye-witness. All the Evangelists relate that in Galilee the people remained with Jesus for days and listened gladly to his long discourses. Matthew's summaries of these discourses are exactly what early Christians were most interested in hearing.

(3) Why should Matthew *not* have recorded what he heard Christ say? It cannot be allowed that a discourse like the Sermon on the Mount or the description of the last judgment, once in possession of Christian churches, could have been "re-edited" by anyone. It is not in the nature of religious men to permit a redactor who knew not the Master to tamper with his very words as reported by an earwitness. Modern critics talk glibly of a Greek translator who amplified, rearranged, and codified the sayings recorded by the original Matthew, uniting them into the five discourses in the Greek Gospel. But such a procedure, once the document was in the possession of any Church, would have caused a protest which would have left its mark on history. Why should Matthew, educated by Jesus for three years and accustomed to the manner of Hebrew oral teaching, have been unable to report a sermon which had held its audience spellbound? Why should a translator at the end of the first century have been better able to report Jesus' moral teaching than was a firsthand witness?

(4) St. Jerome was interested in anything written in Hebrew. He believed at first that the Gospel used by the Nazarenes was the Aramaic Gospel of Matthew; learned later that he was mistaken.[4] History provides no information about the translation of the Aramaic Gospel into Greek; but since the Fathers of the second century quote the Greek Gospel as Sacred Scripture and regard it as part of the canon, they clearly accepted it as inspired and of apostolic

authority. If it was translated by another, the translator must have done his work reverently.

(5) Papias also applies the word *Logia* to the Gospel of Mark, which treats mainly of miracles. And Papias' own five books, as we know from Eusebius, contained stories of miracles as well as sayings of Christ, although they were entitled *Exegesis of the Logia of the Lord*.

(6) Twenty years may have elapsed between the death of Judas and the publication of Matthew's Gospel. The expression "until this day," which was idiomatic among Jews, could be justified by the lapse of that period of time. The expression merely adds emphasis. There is a possibility that the phrase "unto this day" was a gloss added by a copyist.

(7) Peter's confession that Jesus was the Messias and the Son of God was the turning point of the public life of Christ. This text is found in all the ancient manuscripts. No valid argument can be presented against its authenticity; the attempt to consign it to a later date appears to be solely because of its doctrinal importance. Rationalists do not wish to admit that Peter made this confession or that Jesus approved it. Christ's divinity and Peter's authority are too clearly attested. Critics have no reasonable grounds for calling into question the authenticity of this passage; but they do not like it; therefore they say that Matthew did not write it.

(8) There is no contradiction between the "Judaizing" Matthew and the catholic Matthew. During his lifetime, Christ preached only to "the lost sheep of the house of Israel"; he sent his disciples first to preach to Jews. Even after his resurrection the Holy Ghost directed the Apostles

to preach first in Jerusalem. Nevertheless, Jesus had warned the Jews in the parable of the vineyard that God was angry with those who killed his messengers and would give his vineyard to the Gentiles. In the Sermon on the Mount he had said the Jews must bring forth good fruit if they wished to belong to the kingdom of God; that many would come from the East and the West to sit down with Abraham, while the children of the kingdom would be cast out. What does the parable of the marriage feast mean, if not that God would invite Gentiles to a feast to which Jews refused to come? The view that the Greek Gospel contains contradictory documents cannot be sustained. Grandmaison writes:

> Despite, and partly by reason of the conflict which divides the evangelist between his love of his race and his clear view of the changing economy which is substituting a new people for the Israel of the flesh, the unity of the narrative is profound. There is unity of feeling, and still more, there is literary unity.[5]

After Christ's resurrection, he commissioned his disciples to go into the whole world and to preach the Gospel to all nations. With his death, the old covenant had come to an end. The Jews were no longer a separated people. Henceforth, in the sight of God there was to be neither Jew nor Gentile; all men were redeemed and called to the kingdom of God, provided they believed and were baptized.

Among recent critics, Dom Cuthbert Butler claims that Matthew was earlier than Mark and that Q is "an unnecessary and vicious hypothesis."[6] His book provoked other critics to defend the priority of Mark and the validity of Q, but the existence of this controversy in the second half of the twentieth century shows that internal evidence is not sufficient to establish the Two-Source Theory as more than conjecture.

The Gospel According to Mark

We need not defend the authenticity of the Gospel of St. Mark because it is not seriously contested. Except for the skeptical school which will not admit the validity of any testimony concerning the historical Jesus, even Rationalists and Modernists recognize in the second Gospel the recollections of St. Peter, recorded by St. Mark.

The character of Peter, like the character of Paul, is unmistakable. His unsophisticated honesty, his lack of tact, his capacity for wonder, astonishment, and awe at the deeds and words of Jesus reveal a personality hard to duplicate. Literary critics wonder at him as he wondered at Christ. Mark's Gospel has passed through the fiery furnace of literary criticism; and modern critics agree with Christian tradition that it is the preaching of Peter set down in writing for the early Christians of Rome. In Mark's Gospel we have a reliable historical record of the life of Jesus. Further investigation of internal evidence for the authenticity of the second Gospel is unnecessary; it is recognized as unique.

The Gospel According to St. Luke

After a careful examination of Luke's literary style, literary critics reached the conclusion that the third Gospel and Acts were written by the same person. Both books reveal literary genius. The parables of the Good Samaritan, the Prodigal Son and the Lost Sheep, and the two chapters on the infancy, with their canticles, must be included in any collection of the world's best literature. Henshaw speaks of Luke's art in writing in this manner:

> Of the three synoptic authors, Luke is the only one who can be called a stylist, having a command over language and a power of

using it which entitle him to be ranked among the great writers of the world. We have already shown his ability to vary his style at will, but no matter whether he employs the polished rhetorical Greek of contemporary literature, or the vernacular of the Mediterranean world, or imitates the archaic style of the Septuagint, he shows complete mastery of his art.[7]

Father Pope also pays tribute to St. Luke's writing:

> No one can read St. Luke's Gospel through without feeling that he is being afforded a literary treat. His narrative unfolds in a series of pen-pictures of undying beauty. . . . He is a consummate writer of history as well as an artistic delineator of character.[8]

Modern criticism has increased respect for Luke, not only as a writer but as a historian. The "blunders of Luke" in respect to chronology and to historical persons cited by early Rationalists turned out to be blunders of his critics. Luke has been vindicated by careful scholars as a painstaking, careful historian. He went about the composition of his Gospel after the manner of a scientific historian, using all available sources, and entering into details of chronology which allowed of verification. True, he relates miracles as facts—but, say Rationalists, in his time everyone believed in miracles.

"Luke, the companion of Paul," says St. Irenaeus, "set down in writing the Gospel preached by Paul."[9] Because of Luke's close association with Paul, it is easier to establish the date of his Gospel than that of any of the others. *Acts* ends abruptly with the statement: "And for two full years he (Paul) remained in his own hired lodging . . . preaching the kingdom of God" (Acts 28:31). This refers to the first imprisonment of Paul in Rome which lasted from 60 to 62 A.D. Since it says nothing about Paul's second imprisonment or his death, Acts must have been published before Paul died, which was in 64 or 67 A.D. At the beginning of Acts, Luke refers to "a former book in which I spoke of all things Jesus did and taught from the beginning until the day on which he was taken up" (Acts 1:1). This was of course his Gospel. Now, if Acts was published about 64 A.D., then Luke's Gospel must have been published earlier. This also helps to place the date of Mark's Gospel, because critics assure us it was one of the sources used by Luke.

The Synoptic Problem

How do we explain the "obvious similarities and subtle differences" of the Gospels of Matthew, Mark and Luke? Our answer comes first of all from the fact that all of them at times used phrases and sentences from the oral Gospel. They were all preachers of the kerygma or oral Gospel and they were also hearers of it. Sentences and descriptions of events became stereotyped. Moreover, as St. Augustine suggests, St. Mark may have been familiar with St. Matthew's Gospel and St. Luke with both Mark's and Matthew's.

On June 26, 1912, the Biblical Commission directed Catholic scholars to exercise reasonable restraint in regard to the Two-Source Theory. While recognizing the right of literary critics to discuss the origin of the similarities and differences of the synoptics, the Commission objected to the Two-Source Theory on grounds that it showed lack of respect for the authenticity and integrity of the Gospel of Matthew, the substantial identity of the Greek Gospel of Matthew with the primitive Matthew, and the order of time in which, according to Christian tradition, the Gospels were written.

Historical Christianity is founded on the testimony of

the Apostles. The certainty of Christian faith depends on reliable historical records of the preaching of the Apostles. No theory is acceptable if it substitutes for the testimony of Peter, Matthew, John and Paul anonymous writers, editors, and redactors. At no time in the history of the Church was anyone permitted to add to or to subtract from the original oral Gospel preached by the Apostles. Paul indicates this plainly in I Corinthians 15 and in Galatians 1:8. Scholars who do not believe in divine revelation of course do not understand the mental attitude of scholars who do. No anonymous redactor was ever allowed to change Christ's teaching. Glosses may have crept in; translators may have given interpretations; but deliberate alteration was never permitted. A divine message must be transmitted by inspired ambassadors. "Though we, or an angel from heaven, preach a gospel to you besides that which we have preached to you, let him be anathema" (Gal. 1:8). These words reflect the mind of the Apostles. For them, Jesus of Nazareth was the Son of God; the apostolic churches received the Gospels from inspired men; it is incredible to think they would permit uninspired men to amplify, excise, rearrange and develop that doctrine. The point of view of literary critics who see Christianity as no more than a natural religion will always be different from the point of view of those who see it as supernatural revelation.

The Gospel According to St. John

No book of the Bible has been attacked with such ferocity as has the fourth Gospel. To give even a brief account of its enemies and their arguments and methods would require a volume. "It is no wonder we reject this book," says Otto

Schmiedel, "for with it is connected the battle over the divinity of Christ."[10] Since Rationalists deny the existence of a supernatural God, they are logically bound to deny the invasion of the natural order by a divine person. They cannot allow that the fourth Gospel was written by John, son of Zebedee, intimate friend of Jesus, because if they did, there could be no room for doubt that Jesus claimed to be the eternal Son of God. Pantheists and materialists cannot endure the idea of the Incarnation. They hold that Jesus of Nazareth was no more divine than Confucius, Buddha, Zoroaster or Socrates. Hence they say that the narrations of John are not properly history but mystical reflections on the original Gospel; that the discources put into the mind of Christ are theological meditations devoid of historical truth; that the fourth Gospel exaggerates miracles to make Christ appear divine; that the doctrine of the Logos is the work of a philosopher who wrote at the close of the first century. More recently, some critics suggest that the fourth Gospel is the result of multiple authorship, prepared by anonymous authors who drew on "the faith of the community."

Various arguments are brought forth to discredit the historical value of John's gospel. Some critics claim John was put to death with his brother James in 44 A.D. Yet Paul found John alive, with Peter and James, when he visited Jerusalem years after that (Gal. 2:9).

Father Leopold Fonck, S.J., first Rector of the Pontifical Biblical Institute, summarizes the case concerning the fourth Gospel in this wise:

> If we except the heretics mentioned by Irenaeus (Adv. Haer. III, xi, 9) and Epiphanius (Haer. 51:4) the authenticity of the Fourth Gospel was scarcely ever seriously questioned until the end

of the eighteenth century. Evanson (1792) and Bretschneider (1820) were the first to run counter to tradition on this point, and, since David Friedrich Strauss (1834) adopted Bretschneider's views and the members of the Tubingen School, in the wake of Ferdinand Christian Baur, denied the authenticity of this Gospel, the majority of critics outside the Catholic Church have denied that the Fourth Gospel is authentic. On the admission of many critics, their chief reason lies in the fact that John has too clearly and emphatically made the true divinity of the Redeemer, in the strict metaphysical sense, the center of his narrative. However, even Harnack has had to admit that, though denying the authenticity of the Fourth Gospel, he has sought in vain for any satisfactory solution of the Johannine problem. "Again and again have I attempted to solve the problem with various possible theories, but they have led me into still greater difficulties, and even developed into contradictions." If, as is demanded by the character of the historical question, we first consult the historical testimony of the past, we discover the universally admitted fact that, from the eighteenth century back to at least the third, the Apostle John was accepted without question as the author of the Fourth Gospel.[11]

The early heretics referred to by Fonck are called Alogi by Epiphanius. Two groups should be distinguished: followers of Cerinthus who denied the divinity of Christ, and followers of Caius (200 A.D.) who opposed the Montanists. The Montanists imagined a new revelation through the Paraclete. Cerinthus rejected St. John's Gospel because it identifies Jesus with the Logos; Caius conceived a dislike for it because Montanists attempted to prove from it a reign of the Holy Ghost superior to the reign of Christ. Dionysius of Alexandria, in the middle of the third century, suggested that the Apocalypse was written by John the Elder (to whom Papias refers) because the Chiliasts of his time were attempting to prove from the Apocalypse that Christ would reign a thousand years on earth after his second coming. Obviously, such ideas have no historical validity; they died with the heresies that gave birth to them. They are mentioned to illustrate the fact that in the past as now, objections to the writings of John the Apostle sprang from dogmatic, not historical grounds.

Sublimity of the Fourth Gospel

Luke's Gospel has been called "the most beautiful book ever written," and John, because of his Gospel, has been styled "the Divine," and has been traditionally symbolized by the eagle because of the loftiness of his intellectual flight. Certainly no book in the Bible is more highly inspired. Christian commentators from Augustine to our own time have found John the best exponent of the inner life of the Three Divine Persons and the participation through grace in that divine life to which Christ invites his followers. Clement of Alexandria, at the beginning of the third century, characterized the fourth Gospel as "a spiritual Gospel" —not that the synoptics are not spiritual, but they deal with the earthly life of Jesus rather than with his divine life. In his prologue John affirms the identity of Jesus with the Word of God, and throughout remains loyal to this thought.

No one ever wrote like John the Evangelist because no one ever thought like him. From the prologue through the discourses to Nicodemus, the Samaritan woman, the Scribes, Pharisees, and priests, and in Christ's last discourse to his Apostles, John soars to heights inaccessible to the unaided human intellect. "Never did man speak as this man" (John 7:46).

Rationalists assume, with total lack of logic, that neither Jesus nor John was capable of such discourses as are recorded in the fourth Gospel. They prefer to bestow the honor upon an unknown philosopher who lived at the close of the fourth century, or to divide it among a number of unknown writers. One wonders why they presume these un-identified authors could do better than John the Apostle or Jesus himself!

In the Gospel of John, we reach the fullest revelation made by Jesus Christ. It could never have been introduced into the Christian faith had it not agreed with Paul and the synoptics. John the Apostle was not an obscure figure in the early Church. Any fraud which made use of his great name would have been detected and exposed. No anonymous philosopher provided Christianity with its deepest insight into the inner life of God, and man's participation in divine life through grace.

The literary unity of the fourth Gospel flows from the unity of its thought. Grandmaison quotes Weiss as saying that from beginning to end there is "the same type of piety, of religious experiences, and of style." And Grandmaison himself declares:

> We must boldly say that the unity of this Gospel is not contest-able, if we except a few passages. . . . If we cannot write like John, . . . it is because we cannot think and do not feel as John thought and felt. . . . John is a true mystic, and undoubtedly the greatest of mystics. He is this by reason of that realized unification, that consecration of the whole of his being to a single cause, to a single love, to a single faith and finally . . . to a Single Being. . . . That is why all the efforts at dissection and division are fated to remain useless exercises of critical virtuosity.[12]

Historical and Geographical Accuracy

As late as the time of Loisy (in the early part of this century), Rationalists maintained that the author of the fourth Gospel had no idea of writing history; that he was occupied wholly with a spiritual, mystical, allegorical interpretation of Christianity. This is definitely wrong. Everyone who has seriously studied the life of Christ knows there is more precise information in the Gospel of John than there is in the synoptics concerning the chronology of Christ's public life. John tells of journeys to Jerusalem and of teaching in Jerusalem and Judea not mentioned by the earlier writers. Were we dependent on the synoptics alone, we might think the ministry of Jesus lasted only one year and was confined to Galilee except for the final journey to Jerusalem preceding his death. John tells us that Jesus was baptized by the Baptist at Bethany beyond Jordan, and was introduced by him to his first disciples; that he preached in Jerusalem, Judea and Samaria before starting his ministry in Galilee, which did not begin until after the imprisonment of John the Baptist. Jesus' best biographers follow John's chronology. John does not contradict the synoptics; rather, he supplements them, keeping them from being misunderstood, just as the Acts supplement Luke's Gospel. We might think, for example, that Christ ascended into heaven on the evening of the day he rose from the dead; but Luke clarifies this when he tells in Acts that Jesus remained in earth forty days. John's Gospel is a precious historical supplement to the synoptics, and is so recognized by the best historians.

The author of the fourth Gospel was a Jew familiar with the prophecies, types, legal observances, feasts, and customs of the Jewish people. He gives details of topography which are verified by modern scientific research. He distinguishes between Bethany beyond the Jordan where John baptized, and Bethany near Jerusalem where Mary and Martha lived. John baptized in Aennon, near Salim, because "there was much water there." The pool of Bethsaida near the sheepgate, the pool of Siloe, the garden beyond the brook Cedron

—all these are the observations of an eye-witness. No one but an eye-witness would think of recording that Peter swam a hundred yards after he plunged into the lake one early morning; that Christ was broiling fish; that the number of fish taken in the net was one hundred and fifty-three. John knows the number of furlongs the disciples rowed the night Jesus fed the five thousand, how contrary was the wind, how easy the journey after Jesus joined them. "Now there took place at Jerusalem the feast of the Dedication, and it was winter. and Jesus was walking in the temple in Solomon's porch." John is exact. Even Renan was forced to admit that the author of the fourth Gospel could have had no motive other than to write the truth when he says the brethren of Jesus did not believe in him, but challenged him to go up to Jerusalem and manifest himself to the world (John 7:1).

Independence of the Author of the Fourth Gospel

One argument used against the authenticity of the fourth Gospel is based on supposed divergencies between it and the synoptics. Neither the authors of the synoptics nor St. John had in mind writing a complete history of Jesus. Indeed, St. John says this could not be done. The synoptics differ among themselves as well as from St. John. John wrote after the others, and supplied information they did not give, especially in respect to Christ's assertion of his divinity in Jerusalem in arguments with Pharisees and priests. John made it clear that Jesus claimed to be the eternal Son of God. He cited the miraculous cure of the man born blind and the discussion it provoked; also the amazing miracle of raising Lazarus from the dead. These served his purpose.

He was intimately acquainted with the words and deeds of Jesus of Nazareth. He writes that no one could do justice to Jesus Christ if he were to fill the earth with books about him.

On the matter of the date of the Last Supper, one cannot but contrast the restraint of Origen, John Chrysostom, Augustine and Jerome with the self-assurance of modern unbelieving critics who claim that there is a contradiction on this point between John and the synoptics. Lagrange discusses the question thoroughly, showing that there was a certain elasticity about the eve of the Pasch when the 15th of Nisan fell on Saturday. The eve was both Thursday after sundown and Friday. Jesus celebrated the Passover on Thursday night and was crucified on Friday. The 15th of Nisan that year fell on Saturday, and we are told the Jews wanted the bodies of the crucified removed before the Sabbath arrived with sundown. Just as there was elasticity about the third hour (Mark) and the sixth hour (Luke) when Jesus was nailed to the cross, so there was elasticity about the eve of the Pasch. That year, Thursday evening and all day Friday were the eve of the Pasch because the Pasch fell on the Sabbath. There is no contradiction here between John and the synoptics.[13]

The driving of buyers and sellers out of the temple creates no difficulty, either, if we understand that Christ cleansed the temple twice, once at the beginning, once at the end of his public ministry. Critics who insist that John and the synoptics refer to the same event are also sure Matthew and Mark are guilty of error in reporting two multiplications of loaves. They can give no sound reason why Jesus could not have cleansed the temple twice, or twice multiplied loaves and fishes.

Critics also insist there are contradictions between Jesus as he is described in the synoptics and as he is presented in the Fourth Gospel. But as Grandmaison points out,

> The objections made to the historical value of *John* on the score of alleged incompatibility with the Synoptists, which were long looked upon as formidable difficulties, have been little by little demolished by more objective study.[14]

Conclusion

Critics who deny that John the Apostle wrote the Fourth Gospel confess they do not know who did write it. Some of them postulate a mythical group of compilers. But it is inconceivable that the Church at Ephesus should have received the book as the work of John the Apostle if it was not; it is likewise incredible that Polycarp should have misinformed his disciple Irenaeus and the whole of the early Church on such a matter.

From the middle of the second century, the apostolic churches treasured the four Gospels as pillars of their faith. When Marcion came to Rome about 138 A.D., endeavoring to suppress the three other Gospels in favor of Luke's Gospel and Paul's Epistles, he was condemned as a heretic. The known temper of early Christians in respect to non-apostolic sources does not permit us to believe that the early churches would have accepted a book by an obscure or unknown author, or by a multiplicity of authors, making use of a distinguished name. Justin, Tatian, Polycarp, Marcion, Heracleon and Ptolemy all speak of four Gospels which were read in the churches of Rome, Antioch, Edessa, Ephesus and Alexandria. The fourth Gospel would never have been canonized unless its authority was certain.

Nor could it have been altered. Tischendorf writes:

There was no Gospel more difficult to tamper with than St. John's. His Gospel went forth from the midst of the circle of churches of Asia Minor, and spread thence to the whole world. Was this possible if the slightest taint of suspicion had lain upon it? Suppose, on the other hand, that it first appeared elsewhere, then we may be sure these Asiatic churches would have been the first to detect the fraud. It would have been impossible to palm off on them a spurious document as the writing of their former bishop.[15]

NOTES FOR CHAPTER XII

1. Adolf von Harnack, *The Essence of Christianity*, p. 32, quoted by Grandmaison, *Jesus Christ*, Vol. I, p. 118.
2. Grandmaison, *Jesus Christ*, Vol. I, p. 54.
3. Henshaw, *New Testament Literature*, pp. 111-13.
4. See "Matthew, Gospel of," in Smith's *Dictionary of the Bible*.
5. Grandmaison, *Jesus Christ*, Vol. I, p. 66.
6. Dom Cuthbert Butler, "Notes on the Synoptic Problem," *Journal of Theological Studies*, IV (1953).
7. Henshaw, *New Testament Literature*, p. 142.
8. Hugh Pope, O.P., *Aids to the Study of the Bible* (London: Burns, Oates, and Washbourne, 1923), Vol. II, p. 225.
9. Irenaeus, *Adv Haer.* III, 1.
10. Fillion, *Life of Christ*, Vol. I, p. 487.
11. Leopold Fonck, S.J., "John, Gospel of," *Catholic Encyclopedia*.
12. Grandmaison, *Jesus Christ*, Vol. I, pp. 155-59.
13. See M. J. Lagrange, *The Gospel of Jesus Christ*, (London: Burns, Oates and Washbourne, 1938), Vol. I, p. 174.
14. Grandmaison, *Jesus Christ*, Vol. I, p. 174.
15. Constantine von Tischendorf, *Codex Sinaiticus* (English translation, London: The Lutterworth Press, 1934).

CHAPTER XIII

Sources Other Than The Gospels

The four canonical Gospels are the main historical sources of the life of Christ; but they are not the only sources. The Epistles of Paul, for example, are the oldest of all apostolic writings and contain much information about the sayings and doings of the historical Jesus, although they assume knowledge of the oral Gospel. These letters are of the utmost importance in deciding the question between modern Rationalists and defenders of supernatural religion concerning the identity of the Jesus of history with the Jesus of Christian faith. "What think you of Christ, whose son is he?" is the fundamental issue. Is the historical Jesus of Nazareth the originator of the system of thought and worship which bears his name, or has his name been given to a system evolved out of philosophies and religions which preceded and followed his coming? Christianity produced a profound change in the history of the world. The opposition it aroused among Jews and Romans is a conspicuous historical fact attested by pagan and Jewish sources.

Saul of Tarsus, a bitter enemy of Christianity, an educated

272

Pharisee with great zeal for the law of Moses, was converted and became an ardent Apostle. He in his turn stirred up many enemies and defended the doctrine he preached with such passionate power that critics loyal to historical truth have found it impossible to deny the authenticity of his longer epistles. No critic of consequence has rejected Galatians, I and II Corinthians, Romans, I Thessalonians and Philippians. These epistles confirm in the most decisive way such important facts as the human birth of Jesus, his miracles, preaching, death, burial, resurrection from the dead, ascension into heaven, and the expectation by his followers of his second coming as judge of the living and the dead.

Luke, the physician of Antioch, is inseparably associated with Paul. Acts of the Apostles is a historical document whose authenticity is recognized by modern critics. Using their own test of internal evidence, literary critics have demonstrated that the same person wrote Acts and the Third Gospel. No one has ever been seriously proposed as author of these two books except Luke, disciple and companion of Paul. Our proof that the historical Jesus is the originator of the Christian religion is immeasurably strengthened by the fact that the authenticity of the Epistles of Paul and Acts is universally acknowledged.

Epistles of St. Paul

In his Epistles, Paul asserts that Jesus of Nazareth, the eternal Son of God, was born in time of a woman; that he is the Messias and Redeemer of the whole human family, which was set at enmity with God by the son of Adam. Paul stresses the role of Jesus as the scapegoat of the sinful family into which he was born. Through his passion and death, Jesus merited forgivenes for all men, and the privilege of becoming adopted sons of God, destined to see God face to face. Paul supposes that those for whom he writes know the facts about the life, death, and resurrection of Jesus as preached by himself and other Apostles. In I Corinthians he says explicitly that both he and they have taught that Christ died for our sins, was buried, and rose on the third day. Paul was as well qualified as his disciple Luke to write about the facts of Christ's life. Although he was not a disciple of Christ, he was a contemporary.

Galatians, I and II Corinthians, Romans, Philippians and I Thessalonians were written between 49 and 63 A.D., that is, at the time when many eye-witnesses both friendly and hostile to Jesus were alive. Paul was a forceful individual with a mind and style of his own. A Jew zealous for the traditions of his fathers (Gal. 1:14), a Pharisee, the son of Pharisees (Acts 23:6), brought up at "the feet of Gamaliel" (Acts 22:3), possibly acquainted with Christ according to the flesh (II Cor. 5:16), consenting to the stoning of Stephen, pursuing Christians to Damascus, and converted by immediate experience of the risen Christ, Paul's life was dramatically changed by the influence of Jesus. After his conversion, Paul passed three years in Arabia, returned to Damascus, and went from there to Jerusalem to see Peter, with whom he tarried for fifteen days (Gal. 1:18). Fourteen years later he revisited Jerusalem and submitted to Peter, James, and John the Gospel he had been preaching to the Gentiles. They found no fault with it, recommending only that he be mindful of the poor— "which," says Paul, "I was careful to do" (Gal. 2:10). Paul emphasized the efficacy of Christ's death for the salvation of men's souls. God spared not his only Son but delivered him up for all of us (Romans 5:9). Nowhere in the Bible are the doctrines of original sin, vicarious atonement and salvation through faith taught more explicitly than they are in the Pauline Epistles. Men became children of wrath, alienated from their original adoption as sons of God. Adam, progenitor of the family, by his son lost the friendship of God for all his children as well as for himself. Jesus, being both the Son of God and son of man, was qualified to mediate between his divine Father and his sinful brethren. All who are baptized in Christ die to membership in the family of the first Adam and become members of Jesus Christ (I Cor. 12:27). Through his grace men become his brethren, adopted sons of God, living supernaturally. Though we see now through the dark glass of faith, we shall ultimately see face to face (I Cor. 13:12).

The letters of Paul, written between 49 and 63 A.D., expound historical Christianity. There had been no time for its "evolution." As soon as Paul was converted, he began to preach that Jesus is the Christ, the Messias. His doctrine on the Eucharist, original sin, divine adoption through grace, the necessity of baptism, the Trinity, the divinity of Christ is identical with the doctrine of Peter and John. Paul preached not his own theories but the teachings of Jesus Christ. This doctrine must be accepted by faith. Faith is the substance of things to be hoped for, the evidence of things unknown by experience or reason. While emphasizing faith, Paul does not overlook charity, "the bond of perfection," and "the fulfilling of the law." "This is the will of God, your sanctification" (I Thess. 4:3). Men are sanctified through faith, hope and love, justice and generosity. From beginning to end Paul's Epistles teach supernatural religion emanating from the historical Jesus. The seeds of this doctrine are not found in Greek philosophy or in Oriental religions. Its very essence consists in acknowledging Jesus to be the natural Son of God, the image of the Father. Through the operation of the Holy Ghost men become sharers of divine life. This doctrine cannot be reduced to natural theology. Like the other Apostles, Paul says what he teaches has been divinely revealed.

Paul lays no claim to originality. He does not pretend to be a philosopher; he teaches a doctrine that came down from heaven. At sundry times and in divers manners God had spoken to men by prophets; but in Paul's own time God spoke by his Son (Hebrews 1:1). A herald of Jesus Christ, Paul is not ashamed of the Gospel (Rom. 1:16). He does not invent, he does not argue; he dogmatizes. What he received by faith he communicates to men who are willing to believe. "For I received of the Lord that which I also delivered unto you, that the Lord Jesus, the same night in which he was betrayed, took bread, and giving thanks, broke and said: Take ye and eat: This is my body which shall be delivered for you" (I Cor. 11:23). Paul believes that bread consecrated according to the rite prescribed becomes the body of the Lord. And likewise wine becomes, by consecration, the blood of Christ. As often as Christians do this, that is, change bread into the body of Christ and wine into his blood, they "show the death of the Lord until he come." Here is the concept of the Eucharist as the representation and renewal of the sacrifice by which men were redeemed. Wine changed into the blood of Christ after bread has been changed into his living body represents the way Jesus died. Thus in the first century, not more than twenty-five years after the crucifixion, Paul was teaching that the Eucharist represents the sacrifice of Calvary.

Critics talk glibly of the evolution of Christianity under the powerful genius of Paul; but the plain historical fact is that Paul's Epistles were written between 49 and 63 A.D. as a straightforward commentary on the oral Gospel preached by all the Apostles. There was no conflict between Peter and Paul as to the meaning of Christianity. Both of them preached what the historical Jesus had revealed.

Anyone who knows the history of philosophy is aware that systems of philosophy do not originate in the thinking of multitudes of men. The history of Greek philosophy is the history of the thinking of Parmenides, Heraclitus, Socrates, Plato and Aristotle. In the case of Christianity, Jesus is the author.

Jules Lebreton, an authority on Christian origins, shows in his great work on the *History of the Trinity* that those who seek the doctrine of the Trinity in Hellenic philosophy or Oriental religions deceive themselves.[1] This doctrine does not exist in pagan sources, nor in Jewish sources except in embryo.

Paul as Witness of the Resurrection

Paul rendered important service to the history of Christianity by the testimony he bore to the resurrection of Jesus, in the fifteenth chapter of his First Epistle to the Corinthians. No one has ever challenged the authenticity of this Epistle. Strauss was disconcerted to find that not more than twenty-five years after the death of Christ, Paul was preaching his resurrection and appealing to many living eyewitnesses of this amazing event. The resurrection of Jesus Christ after his death and burial is the cornerstone of Paul's preaching. It was the decisive fact in Paul's own conversion: it emboldened him to claim he was not inferior to the Twelve, who understood it was their mission to bear witness to the truth of the resurrection. Realizing that he could not qualify as an Apostle if he were not a witness to this crucial fact, Paul met every challenge hurled against him in this score. Although he had not been a follower of Jesus during his earthly life, Paul insisted vehemently that he had seen the Lord. He had direct personal experience of the glorified Christ on the road to Damascus. Paul's conversion cannot be explained by anything short of the objective reality of this encounter. His whole character was transformed by it. Paul was qualified to be an Apostle because he too had seen the Lord.

In the fifteenth chapter of First Corinthians, Paul argues that Christ's resurrection involves a promise of the resurrection of all men. Greeks found difficulty in believing in the resurrection of the body, although they freely admitted the immortality of the soul. Paul's experience at Athens illustrates this: they heard him respectfully until he began to talk of bodily resurrection, then they refused to listen. At Cornith, too, there was controversy. Paul assures the Corinthians that without this belief there is no Christianity. Christ died for our sins, was buried, and rose again on the third day. "He appeared to Cephas, and after that to the Eleven. Then he was seen by more than five hundred brethen at one time, many of whom are with us still, but some have fallen asleep. After that he was seen by James, then by all the Apostles. And last of all by me."

It is important to note how early Paul preached this doctrine. Karl Adam writes:

If, reckoning from the Epistle to the Galatians (2:1), we assign St. Paul's conversion to the year 33, the earliest testimony to the Easter events, namely Paul's, must date back to at least the year 36, at which time its immediate sponsors, the original witnesses, Peter and James, were at the peak of their powers and activity. A more primitive and reliable testimony is impossible. Paul's account of the first Easter derives, therefore, from what Peter and James had experienced and from whatever had been revealed to himself on the road to Damascus. 2

Paul clearly assumes that all Christians have been taught the bodily resurrection of Jesus as a fundamental fact. Why, then, should the Corinthians doubt their own bodily resurrection? "If there is no resurrection from the dead, neither has Christ risen; and if Christ has not risen, our preaching is vain and your faith is vain" (I. Cor. 15:13). All the Apostles are preaching that Christ rose from the dead. It is plain that Christians believed in the bodily resurrection of Christ from the very beginning; it was the cornerstone of their faith. The first Epistle of Paul to the Corinthians, by laying stress on the fact of the resurrection as well as on the real presence of Christ in the Eucharist, is historically precious.

Monists hold there is only one kind of substance. Paul was a dualist, maintaining that the man Jesus had a substantial soul and a body, separated at death and reunited at resurrection. He instructed his converts that they, too, consisted of a substantial soul and a body, which would be separated at death and reunited at the general resurrection.

Authenticity of Paul's Epistles

We need not enter into an elaborate argument to prove the authenticity of the Epistles of St. Paul, because all competent literary and historical critics acknowledge the authenticity of I Corinthians, as well as Romans, II Corinthians, Galatians, and the letters Paul wrote while in prison to the Philippians, Ephesians and Colossians. The only serious dispute has been over Hebrews and the Pastoral Epistles (I and II Timothy, and Titus). The authorship of the Epistle to the Hebrews was disputed even in early times, some attributing it to Barnabas, some to Clement of Rome. Critics object to the Pastoral Epistles on grounds that they indicate a hierarchical organization of the Church too well developed for the time of St. Paul. This is arbitrary, based on *a priori* reasoning. However, we are not now discussing the orgainzation of the Church. The undisputed Epistles, Thessalonians, Galatians, I and II Corinthians and Romans, suffice for our purpose Grandmaison confirms what we have said as to the acknowledged authenticity of these Epistles:

> The collection of St. Paul's epistles is composed of thirteen letters (fourteen if we include *Hebrews*) addressed by the apostle to various personages, churches, or groups of churches. Their general authenticity is so firmly established that it would be superfluous to go over the ground again; none but II *Thessalonians* and *Ephesians* have been the object of recent attacks which deserve a hearing. . . . The Pauline origin of the spiritual epistles of the time of the captivity (*Philippians, Colossians* and *Philemon*) is now admitted almost universally by even the liberal critics; while those who dispute the Pauline authenticity of the *Epistle to the Ephesians* and of the pastoral epistles (I and II Timothy and Titus), recognize that these epistles are almost as old as, and consequently that their value as testimony is almost equal to, that of St. Paul. As for the great epistles of the time of St. Paul's maturity (*Galatians, I and II Corinthians* and *Romans*), . . . there are no historical documents more solidly established, whether we consider the ancient attestations of which they are the subject, or whether we stop short of their contents. The doubts raised about them by a few *enfants perdus* of the Dutch School have not succeeded in impressing any scholar worthy of the name, and an exegete so radical as Julicher sees in these fantasies nothing but an inoffensive attack of critical delirium.[3]

Concerning the authenticity of I Corinthians, Henshaw writes:

> As regards the first Epistle, Clement of Rome, writing to the Corinthian Church (c. 96 A.D.) tells them "to take up the letters of the blessed Paul the Apostle in which he wrote to them about himself and Cephas and Apollos, because even then ye had made yourselves parties." It was known to Ignatius and to Polycarp, whose writings are so saturated with its thought and language, that he must have known it almost by heart. It is included in Marcion's Canon and the Muratorian Fragment, and is cited by Irenaeus, Tertullian, and Clement of Alexandria. . . . Both Epistles reveal such intimate knowledge of conditions as they existed in an early Christian community that it is inconceivable that they should be the product of invention.[4]

The Epistles of Paul are among the most valuable of all historical documents dealing with supernatural revelation. They have stubbornly resisted all efforts to disqualify them as authentic sources of life and teaching of Christ.

Acts of the Apostles

The Acts of Apostles is the primary source of the history of the organization and spread of the Church during the first thirty years of its existence. It is really a continuation of the third Gospel, by the same author and for the same Theophilus for whom the third Gospel was written. After relating more fully than the Gospel the circumstances of the Ascension, the author tells how the Apostles, with the mother of Jesus, remained in Jerusalem in prayer until the coming of the Holy Ghost, who endowed them with charismatic gifts to enable them to carry out their sublime mission. After Peter's first sermon, three thousand were converted. A few days later Peter and John cured a well-known beggar who had been lame for all his forty years. For this they

were arrested and threatened by the Sanhedrin. Other per-
secutions followed; Stephen was stoned to death; somewhat
later James, the brother of John the Apostle, was beheaded.
In the meantime Peter visited Christians along the coast at
Joppa, Caesarea, and other towns, and performed miracles,
one of them raising a widow named Tabitha to life. Upon
instruction from heaven, he admitted Cornelius, a Gentile,
to baptism. Philip preached the Gospel in Samaria, and
baptized an important Jewish official of the kingdom of the
Ethiopians. Peter was cast into prison in the same persecution that made a martyr of James; but he escaped through
the help of an angel and left Jerusalem. Tradition says that
he moved to Antioch and afterwards to Rome.

Chapters thirteen to twenty-eight describe three missionary journeys of St. Paul, his arrest in Jerusalem and
his imprisonments in Caesarea and Rome. The author
writes as an eye-witness of some of these events. Barnabas,
Silas, Mark and Timothy appear in the history, but Paul
is the principal actor. Acts has been appropriately called
"the Gospel of the Holy Ghost" because of the all-pervading
influence throughout of the Spirit of Jesus.

Purpose

The purpose of the writer was to give Gentile converts
a historical account of the origin of the Church. In his
Gospel Luke instructs Theophilus in regard to Christ's life
and teaching; in Acts he continues this history by relating
how Christ's promise to send the Holy Ghost to his Apostles
was fulfilled; and how they became his witnesses "in Jerusalem, and in all Judea and Samaria and even to the utter-
most parts of the earth" (Acts 1:8). Luke does not aim at

describing the activity of all the Apostles, but rather at explaining the origin of the Christian Church and its extension to the Gentiles. The first twelve chapters deal mainly with Peter's preaching in Jerusalem and the spread of the Church throughout Judea and Samaria as far as Antioch; the last sixteen chapters treat principally of Paul's missionary journeys to Asia Minor and Greece. Whether Peter preaches or whether it is Paul or Stephen or Philip, the same Gospel is everywhere announced. They all speak under the influence of the Holy Ghost, and their doctrine represents itself solely and simply as the carrying out of the commission of Christ to preach his doctrine of salvation to all nations.

Authenticity

From the second to the nineteenth century no one disputed the tradition that Luke, physician of Antioch, disciple and companion of Paul, was the author of Acts of the Apostles as well as of the third Gospel. The Canon of Muratori and St. Irenaeus, in the second half of the second century, mention Luke by name as the author, and earlier writers show by quotations that they were familiar with both books. The heretic Marcion (138 A.D.) was partial to the writings of Luke and Paul.[5] Tertullian, Clement of Alexandria and Origen in the third century, and Jerome in the fourth, testify that Luke wrote two discourses to Theophilus; and this tradition is confirmed by the earliest prologues in manuscirpts of the third Gospel and Acts. Baur, with his Tubingen school, disputed this tradition on philosophical rather than historical grounds.

The Tubingen School, supported by the skeptical Dutch

School, attempted to prove that Acts was not written until late in the second century; but the verdict of history was sustained in a brilliant way by the Liberal School, with Harnack as its spokesman. All Higher Critics accepted the principle of Hobbes and Spinoza that authenticity of the books of the Bible should be determined by internal evidence. Now it so happens that Luke, although he was not an immediate disciple of Christ, was a disciple of Paul, and an intimate friend and a member of his missionary group. Converted about fifteen years after the death of Christ, he accompanied Paul on his second and third missionary journeys and remained with him during the years he spent in prison in Caesarea and in Rome. In Acts 16, 20, 21, 27 and 28, the author writes in the third person plural: that is, as an eye-witness. These "we sections" furnished critics with a rare opportunity to test the unity of authorship of Acts according to internal evidence, to compare the literary style of these sections with the style of the rest of Acts and of the third Gospel.

Sir John Hawkins, in his *Horae Synopticae* (1899), made a careful study of the vocabulary, syntax and style of the "we sections," comparing them with the rest of Acts and with the third Gospel. This was done even more thoroughly by Harnack, whose book, *Luke the Physician,* was published in Germany in 1906. After a minute examination, Harnack found that certain terms occur frequently in all parts of Acts and the third Gospel which are not found in Matthew, Mark, or other books of the New Testament. For example: "The temporal ως is never found in Matthew and Mark, but it occurs forty-eight times in Luke (Gospel and Acts), and that in all parts of the work."[6] Harnack's defense of the thesis that Acts and the third

Gospel were written by one person was a blow to critics who were reluctant to admit that Acts is a primary historical source.

The work of Hawkins and Harnack was continued by V. H. Stanton of Cambridge.[7] In 1923, Stanton replied to Loisy, who had attempted to revive the discredited hypothesis that Acts was not a primary source but a second century compilation. The sober literary judgment of Hawkins, Harnack and Stanton was confirmed by the grammarian J. H. Moulton[8] and by E. Jacquier[9] in 1926. Thus skeptics were signally defeated in their attempt to undermine the historical reliability of these important documents. Harnack deserves respect for honesty as well as for indefatigable labor. As a philosopher, he rejected the supernatural; but he had an intellect that sought truth, and German's capacity for research. His books appeared in the very stronghold of Higher Criticism and did much to silence the Tubingen and Dutch Schools, as well as the followers of Renan in France, and skeptics in England and America.

Sir William Ramsay, by explorations in Asia Minor, also confirmed the reliability of Luke. Henshaw says:

> The famous English archaeologists, Sir William Ramsay, after his excavations in Asia Minor, turned to the study of "Acts" to see what light it threw on the state of that district. Beginning with the assumption that he book was a second-century production, he was gradually forced to the conclusion that it must have been written in the first century, with admirable knowledge. In fact, its contemporary allusions, where first and second centuries differ, are always to the state of things existing in the first century, never those existing in the second.[10]

A sample of this vindication of Luke was the finding of an inscription at Delphi which states that Gallio (the brother of Seneca) was pro-consul of Achaia under Claudius (Emperor 41-54 A.D.). Acts 18:12 says "Gallio was pro-consul of Achaia." From another quarter, searching examination of the Third Gospel and Acts has convinced many that the writer was a physician. Experts say the writer of Acts and the third Gospel used medical terms found in Galen and other medical authorities of that period. For instance, the beggar at the Beautiful Gate was lame from his mother's womb and past forty years of age when cured. The cripple restored at Lystra "had been lame from his very birth and had never been able to walk." Such observations were more apt to be made by a practiced judge of cripples and their chances of being cured.

The outcome of all this scholarly work has been that, with the exception of confirmed skeptics, modern critics recognize that Acts was written by the same man who wrote the third Gospel; that he was a disciple and companion of St. Paul; that he was, to judge from all the evidence, Luke the physician of Antioch. They acknowledge that both books were written, as their preludes indicate, for Theophilus and other cultured Gentiles, to furnish them with a historical background for their faith; that Acts was written after the third Gospel; that it was probably written not later than 65 A.D. (this from the fact that it terminates abruptly after relating Paul's first imprisonment in Rome, 61-63 A.D.). Luke was with Paul during his imprisonments in both Caesarea and Rome. Paul wrote some of his Epistles during this time; no doubt Luke found this enforced leisure conducive to literary activity.

Historical Value

Acts of the Apostles is our main source of information concerning the establishment of the Church of Christ and its growth in the first thirty years of its history; of its spread into Judea, Samaria, Syria, Asia Minor, Greece and Rome. It is therefore of priceless value. It has passed through the fiery furnace of modern criticism, and its authority is recognized. St. Luke is universally esteemed to be a careful, honest, accurate historian. In Acts, he wrote to some extent as an eye witness. For Paul's life, he had Paul's own testimony. During his stay in Rome, he was associated with Mark, from whom he might well have learned the details of Peter's release from prison. In Caesarea he had the opportunity to visit the home of Philip, the deacon. In Jerusalem he met James. From the prologue to his Gospel we learn that he was diligent wherever he went to interview eye witnesses. Acts was written during the lifetime of some of the Apostles. No reasonable man can ask for a better historical source. It testifies clearly that during the thirty years after the resurrection, Christ's Apostles were preaching the doctrines he revealed to them.

The Epistles of Paul, the third Gospel, and Acts of the Apostles are closely related. They carry the history of Christ beyond his death, resurrection and ascension. Paul and Luke are witnesses to the triumphal march of supernatural religion to Asia Minor, Greece and Rome.

The writings of Paul and Luke appeal to the learned. Each writer has an unmistakable style; both of them are cosmopolitan, preaching God's love for all men and the universality of the call to salvation. The vivid description of the storm and shipwreck at the end of Acts belongs to the great literature of the world.

Roman Historians

Suetonius, Tacitus, and Pliny testify that Christians derived their doctrine from Christ or Chrestus, and that in the first century this new religion produced disturbances in the Roman Empire. Suetonius, private secretary to Trajan (98-117 A.D.) and Hadrian (117-138 A.D.) wrote the lives of the emperors from Augustus to Domitian. He says Claudius (41-54) "expelled from Rome the Jews who, at the instigation of Chrestus, stirred up frequent disturbances."[11] Aquila and Priscilla, friends of St. Paul, were obliged to leave Rome (Acts 18:2). Suetonius relates also that Nero persecuted Christians because they introduced "a new and wicked superstition."[12]

Tacitus (55-120 A.D.), a very exact historian, says an immense number (ingens multitudo) of Christians were put to death by Nero (the persecution began in 64 A.D.). He writes:

> Chrestus, the founder of that name, was put to death as a criminal by Pontius Pilate, procurator of Judea, in the reign of Tiberius; but the pernicious superstition, repressed for a time, broke out again, not only throughout Judea, where the mischief originated, but in Rome itself whither everything horrible and disgraceful from all quarters comes to get disciples.[13]

Tacitus realized that Nero persecuted Christians to divert suspicion from himself; but he manifests no sympathy for them. In the reign of Claudius, Christians were considered Jewish dissenters; at the time of Nero they were looked on as forming an international organization. Both Suetonius and Tacitus name Chrestus (Christ) as the founder of the new religion, the latter noting that he had been put to death by Pilate. These Roman historians were not interested in Jesus personally, but regarded him as a source of political and social troubles. From their testimony it is clear that in the first century Christianity had penetrated Rome and was causing a ferment there.

Trajan, a high-minded emperor, appointed Pliny the Younger governor of Bithynia in 111 A.D. Pliny found so many Christians in his province, and their enemies so active in accusing them, that after an investigation of their beliefs and practices he wrote Trajan about the problem. Pliny's letter and Trajan's reply are precious historical documents. About seventy-five years after the death of Christ, his doctrine had so many adherents in Bithynia that the temples of the gods were deserted and services could hardly be conducted. So many of Pliny's subjects were accused of the crime of being Christians that he demurred about proceeding against them. Pliny was governor of Bithynia from 111 to 113 A.D. His letter may be summarized as follows: Bithynia is full of Christians; Pliny is receiving long lists of names, and is expected to proceed against persons accused anonymously without giving them a chance to know who are their accusers. Some of the accused abjured Christ twenty years ago and are now willing to curse him and to offer incense to the gods. But Pliny's investigation has not found the Christians guilty of the crimes alleged against them. All he can discover is that they congregate early in the morning on fixed days, sing hymns to Christ as to God, and in the evening come together to eat a meal in common. They take an oath not to commit certain crimes. Pliny can find nothing reprehensible except their superstition, which is excessive and therefore worthy of blame.[14]

In his reply, Trajan told Pliny: (1) He should not take the initiative against Christians; he should not seek them out. (2) Those who curse Christ, offer incense to the gods or otherwise show they are no longer Christians should be dismissed. (3) Those who are fairly accused and persist in their superstition should be punished. (4) Anonymous accusers should not be heeded, because this is "a system barbarous and out of date."[15]

It is clear that neither Pliny nor Trajan looked on Christianity as an evolution of pagan mystery-religions or as a dissident form of Judaism. The Romans tolerated all gods and all regilions, exempting Jews from the obligation of offering sacrifice to the emperor. In Christianity, they realized they were facing something different. It was mysterious; it was incomprehensible; consequently pagans were disposed to believe the worst that was said of it. Christians had a spiritual life that the Romans suspected because they could not understand it.

Jewish Historians

Flavius Josephus (37-100 A.D.) is a famous Jewish secular historian. His *Jewish Antiquities* is a comprehensive history of the Jews from creation down to 66 A.D. This work was written for the Romans after he was captured by them. One of the most learned men of his time, master of a good literary style, Josephus was highly regarded as a historian by such authorities as Eusebius and St. Jerome. In 66 A.D., when war broke out between Jews and Romans, Josephus was placed in command of Jewish forces in Galilee, where he was defeated and taken prisoner. Vespasian treated him with courtesy, used him as a mediator, and after the war invited him to Rome, where he afterward resided. He appears to have been still active in the reign of Trajan, who became emperor in 97 A.D. He refers to John the Baptist, to James, first bishop of Jerusalem, and to Jesus himself.

The following passage occurs in all extant manuscripts

of *Jewish Antiquities*, and has been commented on by Christian writers since Eusebius:

> Now there was about this time Jesus, a wise man, if it be lawful to call him a man, for he was a doer of wonderful works—a teacher of such men as receive truth with pleasure. He drew over to him many of the Jews and many of the Gentiles. He was the Christ; and when Pilate, at the suggestion of the principal men among us, had condemned him to the cross, those who loved him at the first did not forsake him, for he appeared to them alive again on the third day, as the divine prophets had foretold these and ten thousand other wonderful things concerning him; and the tribe of Christians, so named from him, is not extinct at this day.[16]

This passage has been the subject of controversy. Many critics believe it to be an interpolation, an addition to the original which was silent about Christ. Some Catholic critics are of this opinion. On the other hand, there are eminent non-Catholic historians such as Burkitt of Cambridge, Harnack, Barnes, and others who look on the passage as authentic. Josephus was living in Rome, writing for Gentiles rather than for Jews, and not hostile to Christianity. Those who argue against the authenticity of the passage say that if it were genuine, Justin, Origen and Tertullian would have quoted it. At any rate, Eusebius, Father of Church history, does quote it.

There are actually three opinions: (1) that the whole passage is genuine, (2) that it is partially interpolated, and (3) that the whole of it is an interpolation. We are not qualified to enter into this dispute. Grandmaison gives references to authorities.[17]

The authenticity of the passages in *Antiquities* which refer to John the Baptist and to James "the brother of Jesus" is unquestioned. Both have significance for the early history of Christianity, and therefore deserve attention. The passage concerning John the Baptist says he was

> . . . a good man whom Herod put to death. John urged the Jews
> to practice justice between themselves and piety towards God,
> and then to be baptized. . . . And since no man ran to him, being
> marvelously exalted by his discourses, Herod, fearing the authority
> of such a man might lead some into rebellion—for they seemed
> to do everything according to his counsel—judged it much better
> to crush him before there should be an outbreak, rather than to
> have to bewail a revolution which would place himself in danger.
> On account of Herod's disfavor, John was sent in chains to the
> fortress of Machaerus and there was slain.[18]

The *Jewish Encyclopedia* says John the Baptist was "an Essene saint and preacher; flourished between 20 and 30 C.E.; forerunner of Jesus of Nazareth, and originator of the Christian movement."[19] Jews did not deny the preaching and baptizing of John, his close relationship to Jesus of Nazareth, or the influence he exerted over his Jewish contemporaries. John the Baptist is a historical figure who helps define the historical figure of Jesus.

Josephus also tells how Annas, the high priest, took advantage of the death of Festus to kill James, Bishop of Jerusalem. Festus, Roman procurator of Judea, died in 61 A.D. St. John was tried before Festus in Caesarea about 58 A.D. Albinus, who succeeded Festus, had not yet arrived when Annas (or Hanan the Young) took the bold step of putting to death the Bishop of Jerusalem. Josephus writes:

> Albinus being still on his journey, Annas called together the
> Sanhedrin in judicial session and brought before it the brother
> of Jesus surnamed the Christ (James was his name) with some
> others. He accused them of having broken the Law and handed
> them over to be stoned. Now this greatly shocked the more mod-
> erate men of the town . . . and they secretly sent (agents) to the
> king (Herod Agrippa II), praying him to order Annas to abstain
> from such deeds for the future.[20]

This is important. James "the brother of Jesus surnamed the Christ" was put to death in Jerusalem shortly after the death of Festus, procurator of Palestine. Josephus' record of the deaths of John the Baptist (about 27 A.D.) and James (about 61 A.D.) goes back to the age of the Apostles. Josephus lived at Rome, but is silent about Nero's persecution of the Christians. No doubt he thought it would be imprudent to take sides. The less he said about Christians at that time the better.

In the Talmud and Midrash the general tendency is to belittle the person of Jesus. These Jewish sources relate that Jesus was an illegitimate child; that his mother fled to Egypt to escape being stoned to death; that in Egypt the boy kept company with magicians and became expert in magical arts; that after his return to Palestine he proved a bad influence and was excommunicated as an apostate and seducer. The story was taken from Celsus that his father was not a Jew but a Roman soldier named Panthera or Pandera. Jewish sources often applied opprobrious names to Jesus. It is worthy of note, however, that they never denied his existence.[21]

Modern Jewish opinion—at least among some groups of Jews—is more liberal, and concedes Jesus the position of a good man and a good moral teacher. Among others, the bitterness unfortunately continues.

NOTES FOR CHAPTER XIII

1. Jules Lebreton, *The History of the Dogma of the Trinity* (English translation, New York: Benziger Brothers, 1939), Vol. I.
2. Karl Adam, *The Son of God* (New York: Sheed and Ward, 1934), p. 214. (A new edition was published by Doubleday in 1960).
3. Grandmaison, *Jesus Christ*, Vol. I, r. 21.
4. Henshaw, *New Testament Literature*, p. 248.
5. Grandmaison, *Jesus Christ*, Vol. I, p. 79.
6. Adolf von Harnack, *Luke the Physician*, English translation (? ? ? ?) also *New Testament Studies*, 3 vols. (London: 1907-1912).
7. V. H. Stanton, *The Gospels as Historical Documents* (New York: Macmillan Company, 1920), Vol. II.
8. See Grandmaison, *Jesus Christ*, Vol. I, p. 79.
9. See Steinmueller, *A Companion to Scripture Studies*, Vol. III, p. 216.
10. Henshaw, *New Testament Literature*, p. 185.
11. *Vita Claudii*, XXV.

12. *Vita Neronis,* XV.
13. *Annals,* III, B, XV, 44.
14. *Epistles,* Book X, 97-98.
15. Trajan's reply is preserved in the collection of Pliny's Letters.
16. *Jewish Antiquities,* XVIII, 3, 3.
17. Grandmaison, *Jesus Christ,* Vol. I, p. 190.
18. *Antiquities,* XVIII, 5, 2.
19. "John the Baptist." *Jewish Encyclopedia,* Vol. VII.
20. *Antiquities,* XX, 9, 1.
21. See "Jesus of Nazareth," *Jewish Encyclopedia,* Volume VII; also Robert T. Herford, *Christianity in the Talmud and Midrash* (New York: Bloch Publishing Company), 1904.

CHAPTER XIV

Integrity of The Gospels

The history of Lower Criticism reflects more credit on the ability and honesty of modern scholars than does the history of Higher Criticism. Lower Criticism means textual criticism; it has for its aim to restore, so far as possible, the original text of the Bible. There are no autograph copies of any of the ancient books. Until the fourth century Greeks and Latins wrote on papyrus, a material that went to pieces readily. In the fourth century parchment or vellum began to be used. Parchment or vellum is sheepskin, calfskin, goatskin, lambskin or kidskin, prepared for writing upon. These skins proved very durable; indeed two copies of the Bible written on parchment in the fourth century have survived until the present time and are among the most precious possessions of the scholarly world. Fragments of manuscripts on papyrus have been discovered, but only fragments. Curiously enough, from the point of view of the controversy over the Fourth Gospel, the oldest manuscript of any book of the Bible is Chester Beatty Papyrus 52 which contains verses 31, 32, 33 and 37 of the eighteenth chapter of St. John's Gospel, written in the second century.[1]

We will concern ourselves in this chapter with the text of the Gospels which has been preserved in a great variety of Greek manuscripts. Textual critics examine, collate, compare and prefer readings with a view to approaching the pure text of the originals. Whereas Higher Criticism undertook, on the basis of internal evidence, to determine authorship, date and evolution of the Gospels, textual critics attempted to discover by positive study of the manuscripts how they are related and which is the most primitive. The choice narrows down rapidly, because manuscripts can be classified into families; and sometimes one manuscript can be identified as the head of a whole family.

In dealing with Higher Criticism, we find ourselves in the realm of conjecture. Textual critics, on the contrary, are objective scholars. Manuscripts preserved in the Vatican, Cambridge University, the British Museum, the Louvre, St. Catherine's Monastery on Mount Sinai, Florence, Fulda, Ann Arbor and many other places have been examined with painstaking care by these devoted men. Their inspiration comes from their desire, as enlightened Christians, to possess the best possible text of the greatest of all books.

Higher Critics assumed that the doctrine we find in the Gospels underwent substantial changes until the time the canon was defined in the fourth century, and they drew the conclusion that there remains in our Gospels only faint and uncertain traces of the teaching of the historical Christ. Textual critics find this belief to be without support. No one could have deliberately introduced substantial changes into manuscripts so widely diffused among various nations as the Gospels have been since the close of the second century.

Tatian, the Syrian, harmonized the Gospels in the second century, and in his form they were used by the Church of Edessa for more than a century until the bishops ordered a translation of the separate Gospels. This harmony tended to obscure the text of the separate Gospels, but its very existence in Syria made it impossible to introduce substantial changes elsewhere. Tatian's harmony provided Aramaic-speaking people with a life of Christ that was easy to understand because it was free from divergencies. Substantial errors would not have been tolerated in a popular text; changes would have produced confusion, controversy and strife.

The tendency to popularize the text which existed in Syria and Carthage was not shared by scholars in Alexandria and Antioch. Antioch polished its text; Alexandria allowed the koine Greek to remain. While it is true that every translation involves a certain amount of interpretation, such interpretations do not necessarily affect the substance of what is transcribed. One translator will aim at literal exposition of meaning; another will sacrifice a shade of meaning to turn a fine phrase; another will try to make difficult passages understandable to the common people; still another will wish to soften statements that might seem likely to scandalize pious readers. Such tendencies as these, in addition to mistakes made by drowsy or inattentive copyists, are found in the manuscripts. But substantial changes, never. When in 138 A.D. Marcion attempted to introduce a substantial change he was denounced as a heretic and excluded from communion with orthodox Christians. The widely scattered Christian communities were linguistically and culturally so distinct that the idea of their all consenting to the same changes is fantastic. "Though we or an angel from heaven preach a gospel to you other than that we have preached to you, let him be anathema" (Gal. 1:8).

In copies of the Gospels used in the liturgy, passages like the one about the woman taken in adultery (John 8) or the one which states the relatives of Jesus thought he was mad (Mark 3:21) were sometimes omitted. A bishop might consider such passages undesirable for public reading. No instance can be discovered, however, where deliberate changes were made to develop the doctrine of Christ. The desire to preserve the pure text of the Gospels was as real for Irenaeus, Tertullian, Origen, John Chrysostom, Augustine and Jerome as it is for modern textual critics.

Variant Readings

Printing was not invented until the fifteenth century. Even now, with perfected printing processes and expert proofreaders, it is difficult to publish a book without typographical errors. Inevitably, copyists multiplied errors as they multiplied manuscripts which, for the most part, were not intended to serve scholars but to be read to the people. Copyists made mistakes; the more copyists the more mistakes. Existing manuscripts reveal a number of mistakes fit to terrify the uninitiated. John L. Stoddard says that his faith and the faith of his fellow students in a Protestant theological seminary was shaken when they heard there were 125,000 mistakes in the New Testament.[2] Steinmuller says that in existing Greek manuscripts of the New Testament, there are, 200,000 variants distributed among 4288 manuscripts.[3] But this awful number of variants shrinks to a small fraction if you understand the meaning of the following statistics:

Papyri 97
Uncials 210
Minuscules 2401
Lectionaries 1610

Lectionaries contain Epistles and Gospels read to congregations. Papyri are fragmentary. Minuscules, written in small, cursive script, do not antedate the ninth century. About fifty of these contain the whole New Testament. Uncials are the really important manuscripts for textual criticism. They are also called *majuscules* because they are written in large letters, not joined, each letter standing apart as in print, with no punctuation and no intervals between words.

Among uncials, *Vaticanus,* or B, is outstanding; it belongs to the early fourth century and contains the whole New Testament up to the ninth chapter of the Epistle to the Hebrews. It is supported by *Sinaiticus,* or S, also of the fourth century, which contains all of the New Testament. This manuscript was discovered by Tischendorf, in 1859, in the monastery of St. Catherine on Mount Sinai. *Vaticanus* and *Sinaiticus* stand at the head of the Eastern, Egyptian, or Alexandrian family of manuscripts, and are rated as the most reliable of all manuscripts of the New Testament. They have mightily influenced the history of modern textual criticism. *Codex Bezae,* D, of the fifth or sixth century, is a very important witness to the Western family of manuscripts. It is bilingual, containing the text of the Gospels in Greek and Latin. *Codex Alexandrinus,* A, of the fifth century, is another valuable uncial because of its antiquity, its completeness, and the fact that it is the ancestor of the *textus receptus,* long favored by Protestants. It is preserved in the British Museum. The *Codex Bezae* is in Cambridge;

Vaticanus in the library of the Vatican. *Sinaiticus* was moved from Mount Sinai to St. Petersburg and thence to the British Museum.

Next to these Greek uncials, the most valuable witnesses to the original text of the Gospels are Latin translations. Since the Gospels were translated into Latin in the second century, there are Latin manuscripts which may represent Greek texts older than some existing Greek uncials. St. Jerome, at the end of the fourth century, using both Latin and Greek manuscripts, edited a critical text which gradually superseded the Old Latin. *Codex Amiatinus* is the most famous manuscript of St. Jerome's text; it is said to be one of the finest and best preserved books in the world. It is kept at Florence. Syriac and Coptic translations of great antiquity also possess authority as witnesses to the text used in the early Church. Supplementing these texts are numerous quotations in the writings of early Fathers. Irenaeus is a witness to the state of the text at the close of the second century; Origen to the text used in Egypt in the third century. According to Tischendorf, Irenaeus quotes from the Gospels about four hundred passages, and the text he used resembles the Old Latin, the *Codex Bezae*. Origen's text appears to have been like *Vaticanus*.

The Problem of Textual Criticism

When we read that there are 200,000 variant readings distributed among the 4288 manuscripts of the Greek New Testament, we may feel that this is an astonishing number. It is less significant, however, when we recall that there are only 210 uncials. The 2401 minuscules (cursives) are no earlier than the ninth century. They multiply variant readings without causing added confusion with regard to the original text. The more manuscripts discovered the more errors, but most of them are such things as omissions of lines, changes in spelling, and transposition of words, due to the carelessness of copyists. They do not affect the meaning of the text. Copyists do not make the same mistakes, and their errors may be corrected by comparing manuscripts. Copies of copies may be ignored. Certain manuscripts known to be heads of whole families of manuscripts merit special attention.

In the work of copyists, ancient and modern, it frequently happens that if two lines begin or end with the same word or phrase, one is likely to be left out. Words that are misspelled, synonyms that are substituted, grammatical constructions that are changed in one family will not be similarly altered in other independent families. Such errors as these are inconsequential. Textual critics eliminate most of them when they collate and compare manuscripts after discovering which uncial stands at the head of the family.

The most serious problem arises from the early tendency to harmonize and popularize the Gospels. Tatian did this as far back as 172 A.D., and his *Diatessaron* was used in and around Edessa until the time of St. Ephraem (d. 373), who wrote a commentary on it. *Codex Bezae,* D, is of extreme interest to critics because it is a Greek codex of the fifth century whose text corresponds to the Old Latin which in turn agrees with quotations of St. Irenaeus. Theodore Beza, friend and successor of Calvin, gave this bilingual uncial of the fifth or sixth century to the University of Cambridge. In the letter accompanying the gift he said it had been obtained from the monastery of St. Irenaeus in Lyons in 1562. The Huguenots were at that time waging war against

Catholics. A text similar to *Codex Bezae* was used by St. Cyprian in Africa and by Latin writers generally until the time of St. Jerome. Textual critics say that it has some tendency to harmonize and popularize the Gospels. It was intended as a text for the people, to read or hear read, and to be easily understood. Explanations and marginal glosses may have crept into it.

The existence of slight changes or marginal glosses is explained by Lagrange as follows:

> It wishes to be understood by everybody, and this entails the addition either of explanatory glosses, or, on the contrary, the suppression of difficult terms, or at least some modifications in them. Hence a striking expression, too pregnant with meaning to be universally understood, is replaced by a commonplace phrase. Simple souls were apt to be amazed that Jesus' own people thought that he was beside himself (Mark 3:21), and therefore Type D introduces the scribes by way of substitution. . . . This does not mean that we should impute to the reviser the pretention of correcting the Holy Spirit. He perhaps considered he was doing a useful and pious work.[4]

Alexandrian Type B does not harmonize the Gospels and does not gloss the text. *Vaticanus* is the oldest extant manuscript of this type, containing the complete text of the Bible except the first chapters of Genesis and the end of the New Testament from Hebrews 9:15. Westcott and Hort named it the *Neutral Text* because they considered it free from popularizing and harmonizing tendencies. The greatest modern textual critics: Tischendorf, Westcott, Hort, Nestle and Merk have used B, *Vaticanus,* supplemented by S, *Sinaiticus,* as the basis for their critical editions. They excluded readings peculiar to Type D and also to the Antiochene, Byzantine, Lucian revision known as *textus receptus.* This does not mean that B is always followed; but it has been preferred and has served as the basic text for the best modern critical editions of the New Testament. If it has a fault it is that it is too brief. It omits the account of the adulteress (John 8:1), the end of Mark (16:9), the bloody sweat (Luke 22:43), and the prayer of Christ on the cross for his enemies (Luke 23:24).

History of Textual Criticism

St. Paul tells the Christians of Corinth that among them: "There are not many wise according to the flesh, not many mighty, not many noble" (I Cor. 1:26). This gives us a hint why a harmonized text appeared so early in Syria and a popular text in Latin was used in Carthage and Lyons toward the end of the second century. Tatian's *Diatessaron* was really a brief life of Christ rather than a critical text of the Gospels. The Western text represented by *Codex Bezae*, D, was glossed for popular understanding. The churches of Edessa, Carthage and Lyons were composed not of intellectuals but of ordinary people. Rome was bilingual for the first two centuries of the Christian era and there the Gospels were read in Greek because the liturgy was carried out in Greek. The first Latin translations were used in Africa, that is, in and around Carthage where Latin alone was understood. Tertullian seems to have known the Latin translation and St. Cyprian, Bishop of Carthage from 248 until his martyrdom in 258 A.D., certainly used it. This text was a popular translation; it contained no substantial errors, no deliberate falsifications or developments of doctrine but took some liberties in the way of eliminating difficulties by harmonizing and glossing. For example, the Lord's prayer in Matthew is longer than in Luke. The Old Latin supplied

Luke's text with petitions taken from Matthew. The situation was different in Alexandria, Antioch and Caesarea where there were schools and scholars engaged in exegesis and controversy.

The harmonizing and poularizing tendencies of Tatian's *Diatessaron* were checked by the command of the Syrian bishops who replaced the *Diatessaron* with the separate Gospels in the third or fourth century. Tatian's *Diatessaron* was really a life of Christ compiled from the four Gospels; it had great advantages as a popular textbook, but tended to corrupt the text of the separate Gospels. Consequently bishops engaged in active teaching and defense of doctrine preferred to use the original separate texts.

The Eastern, Alexandrian or Neutral text, represented by *Vaticanus*, B, and *Sinaiticus*, S, of the early fourth century, is critical and conservative. Westcott and Hort considered it free from harmonizing and popularizing tendencies. Neither does it alter grammar or syntax in the interests of elegant language. It has some omissions. Its brevity, chastity and lack of adornment have made it the preferred text of modern critics. Its difficult readings, they say, repay careful study and yield secrets to those who familiarize themselves with the environment in which the Gospels were written.

Codex A, Alexandrinus, is closely related to *Codex B, Vaticanus*. During his life at Caesarea, Origen or his disciples put an elegant finish on Text B. It was done to please those who did not like the rough Greek of Type B. It brought the grammar and syntax of koine Greek nearer to pure Attic. Lagrange says: "One might say it was written to please Erasmus."[5] Lucian, a scholar of the school of Antioch, who died a martyr in 312 A.D., revised the text used by Eusebius of Caesarea. Lucian attempted to improve the text by conflating, that is, by combining or fusing variant readings. Lucian's text was adopted by the church of Constantinople, and was brought to the West by scholars who fled from the Turks when that city was taken in 1453. Thus the Byzantine, Antiochene, Lucian text came to the notice of Erasmus and other humanists who liked its eloquence. It was adopted by the printer Stephanus of Paris. The Elzevirs, Dutch printers of Leyden, advertised it as *textus receptus,* and as such, it appealed to Protestants. It served as the basic text for the King James Bible.

Origen

Editing a book as big as the Bible requires leisure and scholarship. The first Christian school of exegesis developed at Alexandria. Origen, who succeeded Clement as head of that school, lived from 185 to 254. Great scholar and indefatigable worker that he was, Origen set himself the task of obtaining the purest possible text of the whole Bible. His predecessor Clement seems to have been careless on this score, not quoting the precise words of the text but giving their sense in his own words. A convert from paganism himself, he feared the effect of some of his hearers of the Semitic way of saying things. He explained his procedure in this manner:

> If among the body of the faithful my choice of words is considered to be sometimes different from the actual expressions employed in the Gospel, let everyone remember that my language draws its breath of life from the Scriptures themselves. My words are founded on Scripture, and I claim that they remain faithful to the biblical thought even when they do not reproduce the actual Biblical expression.[6]

Clement took liberties with the text; he interpreted it rather than quoting literally. Origen was a greater scholar. He realized the importance of fidelity to the very words of the Evangelists. His method of teaching was to cite and comment on a text. He was a positive, not a speculative theologian, although out of deference to the tradition of Philo he indulged in allegorical interpretations. While teaching in Alexandria, Origen used the *Vaticanus* text; after he moved to Caesarea, he seems to have used the text represented by *Alexandrinus,* which put a literary finish on the rough style of the former.

St. Jerome

Pope Damasus (366-384), worried by variations in Latin texts, sought a uniform text and decided the way to secure it was to appoint the best scholar he could find to furnish one in both Greek and Latin. His choice fell on Jerome (Hieronymus), an eloquent man, thoroughly disciplined in Latin and Greek, who had devoted attention to exegesis under the best masters in Antioch and Constantinople. Jerome was not only a scholar but an intellect well balanced and sensitive to the temptations besetting a translator. Although a lover of eloquence, he had too much respect for truth to sacrifice meaning to form. He realized the harm done by harmonizing and popularizing texts of the Gospels. What was gained in making them easily understood by the people was more than offset by obscuring meanings for scholars. Lagrange tells us:

> Jerome took as his basis the unpretentious Latin of the first translators, but always with due regard for correct Latin expression. He aimed above all else at approaching closely the authentic Greek original which he thought was contained in Type B, al-

though sometimes corrected in the interests of elegance by Type A. This work, performed by a master hand, imposed itself on the Christian clergy rather through its own intrinsic value than through the patronage of the pope. Augustine adopted it so far as the Gospels are concerned, although he felt free to correct it.[7]

Codex Alexandrinus is the ancestor of the Lucian, Byzantine, *textus receptus*, but is more conservative. Jerome himself admired Ciceronian Latin, but resisted his love of eloquence in the interest of accurate interpretation of the Latin text. It is to his undying credit that he preferred *Vaticanus* to more popular and more elegant texts.

The new text did not win out at once over older Latin translations; it existed side by side with them, and, as was natural, some manuscripts of Jerome's version became infiltrated with passages from the older Latin versions. Among the purest manuscripts of St. Jerome's New Testament is *Codex Amiatinus,* presented to the pope in the eighth century by monks of a monastery of Northumberland, England, and now in Florence. It is celebrated because of its exquisite craftsmanship, as well as because it is one of the best witnesses to the original text of the Vulgate. *Codex Fuldensis,* written about 545, is another good witness; it is older by two centuries than *Amiatinus.*

Humanism and Printing

The revival of interest in Greek classics in Italy and Germany and the exodus of Greek scholars to the West after the fall of Constantinople helped to popularize the Byzantine or Antiochene text in the West. Humanists favored it because of its elegance of diction. Literary men like Erasmus appreciated form in writing even more than they did loyalty to delicate shades of meaning. Humanists used Hebrew as well as Greek texts of the Bible and thus promoted the tendency to conflate various texts. Erasmus himself translated the Gospels into graceful Latin.

With the invention of printing in 1452, a new era began in the history of the text of the Bible. A hundred printed editions of the Latin Bible appeared before 1500. Competition among printers was keen; they took account of the literary tastes of humanists. Erasmus' translation of the New Testament was printed in 1511. In 1528 Stephanus, a Parisian printer, adopted the text used by Erasmus; in 1633 the Elzevirs of Holland printed this text prefixing the statement: *Textum ergo habes nunc ab omnibus receptum.* Thus a telling blow was struck for the Antiochene, Lucian or Byzantine text. The *textus receptus* became popular with the Reformers. Through the King James Bible it was made the text of English speaking Protestants, until in 1881 when Westcott and Hort brought about a revision in the direction of Type B. This was a vindication for the Vulgate. In 1881 Westcott and Hort published their *New Testament in the Original Greek,* a text that has been held in the highest esteem by the best textual critics of the twentieth century.

The Council of Trent

The great variety of early printed texts and the tendency of Reformers to slant texts with notes that favored their positions led the Council of Trent to insist, in 1546, on a uniform text for Catholics. St. Jerome's text, long in general use, had come to be known as the Vulgate, and the Council proclaimed it the official Bible of the Latin Church. It was not the intention of the Council to deny scholars the use of Greek and Hebrew texts. It simply declared that the Vulgate is substantially in agreement with the autographs, that it contains no dogmatic errors, and is therefore eminently fitted to serve as a text for use in public disputations and in lecture rooms and pulpits. However, theologians of the Council realized that St. Jerome's text had, through indiscriminate copying, become corrupted, and they respectfully petitioned the pope to provide an edition of the Vulgate as close to the original as possible.

A serious effort to comply with this request was made by a papal commission under the presidency of Cardinal Carafa. The Carafa Commission made its report to Pope Sixtus V, who was displeased with what he considered too many changes. He made an unsuccessful attempt to get out an edition of his own. After his death, a definitive edition of the Vulgate came out under Clement VIII, in 1592; and this became the standard to which other Bibles used in the Latin Church were required to conform. Pius X appointed the Benedictines to edit a new edition of the Vulgate, using all the resources of modern scholarship. Pius XII granted new liberty for translations to be made directly from the Hebrew and Greek.

Modern Textual Criticism

With the rise of Naturalism, as we have seen, came disrespect for the Bible. Rationalists and Higher Critics made a determined attempt to expunge supernatural events from Scripture. Protestant scholars who believed Christ to be divine and the Bible to be the inspired word of God devoted lives of great labor to examining, comparing, and classifying manuscripts in order to secure the closest approximation to the original text. From 1707 to 1830, Mill of Oxford, Bengel of Tubingen, Wettstein of Amsterdam, Griesbach of Halle, Scholz (a Catholic) of Leipzig and others collated and compared manuscripts to clear the way for later scholars.

In 1831 Lachmann of Berlin published the results of his efforts to determine what texts were in general use toward the end of the fourth century. In 1857 an English Quaker, Tregelles, continued the work of Lachmann by collating many more manuscripts and consulting quotations in the writings of the early Fathers. After Tregelles came Constantine von Tischendorf, who established his reputation as a textual critic by deciphering *Codex Ephraemi,* a palimpsest preserved in the Louvre which was brought to Italy after the fall of Constantinople. He exhibited splendid talent and tireless energy in searching for the pure text of the New Testament. His first edition was published at Leipzig in 1841 and his eighth edition in 1870. After he made his famous find of *Codex Sinaiticus* in a monastery on Mount Sinai, he was confirmed in his preference for Text B which is also the type of text found in S. His work was continued by his disciple C. R. Gregory.

B. F. Westcott (1825-1901) and F. J. Hort (1828-1892), Anglican clergymen trained in the tradition of Bishop Lightfoot, devoted twenty-eight years to the preparation of their *New Testament in the Original Greek,* published in 1881. This was an outstanding achievement in the history of textual criticism, and it has been followed as a basic text by the best editors ever since. Lagrange says of this text:

> The recent discoveries of manuscripts and papyri have been numerous and extremely valuable. Never has textual criticism been practiced with such ardor. In our opinion, however, it is difficult to imagine that a more informed criticism will depart very far from the text of Westcott-Hort.[8]

The Westcott-Hort New Testament is based on the text of *Vaticanus,* supported by *Sinaiticus.* Nestle published a critical edition founded on the work of Tischendorf, Westcott, Hort and Weiss, giving the readings preferred by at least two of these.[9] In 1948 the eighteenth edition of this excellent text was printed at Stuttgart. So well thought of in Rome was this text, although Nestle was not a Catholic, that it was recommended for use by theological students until the appearance in 1933 of Merk's New Testament, which follows the tradition of Tischendorf, Westcott, Hort and Nestle. Merk is a Jesuit.

Value of the Text

Eberhard Nestle, one of this century's outstanding textual critics, has an article on the New Testament in Hastings' *Dictionary of the Bible.* In this article he says that however much readers may be startled at reading of the mass of variations in the New Testament text, these variations should no longer cause anxiety, as they did to early critics. Nestle agrees with Westcott and Hort, who state, in their critical edition: "In all the books of the New Testament the substance (*ipsa summa*) has been saved by the providence of God." The variations do not affect essential meanings. No one need doubt that the Gospels furnish us with a reliable record of the life and teaching of Jesus Christ, as delivered by his Apostles.

Westcott and Hort say that 7000 of the 8000 verses that comprise the New Testament are definitely established; and no serious doubt exists about fifty-nine sixtieths of the whole. No dogma is dependent on any disputed reading. From the historical standpoint, a disputed passage such as the ending of St. Mark's Gospel is valuable because, even if written by a contemporary, it is confirmation of the history of Christ as it was preached in the early Church. The passage does no more than summarize what is taught more fully by Luke and Paul concerning Christ's appearances after his ressurection, and his commission to his Apostles to teach all nations, which is attested by Matthew.

The substantial integrity of the text is defended by Steinmueller:

> Since . . . the greater part of the text shows perfect uniformity, we can say with Westcott and Hort that seven-eighths of the Greek New Testament is critically certain. Of the remaining one-eighth many of the variant readings concern the same word or phrase, and most of these readings consist merely in changes of spelling or particles, in the order of words, in grammatical differences and the usage of synonyms, or in the conscious or unconscious faults of copyists. However, all these are immaterial changes, which do not obscure the meaning of the text. Of the variants which remain, there are hardly 200 which affect the meaning of the text, and of these only 15 are of major importance. Yet, these and the other variants neither add to or detract from a single dogma of the Church.[10]

NOTES FOR CHAPTER XIV

1. Steinmueller, *A Companion to Scripture Studies,* Volume III, p. 147.
2. *Rebuilding a Lost Faith,* p. 37.
3. Steinmueller, *A Companion to Scripture Studies,* Volume I, p. 182.
4. Lagrange, in Robert and Tricot, *Guide to the Bible,* Vol. I, p. 379.
5. *Ibid.,* p. 381.
6. Clement, *Hypotyposes,* quoted by Eusebius; see Rene Cadiou, *Origen,* (St. Louis: B. Herder Book Co., 1944), p. 30.
7. Lagrange in Robert and Tricot, *Guide to the Bible,* Vol. I, p. 385.
8. *Ibid.,* p. 391.
9. Steinmueller, *A Companion to Scripture Studies,* Vol. I, p. 182.
10. *Ibid.,* pp. 182-83.

"Concerning the knowledge of the witness we may ask: Did he live at the time when and in the place where the fact occurred, and was he so circumstanced that he could know it? Or at least, are we sure he obtained his information from a good source? . . . It is the duty of a critic to enumerate and weigh all the influence which may have altered more or less the sincerity of the witness."

Charles DeSmedt, S.J.

"I do not hesitate to believe witnesses willing to die for the truth of their testimony."

Blaise Pascal

CHAPTER XV

Veracity of The Gospels

"It would be of decisive weight for the credibility of biblical history if it were demonstrated that it has been told by eyewitnesses,"[1] said D. F. Strauss in 1835 when Rationalists were setting out to discredit the truthfulness of the traditional account of the origin of Christianity. Strauss, was distressed because he could not deny that the First Epistle to the Corinthians is authentic. He recognized it to be the work of Paul, the converted Pharisee who had astonished both friends and enemies of Christ when he became a Christian. And in this Epistle, written no more than twenty-five years after the death of Christ, Paul asserts that he himself saw Jesus of Nazareth after he rose from the dead; that five hundred other persons saw him, of whom many were yet alive to corroborate the statement. Therefore, Strauss was obliged to admit that whatever might be said of other sources, the First Epistle to the Corinthians had solid historical authority.

Paul fulfills ideally the requisites for a historian. He lived in the midst of the events he wrote about, and his own life

317

was transformed by them. Men do not lie without a motive. Paul was intelligent, informed, and sincere; he had to overcome the strongest of prejudices when he accepted Jesus as the Messias. He had been a fanatical persecutor of Christians. He was converted by a personal encounter with the risen Christ. In testimony to his sincerity, Paul laid down his life for his conviction. He comments on his testimony to the resurrection of Christ: "If with this life only in view we have had hope in Christ, we are of all men the most to be pitied" (I Cor. 15:19).

From the point of view of worldly prosperity, Paul had nothing to gain and everything to lose by becoming a Christian. He incurred the implacable hatred of his former associates; some of them vowed not to eat or drink until they killed him. Wherever he went he was singled out for special persecution. He was beaten with whips and rods; he was stoned and imprisoned. Paul certainly should be believed. The otherworldliness of the doctrine he preached precludes the charge that he became a Christian to gratify any secular ambition. His manner of life as well as his doctrine has left an indelible impression upon mankind.

The intellectual world was shocked when Reimarus charged Christ and his Apostles with being willful deceivers.[2] Jean Jacques Rousseau scorned such "base and senseless explanations of Jesus given by men the least worthy to understand him."[3] The accusation that Christ and his Apostles were willful deceivers has never won supporters. The later and more successful technique developed by Rationalists was to shroud the historical Christ in a cloud of obscurity, proposing that our sources of information about him are mythical, legendary, or apocryphal.

The veracity of a historian is judged by his competence and honesty. DeSmedt spells out the criteria:

> Did he live at a time when and in the place where the fact occurred, and was he so circumstanced that he could know it? Or at least, are we sure that he obtained his information from a good source? The more guarantees he gives in this respect, all else being equal, does he prove himself trustworthy? As to the question of sincerity, it is not enough to be satisfied that the witness did not wish to utter a deliberate lie; if it could be reasonably shown that he had a personal interest in warping the truth, grave suspicion would be raised as to the veracity of all his statements.[4]

St. Paul is a witness who knew the facts of which he spoke, and who willed to tell the truth. More cannot be asked of a witness. Many witnesses were available, moreover, while Paul was preaching in Antioch, Ephesus, Corinth, Caesarea and Rome. No one contradicted what he said. Paul and the Apostles preached openly to the Jewish and Roman world; the full light of history shines on the origin of Christianity.

St. Luke

Luke is a witness closely associated with St. Paul. A convert from paganism, a literary man of genius, impressed by Christ's life and doctrine, Luke took every precaution to inform himself accurately concerning the events he undertook to relate. He consulted Jesus' Apostles and disciples, and, for the account of the infancy, Jesus' mother, to whom Luke refers several times as having "kept all these words in her heart." The sheer excellence of Luke's two books is support for his veracity. By every test of criticism, his writings have been accredited. He is amazingly accurate in his reports. Sir Arnold Lunn tells of a man who sailed over the course of St. Paul's voyage as recorded in Acts, and verified, by "a number of minute coincidences," the authenticity of the narrative.[5] Professor F. F. Bruce notes Luke's thorough familiarity with the proper titles of persons mentioned in his writings. He never gets the Roman titles wrong—this despite the fact that titles changed frequently: a province governed at one time by a proconsul, at another by an imperial legate.[6] In reporting discourses of others, Luke faithfully reflects their individual manner of expression. Cities visited are accurately described. A masterful narrator, Luke is recognized to be an exact recorder of facts. An intimate friend and companion of Paul, he reflects the intellectual honesty and the zeal for truth that characterized the Apostle to the Gentiles. No reputable scholar denies the historical value of his writings.

St. Mark

Mark is no legendary figure. His mother owned the house in which the disciples assembled in Jerusalem at the time of Peter's imprisonment. He was a companion of Paul and Barnabas on their first missionary journey; later became attached to Peter as his secretary. He was probably the young man mentioned in Mark 14:51, who fled when Jesus was arrested in the Garden of Gethsemane. According to the testimony of Papias, Irenaeus and Clement of Alexandria, Mark wrote what Peter preached. In Mark's Gospel, therefore, we have not only his own testimony but Peter's; and no witness could be better circumstanced than Peter to testify to the events of the public life of Christ. Peter's honesty shines forth brilliantly in Mark's Gospel; indeed it is sometimes even disconcerting. Not a few Christians were shocked to read in Mark's Gospel that some of Jesus' relatives thought he was mad, or that Jesus said he did not know the day when the world would come to an end. Such statements reveal the transparent honesty of Peter's mind. No imposter would insert them in a book whose aim was to present Jesus as the Son of God.

The veracity of St. Matthew's Gospel depends on its authenticity: its authorship by an eye-witness. To Matthew and John we are indebted for preserving the longer discourses of Christ. They were better circumstanced to do this than were Mark or Luke. Speeches, moveover, are more difficult to report than actions. A striking event is calculated to arouse attention and to leave an impression on the memory of witnesses, but accurate reporting of speeches requires disciplined attention. The repeated hearing of a discourse is of course a great aid to remembering it. Matthew and John heard Christ speak almost every day for three years, and were well equipped to give a good account of his discourses.

St. Matthew

Matthew was by occupation a tax-gatherer, accustomed to keeping records and making careful reports. He must have had the education available in Galilee at the time. Hebrew teachers used the oral method and demanded memorizing; they sought to make a vivid impression through repeating essential ideas. Matthew follows this method. Grandmaison says he wrote for Jews accustomed to the art

> . . . of developing the leading idea through opposition and parallelism, and then establishing it by a kind of rhythmic cantilena or ballad which stresses salient words. Veritable landmarks of verbal

development, these words sharpen the memory, and almost automatically bring to the lips of the reciter a given passage or antithesis. . . . These rhythms are especially numerous in St. Matthew's report.[7]

Matthew had the gift of economizing on words. For example, in telling about the raising from the dead of Jairus' daughter and the associated cure of the woman with the issue of blood, St. Mark's account is three times as long as Matthew's and Luke's is twice as long. Mark gives details which make his story of the miracles vivid and picturesque. Matthew condenses. He does not mention the time of the girl's death or her age, the woman's unfortunate experience with doctors, or the admission of the Apostles, with the father and mother, to the room where the dead girl lay. Less lively as a narrator than Mark, less artful as a describer than Luke, Matthew excels as a reporter. He is preeminently an earwitness.

Because of his habit of reporting briefly, Matthew compressed into his Gospel, besides discourses and sermons, more miracles than are found in Mark or Luke. He is quoted more by ancient authors than is any other Evangelist.

Since Matthew wrote for Palestinian Jews, his work abounds in references to the religious beliefs, legal formalities, and political and social conditions of the Jews of Palestine during the first half of the first century. His account of Pharisees, Sadducees, and Scribes; of Herod, John the Baptist and the individual Apostles, is matter-of-fact, with no effort at rhetorical effect. His Gospel bears evidence of its author's willingness to let facts speak for themselves. He does not hesitate to note that among the friends invited to his banquet were "many publicans and sinners" (Matt. 9:10).

The intrinsic merit of the Sermon on the Mount proclaims it a product of the genius of Jesus Christ. No other hypothesis makes sense. This discourse, together with the parables of the kingdom of God reported in chapter 13, are among the great cultural treasures of mankind. In the Sermon on the Mount, Matthew recorded the words of the Son of God.

St. John

John the Apostle, called by Christ a "Son of Thunder," was a lover of truth and a hater of lies; his competence as a witness to the sayings and doings of Jesus cannot be challenged. A disciple of John the Baptist, he, along with Andrew, was the first to follow Jesus, and he continued to follow him during his whole public life. John, with his brother and St. Peter, were allowed to witness some happenings from which the other Apostles were excluded. John was the one whom Jesus entrusted the care of his mother. He outlived the other Apostles and hence was a witness of the growth of the Church until the end of the first century. We took great pains to establish the authenticity of his Gospel, and in so doing we virtually established its veracity. No document in the possession of the Church outranks it in historical value.

John's Gospel is different from the other three, but the difference is what we should expect from one who wrote years after the death of the others. The Church was well established not only in Palestine but in Greece; it was already in possession of the other Gospels. But there were many things Jesus had said and done which no one had recorded. John emphasizes Christ's divinity: the identity of Jesus of Nazareth with the Word of God.

Biographers of Christ find more exact information in John's Gospel concerning the length of Jesus' public life, his comings to Jerusalem and his goings to Galilee, than they find in the Synoptics. And, surprisingly enough, John is the most definite concerning the human limitations of the Word made flesh. Jesus grew hungry, thirsty, and tired. "Jesus, therefore, being weary with his journey, sat thus on the well" (John 4:6). "Jesus said to her: Give me to drink" (John 4:7). "In the meantime the disciples besought him, saying, Rabbi, eat" (John 4:31). It is John who relates this human detail: "And Jesus wept" (John 11:35). And he tells of the anguish that overpowered Jesus in the Garden of Gethsemane. "Now is my soul troubled. . . . Father, save me from this hour" (John 12:27). John's information was derived from his intimate daily companionship with Jesus. Burkitt declares: "In no early Christian document is the real humanity of Jesus so emphasized as in the Fourth Gospel."[8]

If Peter's undiplomatic effusions bear clear evidence of truthfulness, so does the following statement in which John quotes Christ: "You have heard that I said to you: 'I go away and I come unto you.' If you loved me you would indeed be glad, because I go to the Father: *for the Father is greater than I*" (John 14:28). No forger, trying to make Jesus divine, would have recorded these words. The Arians pounced on them as evidence that the Logos was subordinate to the Father. There is only one possible explanation why this statement was recorded: that John had such great reverence for Christ that he was not ashamed to quote hard sayings or mysterious utterances.

Careful study of St. John's Gospel should convince the most hostile critic of its geographical and historical correctness. John makes twenty-four topographical references that are not found in the Synoptics, and none of these references have proved wrong when tested by modern experts.[9] John tells exactly where and when events occurred. Both the Gospel and the First Epistle insist that the author was an eyewitness of the life, death and resurrection of Jesus of Nazareth. "And he that saw it has given testimony; and his testimony is true" (John 19:35). "That which we have seen and heard, we declare unto you" (I John 1:3).

Supernatural Events

If, in the Gospels and in the Epistles of Paul, we have reliable history of the primitive, Judaic period of Christianity, written by men whose competence and sincerity cannot be doubted, why do many modern scholars call their accuracy into question? The answer is simply this: because they do not acknowledge the existence of a supernatural order. Their position is clearly stated by J. B. Bury, a British historian, who believes that supernatural phenomena are not verifiable. He writes:

> The distinction may seem so obvious as to be hardly worth making. But it is important to be clear about it. The primitive man who had learned from his elders that there were bears in the woods and likewise evil spirits, soon verified the former statement by seeing a bear, but if he did not happen to meet an evil spirit, it did not occur to him unless he was a prodigy, that there was a distinction between the two statements; he would rather have argued, if he argued at all, that as his tribesmen were right about the bears they were sure to be right also about the spirits.[10]

Bury assumes that because he has not seen any supernatural

phenomena, they cannot exist. A historian who is a positivist or an agnostic is bound by his philosophy to deny, *a priori*, the truth of all manifestations of the presence and efficient causality of God, angels, devils, and disembodied souls. Although spiritual phenomena have been perceived by many witnesses, they are rejected because the historian himself is limited by his materialistic theory of knowledge: that is, that man *cannot* perceive such phenomena; that they cannot, in fact, exist. Such an attitude is unscientific. Any fact is verifiable which is evident either to the senses or the intellect, or the reasonable inferences of man. *A priori* theories concerning the non-existence of metaphysical and supernatural worlds contradict the inductive method of science.

Miracles are as verifiable by observation as are any natural phenomena. Indeed, they attract more attention and interest than ordinary occurrences. Bury never encountered a man risen from the dead; but St. Paul did. This was the reason for his complete transformation, and the explanation of his marvelous career after the experience. St. Augustine said if you deny that miracles accompanied the preaching of Christianity, you must explain its spread without miracles —in which case, Christianity becomes itself a miracle.

History depends upon the testimony of reliable witnesses. If we do not accept such testimony, there can be no history. To challenge every statement made by historians who have recorded events of the past would bring us to cultural barbarism. Man's knowledge would be extremely limited if he were to confine it to what he can verify through his own experience. The crises that have changed the course of history and have most deeply affected human society may not occur again. They can be verified only by history and by their effects.

Testimony of the Christian Community

In discussing the trustworthiness of the Gospels, Karl Adam stresses the fact that the Evangelists were not isolated witnesses; but that the facts they reported were witnessed to by the whole community of early Christians. Many early Christians lost property, reputation, and even life for their faith in Christ. Their otherworldliness is a colossal historical phenomenon with no explanation other than their conviction that Jesus did and said what the Gospels relate—that he did and said what was preached to them orally by eyewitnesses. Karl Adam writes:

> In the fact that the primitive Christian message was never restricted to individuals or to individual groups or schools, but was always attached to the whole body which was fast anchored to the apostolic teaching transmitted to it, and that the message was passed on as an apostolic belief held in common by the body, lies the strongest guarantee that the Christian faith from its first beginnings invariably remained true to itself, and also that in its preliterary period it was not tampered with; that we have therefore in the Gospels the primitive message of Jesus in all its wealth and purity.[11]

Humility of the Evangelists

Peter's denial of his Master is told by all the Evangelists, Mark supplying the most humiliating details. The ambition of John and of his brother and mother is not concealed. Luke does not suppress the part played by Paul in stoning Stephen, or his violence against other Christians. The four writers are not working together to avoid discrepancies;

each gives his own account in a straightforward, objective way. They narrate the same facts; they do not contradict each other; yet they differ enough to make it plain that there was no collusion between them. Their veracity is evident from their simplicity and candor. They make no effort to color or slant their testimony; they do not try to make an impression through clever use of rhetoric. They are themselves awed by what they have to tell.

St. John Chrysostom says, with regard to the differences in the Gospels:

> Many passages show discrepancies. This is still another proof of their credibility, for if they were in exact accord as to time and place, and even the form of expression, our opponents would never believe that they wrote without a previous understanding, without a purely human agreement. . . . But the apparent contradiction in a few small details protects them from such a suspicion and is the finest defense of these historians.[12]

Proof of Their Sincerity

There is no reasonable argument for invention or deception on the part of the Evangelists. They could hope for no worldly advantage through being Christian witnesses; quite the opposite. They were willing to sacrifice worldly advantage, setting their sights on an otherworldly reward—the treasure in heaven that was promised to them by Christ. They were prepared to die for the Christ in whom they believed—the most conclusive proof of their absolute sincerity.

Why Disbelief?

There is growing disbelief in the world today; we are constantly being told: "Modern man will not accept the teachings his forebears did." The truth is that modern man has little chance to hear them. New theologians blithely reconstruct Christianity, attempting to tailor it to fit evolutionism and existentialism, and to limit it to a this-worldly outlook. The result is, quite naturally, unbelievable. As Sir Arnold Lunn wrote some thirty-odd years ago: "Of all irrational creeds, the non-miraculous Christianity of the modernists is the most irrational."

We also hear a great deal today about "new approaches" to Bible study. We are frequently given to understand that new discoveries have confirmed the theories of the Rationalist and Modernist critics. Certain biblical scholars claim insights, gained from new knowledge, which enable them to know much better than was known before what the sacred writers really meant. Such writers are generally ready to discredit prophecy and miracle, and to find the Gospels merely a reflection of "the thinking of the community" rather than accurate, eyewitness accounts.

The Logical Conclusion

The fact is that archaeological findings have done much to confirm traditional beliefs; to support statements made in the Bible. Many strange theories produced by scholars have been demolished by more thorough and more objective scholars. It is wise to distrust those who lay claim to new and startling "insights" never known to man before. The historicity and authenticity of the Bible has been thoroughly studied and affirmed by men who were giants in the field of Scripture scholarship.

We have every reason to believe the Bible as the word of God. The Second Vatican Council did not hesitate to reaffirm the traditional stand of the Church: that the Bible teaches "firmly, faithfully, and without error"; that the Gospels are by eyewitnesses or disciples of eyewitnesses; that they "tell the honest truth about Jesus."

NOTES FOR CHAPTER XV

1. D. F. Strauss, *Leben Jesu,* I, sec. 13.
2. Wolfenbuttel Fragments of Reimarus, published by Lessing between 1774 and 1778.
3. Confessions VIII.
4. Charles DeSmedt, "Criticism (Historical)," *Catholic Encyclopedia,* Vol. IV.
5. Arnold Lunn, *Is Christianity True?* (Philadelphia: J. B. Lippincott, 1933), p. 287.
6. F. F. Bruce, *The New Testament Documents: Are They Reliable?* (Grand Rapids: Wm. F. Eerdmans Company, 1954), p. 82.
7. Grandmaison, *Jesus Christ,* Vol. I, p. 62. Grandmaison refers to Plummer as a commentator who has treated this feature of Matthew's Gospel in detail.
8. John Burkitt, *Gospel History and Its Transmission,* p. 232, quoted by Grandmaison, *Jesus Christ,* Vol. I, p. 173.
9. Grandmaison, *Jesus Christ,* Vol. I, p. 176.
10. J. B. Bury, *History of Freedom of Thought* (New York: Oxford University Library, 1952), p. 16.
11. Karl Adam, *The Son of God,* p. 77.
12. St. John Chrysostom, *Homily on St. Matthew,* Introduction I, 2.

Index